The Which? Guide to
Making the Most of Retirement

About the author

After working on consumer involvement and patient information in a number of London health authorities, Thalia Thompson spent six years at Consumers' Association. As head of Services Research for *Which?* magazine there, she specialised in topics ranging from health to retail and computing. She is now a freelance journalist on consumer issues.

Acknowledgements

The author and publishers would like to thank the following organisations and individuals for their helpful comments on the text: Age Concern, Carers UK, Elderly Accommodation Counsel, Help the Aged, Ricability, Frances Blunden, Jon Cole of the Association of Chief Police Officers, Jennifer Conti, Emma Copeland, Teresa Fritz, Melanie Green, Julie Lennard, Julie Mendis, Ajay Patel, Felicity Porritt, Howard Price of the Chatered Institute of Environmental Health, Dr Ann Robinson, Tessa Russell and Pete Tynan.

The Which? Guide to Making the Most of Retirement

Thalia Thompson

 CONSUMERS' ASSOCIATION

Which? Books are commissioned by
Consumers' Association and published by
Which? Ltd, 2 Marylebone Road, London NW1 4DF
Email: books@which.net

Distributed by The Penguin Group:
Penguin Books Ltd, 80 Strand, London WC2R 0RL
First edition September 2003

British Library Cataloguing in Publication Data
A catalogue record for this book is available from the British Library

ISBN 0 85202 932 2

For a full list of *Which?* books, please write to Which? Books, Castlemead, Gascoyne Way,
Hertford X, SG14 1LH or access our website at www.which.net

Editorial and production: Joanna Bregosz, Mary Sunderland
Original cover concept by Sarah Harmer
Cover photograph by ROM-RO-MA STOCK/A1PIX

Typeset by Saxon Graphics Ltd, Derby
Printed in Great Britain by Creative Print and Design, Wales

Contents

Introduction   7

Part 1: House and home

1   Moving house   13
2   Getting the best deal on household utilities   26
3   Safety and security in the home   42
4   Your rights as a householder   58

Part 2: Enjoying your retirement

5   Employment and voluntary work   75
6   Leisure and learning   84
7   Computers and the Internet   93
8   Getting around   104
9   Holidays   121

Part 3: Your very good health

10 You and the health service   133
11 Healthy eating   149
12 Keeping fit and active   163
13 Common health problems   173

Part 4: Planning ahead

14 Becoming a carer   215
15 Adapting your home   226
16 Sheltered housing and care homes   232
    Addresses*   239
    Index   250

*An asterisk next to the name of an organisation in the text indicates that its address or contact details can be found in this section.

Introduction

The old stereotypes of retirement just don't hold true anymore. To hear some people talk, you would think that once a person gives up work, he or she suddenly has to start wearing carpet slippers, take up bowls and write angry letters to the local newspaper. But with almost 20 per cent of the population being over pensionable age, it's impossible to generalise about 'retired people' as if they're a single homogeneous group – they encompass probably the widest range of lifestyles that you'll find in any age group.

They cover a broad age range, too. We're all living longer – according to National Statistics, a man aged 60 in 1999 could expect to live for another 19.2 years and a woman of the same age for 22.8 years. Retirement is sometimes described as your 'third age', and you may well find that this lasts longer than your first two.

This book is intended as a resource to help you get the best out of this time, whether you are just coming up to retirement or whether you've been retired for some time already. It focuses on four areas that may be becoming more important to you – your home, your leisure time, your health and planning ahead.

Retirement is a good time to review your living arrangements – many people consider moving house or will be spending more time at home than they have before. This book is full of practical information to help you make the right decisions throughout your retirement, whether you are moving to another part of the country, saving money on household utilities or improving your home security.

The best thing about reaching your third age is the opportunity to do all those things you never had time to do before. It's important to keep as fit and healthy as possible to enjoy them: regular exercise is highly recommended and can be fun. This book contains practical advice and information to help you make the most of the leisure and fitness options available, whether this means compiling a reminiscence scrapbook, starting a lunch club, or taking up a class in yoga or the martial arts. It also gives advice about the symptoms and treatment of common health conditions.

Of course, an active mind is as important as an active body. In 2002, 20 per cent of people aged between 65 and 74 – and 10 per cent of people aged over 75 – took part in some sort of adult learning, according to a 2002 study by the National Institute of Adult Continuing Education (NIACE). Even more older people take part in unpaid or charity work, with the Institute of Volunteering Research finding in 1997 that 45 per cent of those aged between 65 and 74 – and 35 per cent of those aged over 75 – had participated in some sort of voluntary work over the past year.

Opportunities in this sector are as varied as you want them to be. This book can point you in the right direction, whether you're interested in becoming a trustee of a charity, spending a few weeks – or years – doing voluntary work abroad, or simply want to take up a new hobby or gain a new skill.

One increasingly popular interest – part leisure activity, part vital information tool – is using a home computer and Internet connection. Over a third of people aged over 60 have a home computer, according to the most recently published General Household survey (2000). And this group – the so-called 'silver surfers' – are taking to the web in ever-increasing numbers. The 2002 Which? Online annual Internet survey found that web usage amongst older people is increasing at the greatest rate of any age group, with the proportion of Internet users aged over 55 increasing by 40 per cent compared with the previous year. This book gives you the facts you need to know in order to get started, as well as useful tips for more experienced users.

If one of your reasons for getting interested in computers is to keep up with your grandchildren, you may appreciate the section on mobile phones. In February 2003, Oftel found that 53 per cent of people aged between 65 and 75 – and 24 per cent of people aged over 75 – owned a mobile phone, and this number is increasing fast. Whether you want a mobile phone just to use in emergencies or want to be able to keep in touch with friends and family when you're out and about or even abroad, we explain what to look for and how to make sure you've got the right tariff for you.

You will probably be managing a change in your income. While the companion volume to this book, *The Which? Guide to Money in Retirement,* will help you plan your overall financial strategy, this book also contains useful information on the 'perks' of the third age which can help your money go further. This includes grants for home improvements or help with fuel bills, discounts on travel fares, reduced-price leisure activities and savings on adult education classes. And there is a host of money-saving tips for getting the best deal on everything from your phone bill to booking a cheap flight to the sun – for instance, changing your gas and electricity companies could save you up to £100 a year, while the tips on cutting the cost of your motoring could save you even more.

While everyone's third age is different, it can be prudent to plan ahead, and this book gives helpful advice on the best ways of dealing with responsibilities the future may bring. Older people are increasingly taking on the demanding but valuable task of being a carer; the 1995 General Household Survey revealed that more than 25 per cent of people caring for someone else in their own home were themselves aged over 65. This book has information on the support systems that are available, adaptations that can help people maintain their independence, and advice on choosing sheltered housing or a care home.

Retirement is the ideal time to expand existing interests and develop new ones. Learning a new skill and opening yourself up to new experiences are key parts of keeping yourself at the peak of your potential. Whatever your retirement holds, this book will be an invaluable reference to help you meet any challenges and make the most of the freedom and opportunities your third age can bring.

Part 1

House and home

Chapter 1

Moving house

For a lot of people, retirement is a time to think about moving house. Perhaps a rose-clad cottage in the country beckons? Or maybe growing your own grapes in Spain? If you're planning a move then some careful thinking up front can help turn your dream into a reality – and make sure it doesn't become an expensive nightmare.

Be clear about what you are trying to achieve first of all. What are your priorities? Do you want:

- to live in an area you've always dreamt about but have previously been unable to consider because of work or other commitments?
- to be nearer family (either children or parents) or friends?
- to get more money for your retirement by realising some of the capital that has appreciated on your current property?
- to get somewhere easier to maintain – possibly smaller, with more labour-saving features?
- the security of being settled in accommodation that offers you facilities you may want as you become older?

Staying put

If you decide your current home isn't right for you but want to stay in the area, then consider if you actually have to move to achieve what you want.

Space

Don't automatically assume you will need less space once you have retired. Spending more time at home could mean you appreciate the chance to spread out and cultivate personal interests. If you can afford it and have the capacity, you (and your partner) could create a separate study or hobbies room. And a spare room will come in handy to accommodate visiting grandchildren, family and friends.

Changing rooms

If you want to stay put, but are concerned that your house will become increasingly unpractical as you get older and perhaps less mobile, it's worth considering whether you could make adaptations as a simpler and cheaper alternative to moving. There's a whole host of gadgets and adaptations to suit your needs – you'll find more information in Chapter 15.

In general however, it's well worth thinking about function as well as form whenever you're carrying out routine work on your house. Incorporating features that might make your house more comfortable for you in years to come can often be done without too much extra trouble or expense. For instance:

- review your home security when you decorate a room. An example might be to consider adding window locks if you're painting window frames. See Chapter 3 for more on home security
- if you're re-wiring or re-plastering, consider having some sockets fitted at waist height
- installing a downstairs toilet or bathroom can be a wise investment. At present it may just be useful when you've got visitors, but in the future it could make all the difference
- lever-controlled taps can be easier to turn on and off as well as looking stylish. In the same way, lever door handles can be easier to operate than door-knobs, and you may find D-shaped handles easiest on cupboard doors
- overhauling heating and insulation makes good economic and environmental sense as well as making the house more comfortable in the long term. For more information, see *The Which? Guide to the Energy-saving Home*, from Which? Books*.

Making money from your home

Soaring house prices in some areas of the country may mean you have the opportunity to capitalise on the value of your property. Of course, to take advantage of this you have to be able to buy something which costs less – either a smaller property or one in a cheaper part of the country. If you don't want to move to another area and like the amount of space you have, there are other ways of making money from your house.

One option is taking in a lodger. Under the government's 'rent-a-room' scheme you can currently receive up to £4,250 a year in rent from lodgers, without having to pay tax on this income. You could even convert your house so you have a self-contained bedsitter that will give you and your tenant more privacy and perhaps even be suitable for a granny-flat in the future. (If considering this type of conversion, get professional advice – not only on the building work but also on any implications for capital gains tax if you make the flat completely self-contained.)

You can advertise a room locally, or try the accommodation office of colleges and universities if you live near any, as they may be looking for suitable housing for students. If you live near a language school, it may be seeking host families for language students – these can range from children to business people. These are usually fairly short-term placements, so it can be a good way to find out whether someone else living in your house suits you. If you do decide to rent a room or bedsit make sure you have a proper tenancy agreement: *The Which? Guide to Renting and Letting* contains sample contracts.

You could also think about taking in guests on a bed-and-breakfast basis. This can be fun and financially rewarding, but don't underestimate the amount of work involved. As a first step, contact your local authority to find out about any regulations you need to meet.

Another option for raising cash from your home is an equity release scheme which lets you use the capital in your home while retaining the right to carry on living there. You should always take independent financial advice before entering into this type of scheme. Find out more from *The Which? Guide to Money in Retirement*.

Moving house

If you do decide your current house isn't right for you, then you might move house in the same area or to a new area altogether. If you're buying a new house, it's definitely worth planning ahead for

15

possible future needs. Moving rates alongside getting married or divorced among the chief causes of stress so you want everything to go as smoothly as possible – and to be prepared for all eventualities once you are settled.

That doesn't mean you should look only at houses set up for very elderly people – but you'd be wise to keep an eye on how you might want to adapt things in the future. For instance, perhaps you love gardening and retirement offers the time to indulge your passion. You shouldn't feel you have to sacrifice 20 years or more of pleasure by rejecting anything but the most maintenance-free of gardens just in case it becomes a burden in the future. Pick a house with a large or interesting garden by all means, but at the back of your mind think about how you might manage it in the future. Maybe the paved patio area could be extended, or that herbaceous border could become a shrubbery?

Moving from a house to a flat

If you're considering scaling down from a house to a flat, here are some points to consider.

- Check how sound-proof the flat is – try to look round the flat in the evening and at a weekend when most of the other flat-owners will be at home.
- Upper-floor flats may be more secure than ground-floor flats, but think about accessibility if there is no lift.
- Look carefully at the terms of the lease. If you've been used to living in a freehold house you may be surprised at the number of rules and conditions that some leases contain.
- In particular, check how any shared areas are maintained. Is there a management company? What have the service charges been in the past? Are there any proposals to increase these or to increase the ground rent or to carry out major building works?
- If the flat-owners share the ownership of the freehold, find out how decisions are taken on this type of work and ask to see records of meetings or agreements.

It's worth remembering that groups of leaseholders now have the right to buy the freehold of the building they live in, and individual leaseholders have the right to extend their leases at market price.

From August 2003, leaseholders have had the right to take over the management of the building from the landlord (the Right to Manage). Conditions apply for all of these and you should contact the Leasehold Advisory Service★ for further details.

Moving to a new area

Maybe you're considering a move to an entirely new area. If so, it's a good idea to list all the pros and cons before you decide. These might include:

- **family and friends** You might be moving to be closer to your family, but what about friends? Think about ways you might meet and make new friends in your new local area
- **transport and facilities** Will you be absolutely dependent on a car? Will there be shops, a post office, libraries, pubs, entertainments or services within walking distance? What public transport is available? Is there adequate street lighting?
- **healthcare** How accessible are the healthcare facilities? If you're moving to an area that's traditionally been a popular place to retire, such as the south coast of England, bear in mind that health services may be overstretched
- **holiday homes** If you're planning to return to a place where you've spent idyllic holidays, make a return trip at a different time of year first. Places can look very different on a wet Sunday in November and a peaceful beauty spot can be unrecognisable on a busy bank holiday. Take a self-catering let for as long as you can and try to treat it as a test run for living in the area rather than a holiday.

Moving in with family or friends

Rather than just moving to be nearer family or friends, you may be considering going a stage further and moving in with them. With families, this may mean moving in with children or it may mean moving in with your own parents, perhaps to provide care (for more information on becoming a carer, see Chapter 14). You may be moving into an existing house or pooling money to buy a bigger property that's suitable for all of you. All these options require careful thought (see box overleaf).

Tips for a happy coexistence

- Consider whether an existing house could be extended: one of the provisos for successful integration between different generations is plenty of living space. A kitchenette, or at least the facility to make a snack or hot drink safely without having to use the main kitchen, can help too.
- Building an extension gives you the opportunity to design in features that take account of any existing or potential future needs. There may be grants available – see page 230–1 for more details.
- It's an excellent idea to organise a trial run to give you a taster of what daily life will be like before committing yourself absolutely.
- It helps to create an atmosphere of home if the person moving in can furnish his or her room with his or her own bed and other possessions as much as possible.
- Discuss what you would do if either party wanted to end the agreement. If you've pooled money to buy a place, you should make a formal agreement covering this contingency.
- Try to think through any potential problem areas in advance; for example, will you share meals or cars, will you go on holiday together, will you have a pet or friends to stay?
- Decide how day-to-day chores will be shared out. If you're moving in with children, you may welcome the chance to help out, but everyone needs to know what's expected.
- Don't fall out over bills – work out how you'll divide them in advance. It may be worth installing an extra telephone line, say, so you each have your own number and your own bill.
- If one of you is paying rent, have a formal agreement about how much it is and whether and how it will be increased.
- If you're converting a property to incorporate a self-contained flat, take professional advice. If you make the flat completely self-contained, you may make yourself liable for capital gains tax when the property is sold.

Moving abroad

If you're thinking of moving abroad, it's even more important that you research your plans thoroughly.

You can get a lot more house for your money in most other countries than in the UK. Spain and France are by far the most popular countries for UK buyers and apart from certain very expensive areas like Côte d'Azur or Marbella, you should find a good selection of properties for under £100,000. However, you should think very carefully about whether you want to live permanently in a foreign country, especially if you are not all that familiar with its language, customs and culture and the majority of your family and friends are in the UK.

Doing your homework

If you're thinking of a move abroad, the advice about a trial period of residence holds good in spades. Try to make this visit during off-season or in the season you know least. Use this trip to check prices of a wide range of goods to give you a true picture of the cost of living. If there are other British people living in the area, talk to them about their experiences. The foreign embassy of the relevant country in the UK may offer useful advice, and you can consult the local British Consul overseas.

Most important of all, research the local health facilities and whether you are eligible for free health care. If you move to a country in the European Economic Area (EEA – all the European Union (EU) countries plus Iceland, Norway and Liechtenstein), you will generally be entitled to the same health services as nationals of that country. But check what this includes as it may not be the same as that provided by the UK health services. You can get further information about entitlement to health care in other countries from the Department for Work and Pensions (DWP) Pensions and Overseas Benefits Directorate★. If you have private health insurance in the UK, check the policy to see if it will cover you abroad.

Make sure you have done some very careful financial planning before you go, and that you are prepared for changes in exchange rates, different levels of inflation and any unforeseen changes in your own health.

Check the pension arrangements too. Your pension provider should be able to tell you about arrangements for having your occupational or personal pension paid to you if you move abroad. You can normally receive your UK state pension in any country but at the time of writing you are not entitled to subsequent increases unless you are living in an EU or EEA country or a few others (including the USA but not including New Zealand or Australia). You can get more information from the DWP Pensions and Overseas Benefit Directorate*.

If you move abroad, you won't be entitled to carry on receiving most UK benefits (exceptions include Bereavement Allowance and Industrial Injuries Disablement Benefit). In EU or EEA countries and some other countries, you also may be entitled to claim benefits available to the nationals of that country. Ask at your local Social Security office or contact the DWP Pensions and Overseas Benefits Directorate* for more details. You can also obtain a range of leaflets including GL29 *Going abroad and Social Security benefits* from the DWP.

Remember that you will still count as a UK resident for tax purposes if you return to the UK for visits which average a total of 91 days or more in a tax year. And even non-residents may have to pay some UK tax – for example, on investment income arising in the UK. See Inland Revenue (IR) booklet IR20 *Residents & Non Residents Liability to Tax in the UK*; copies are available from the IR telephone orderline on (0845) 900 0404, or see the website *www.inlandrevenue.gov.uk*. You should take professional legal and financial advice about inheritance tax and your will.

Finding the right property

There are many 'tumbledowns' in abandoned rural areas of France which may be temptingly cheap, but don't underestimate the time, money and effort it takes to do them up. Much Spanish property is sold 'off-plan' in new developments or 'urbanisations' that have yet to be built. Many of these are designed as holiday homes and are not suitable for a permanent base. Most properties that are part of a development are run communally by the owners; you own your home plus a share of the common aspects such as pools, gardens and lifts.

If your proposed home is in one of these developments, make sure you check the annual maintenance fee and are happy with the rules and regulations that will apply. Whatever you choose, make sure the property is big enough to put up visitors.

Case history: Gwen and Richard

Gwen and Richard spent many happy holidays in Normandy over the years. Now in their mid-fifties, they've taken the plunge and bought a house in a small coastal town there. Gwen took early retirement but Richard still works, and for the moment they're planning to use the property partly for their own holidays and partly to rent out. This doesn't bring in a huge income, but it's a useful extra. 'We could have afforded a more rural property with some land attached, but we wanted something simple to maintain,' says Gwen. 'If we're not going to be there permanently we wanted something that would be easier to look after.'

The couple spent their first Christmas there this year, along with their daughter, son-in-law and their grandson Ryan. 'One of the reasons we like this area is that transport back to the UK is so good. Ryan's our first grandchild and we don't want to miss out on him growing up. We're not sure yet whether we'll move here permanently or not. When Richard retires we'll start spending more and more time here and see how we feel then. For the moment though we're just looking forward to getting to know the place properly.'

There are specialist magazines, such as *France Magazine* and *Daltons Weekly*, that will help you get a feel for what's available in your budget range and give you contacts to follow up including adverts for specialist estate agencies which often have websites to browse. Look out for supplements in the press too. When making enquiries, you may even be offered a subsidised viewing trip by an agent or property developer keen to sell housing stock, but it's wise to avoid putting yourself under this kind of pressure, and paying your own way.

Dealing with the technicalities

If, after doing this research, you decide going abroad is the right move for you, it is essential you get legal advice to help you through the buying procedure. Many buyers prefer to hire a UK law firm that specialises in overseas purchases rather than trying to find a local firm. The advantage of this is that there won't be any language barriers and you can get compensation through the British courts if your lawyers make a mistake. You can get lists of UK solicitors who deal with foreign property legislation from the Law Society★.

Go and see your lawyer before you visit properties and make sure he or she informs you about the legal position with regard to inheritance, briefs you on what constitutes a legally binding offer and tells you about any contracts you may be asked to sign when you agree to buy.

The moving process

If it's been a long time since you last moved house, it's worth refreshing your memory about how the process works. For a full explanation consult *Which? Way to Buy, Sell and Move House* from Which? Books★. Meanwhile, the tips below will help smooth the way.

Using estate agents
- When selling your property, shop around, but don't automatically go for the estate agent who gives you the highest valuation. If it's so high as to be unrealistic, you may end up reducing the price anyway.
- It will probably be cheapest if you give one agent sole agency, at least for an initial period, but having the property on the books with several estate agents may result in a faster sale.
- If you do opt for sole agency, read the contract carefully and make sure you're aware of any notice you need to give before instructing other estate agents if the house fails to sell.

Mortgage deals
You should obtain independent financial advice before you take on a mortgage once you're retired. Some banks and building societies have special mortgage deals for older people.

Getting a survey
It's important to get a proper survey done. If the property is old or in any way unusual you need a building survey (sometimes called a full structural survey). A Homebuyer's Survey and Valuation

(HBSV) will be a bit cheaper and should be sufficient for straight-forward, newer properties. Don't rely on a mortgage valuation – this doesn't tell you enough about the condition of the property.

Timing your move
You may find you have greater flexibility over when to arrange completion now you are retired. There's a greater choice of removal companies and even cheaper prices at less popular times for moving (for example, weekdays and the middle of the month).

Do-it-yourself house buying
Now you're retired, you may have the time and energy to consider handling the sale or conveyancing yourself. This could save you hundreds or thousands of pounds – but don't underestimate the work involved. Below are some of the pros and cons of taking this course to help you decide if it's something you want to explore further. For more information see *Which? Way to Buy, Sell and Move House* and *The Which? Guide to Doing Your Own Conveyancing*.

Handling the sale yourself

✔ Control over the selling process, including setting the sale price, drawing up the particulars and meeting all prospective buyers.

✔ Potential for substantial savings. Estate agents' fees are usually the largest single cost of moving home – typically anything from 1.5 per cent to 3 per cent of the sale price.

✘ Security. If you sell through an estate agent, you can ask for the agent's representative to accompany all viewers. You don't have this safeguard if you sell privately, but you can take basic safety precautions such as taking a telephone number and always calling back to confirm a time for a viewing.

✘ If you advertise your house extensively and don't manage to sell, you may have trouble getting an agent to take over, as a house that has been on the market for a long time is likely to be difficult to sell.

Doing your own conveyancing

The conveyancing process for buying a property is more compli-cated than for selling a property. If you're selling one property to buy another, it may be worth employing a professional to do the conveyancing for both.

✔ You will probably save time by doing the work yourself – and if you don't need a mortgage you'll save money as well.

✘ If you are getting a mortgage, the saving may not be so great as you will still have to pay for the lender's solicitor.

✘ If the property is leasehold or there are any complications – for example, it's being sold by a separating couple or is not wholly occupied by the seller – then you'd be well advised to employ a professional to handle your conveyancing.

Sheltered housing

If you're looking for somewhere smaller and more manageable and want the peace of mind that comes from a warden on call, then you might consider a sheltered housing development. These are oper-ated by both local authorities and private developers. Some shared ownership schemes (where you part-rent, part-buy) also exist. Shared facilities, such as a laundry or dining room, may be available. You should find out if you can take your own furniture, and enquire about service charges.

If sheltered housing appeals to you, even if you're not ready to move yet, it's worth making some enquiries as to likely develop-ments – there can be long waiting lists. But also consider whether you can get any of these features without having to move – see pages 228–9 for more on community alarms and pages 232–5 for more on sheltered housing.

The Advice Information and Mediation Service (AIMS)★ advises people about sheltered and retirement housing.

Local authority and housing authority tenants

If you don't own a home and can't afford to buy one, or if your home isn't suitable for your needs (for example, because you have a disability) and isn't worth enough to enable you to buy somewhere more suitable, you may be eligible for local authority housing. Local authorities must give priority to certain groups of people including those whose current housing is unsuitable because of a disability. To find out more about local authority or housing association housing, including their sheltered housing schemes, contact the housing department of your local authority.

If you live in local authority or housing association housing and want to move, there are services to help you swap with tenants in other parts of the country. As we went to press, the arrangements for these swaps were under review. Your local authority or housing association will be able to give you up-to-date details.

Chapter 2

Getting the best deal on household utilities

Retiring may mean that you're spending more time in your home, so you will want your home environment to be as comfortable as possible. If you're going to be using the heating, lighting or phone more than when you were out at work all day, you should make sure you're getting the best deal possible on these basic utilities. Compared to a few years ago, there's a wide choice of companies so it can pay to shop around.

Price-comparison websites

If you have Internet access (see pages 96–103) there are many sites offering price-comparison calculators. Usually you enter details about your current bills and your postcode and the website calculates the cheapest service in your area. Some of the best-known sites are mentioned in this chapter, but note that sites change rapidly. Before using one ask yourself:

- How comprehensive is the site? Does it cover the entire market or only selected companies?
- When was it last updated? A good site should have this information clearly displayed
- Does it have approval from any regulator or consumer body? Most of the utility regulators (listed below in each section) have a scheme which approves websites that meet certain criteria.

Case history: Hywel

Once Hywel retired, he went through all the household files. After checking the rates on his savings accounts, he turned his attention to the utility bills. Like many people, he'd never got round to changing utility companies and decided to check out the deals on offer. He doesn't have Internet access, so he had to phone around first to get tariff information for gas, electricity and phone companies.

'Once I'd got all the information in the post, it took a while to go through, but most of the calculations were pretty straightforward and I reckon I'll save around £75 a year.' Hywel did find it more difficult to work out the best deal on his phone line. He ended up not changing from BT, but decided to try an indirect operator for some calls.

He hasn't had any problems with setting up the new accounts and so far has been perfectly happy with their service. He plans to keep an eye on prices though. 'I've put the date in my calendar, and next year I'm going to do the same thing to make sure these are still the best deals.'

Gas and electricity

You can now choose a gas and electricity supplier from 20 or so companies. If you switch both gas and electricity you could save up to £100 a year. It should be relatively simple to switch supplier since all that changes is the supply company – there's no change to the gas or electricity you receive or the pipework. (Gas safety and pipework remain the responsibility of Transco – you should contact them immediately on (0800) 111999 if you think you have a gas leak.)

Unfortunately, tales abound of unscrupulous door-to-door salespeople who promote energy companies which aren't really the best value, and even trick people into signing contracts unawares. Of course, not all salespeople are dodgy, but with so many companies out there, relying on the word of a representative of just one of them isn't the best way to make a choice.

Working out the best deal

The smart way to choose an energy company is to do the home-work yourself. There's no single best-buy company as tariffs will depend on the amount of fuel you use. For example, if you live alone and don't use much fuel, you may find that one of the companies that offers a low standing charge but a higher tariff for energy used is cheaper for you than a company with a lower tariff but high standing charge. In addition, not all companies operate in all areas of the country – and those that do sometimes charge different rates in different areas.

Working out the best deal should be relatively straightforward. If you've got Internet access, it's easy, as there are several websites that will compare prices for you. A good starting point is the Switch with Which? website (*www.switchwithwhich.co.uk*). This has research reports on energy companies and links to the price-comparison sites that have been approved by energywatch★, the independent consumer body for gas and electricity.

If you don't have Internet access, contact energywatch which will send you factsheets setting out up-to-date tariffs for companies operating in your area, along with a worked example showing you how to calculate the best deal.

Dual fuel and special deals

Many companies offer dual fuel deals, offering extra discounts if you buy both your gas and electricity from them – but don't auto-matically assume this will be the cheapest option. When *Which?* researched the best deals in November 1999, it found that if a company was particularly good value for one fuel, it tended to be more expensive for the other so that dual fuel deals rarely worked out as the best value.

There may be special deals available for older people. One of these is Staywarm from Powergen, a 'peace of mind' energy deal where customers pay a fixed fee for gas and electricity each month, regardless of how much they use. To qualify for Staywarm you must be aged over 60, with a maximum of four people and three bedrooms in your household. The charge varies according to the size of your household. You can find out more about the scheme by ringing (0800) 1694694, or look up *www.staywarm.co.uk*.

At the time of writing, Staywarm was the only deal of its kind, but energy tariffs change frequently, so it's worth checking out what's on offer from other companies too. And of course, while packages like these might save you money, they're not necessarily the best deal for everyone and you should still compare costs with your previous bills.

How to pay

Generally you'll find it cheapest to pay by monthly direct debit. This is the most efficient way for the companies to collect your money and they will usually charge lower rates to encourage you to opt for it.

Direct debits are usually for a fixed amount based on the amount of energy the company estimates you will use over a year. Compare this with your own meter readings to make sure you're not paying too much or too little. If the company's estimate is inaccurate, let it know.

If you pay quarterly, your energy company may offer you a discount for paying promptly but this is likely to be less than the discount for direct-debit payments.

Pre-payment meters are generally best avoided if possible – they tend to be much more expensive than standard rates. If you have a pre-payment meter, it's worth contacting other companies to see if you can find one that will allow you to pay by direct debit or quarterly bill, although you may have to pay them a substantial deposit to do so.

You can pay almost all utility bills at PayPoint locations in many newsagents, supermarkets and convenience stores; contact your utility company for more information.

Making energy services more accessible

All energy companies must ensure that their services are as accessible as possible to people who are older or chronically sick and those with disabilities. They do this through a Priority Service Register; all older people as well as people with disabilities can join these free and confidential registers. Services on offer include:

- a free gas safety check if everyone in your household is a pensioner

- bills in large print or Braille
- a password to confirm that company staff who call on you are genuine
- arranging to send your bills to a friend or relative if, say, you are going to be in hospital
- help if you find it hard to read the meter.

Ring your energy supplier to ask for an application form. A free brochure about this scheme is available from energywatch★.

Your energy company may also be able to help if you are having difficulty with the controls on your appliances; these can be adapted to make the knobs easier to turn or made more visible for people with poor sight. These adaptations are free – contact your energy company's customer service department for more details.

Complaints about energy companies

You are entitled to fixed amounts of compensation if energy companies do not meet certain standards of service: for example, failing to keep an appointment or in the event of supply interruptions. You can get full details of the standards and relevant criteria from your supplier.

If you have a complaint, contact your supplier first. If this does not resolve the problem, contact energywatch★ for further advice. Ofgem★ and, in Northern Ireland, Ofreg★, are the regulators of electricty and gas companies. These independent bodies monitor energy companies to make sure they comply with their statutory obligations.

Energy efficiency

Making your home as energy-efficient as possible will save you money on your fuel bills, improve the comfort of your home, and is good for the environment as well.

For in-depth advice consult the *The Which? Guide to the Energy-Saving Home* from Which? Books★. The Energy Saving Trust★ (EST) has lots of information about energy efficiency on its website, and staff can give you free guidance either over the phone or face to face at one of the EST's network of local Energy Efficiency Advice Centres – contact the EST for more details.

Simple ways to save energy

These energy-saving measures from experts at the EST are easy to put in place and can cut down your bills.

- Replace light-bulbs that you use for an average of four hours or more a day with an energy-saving equivalent. Energy-efficient bulbs cost around £5 each, but will give you a saving on your bills of £10 over the year.
- To eliminate draughts and wasted heat use an easy-to-fix brush or PVC seal on your exterior doors – this costs around £5. Remember, however, that ventilation is also important, especially if you have open fires, gas fires or a boiler with a flue (see pages 53–4 for more details).
- Appliances such as TVs and stereos continue to use electricity when they're on stand-by. Switch them off properly when you've finished using them unless the manual advises otherwise.
- While you want hot water to be hot, it needn't be scalding. For most people, setting the cylinder thermostat at 60°C is fine and can save you up to £10 a year.

The EST can also give you advice about the cost-effectiveness of more expensive energy-saving measures such as double-glazing, cavity wall insulation and central heating systems.

Help with costs

The **winter fuel payment** is available to almost everyone aged over 60 (it is not means-tested). Currently you are paid either £200 or £100 depending on your household circumstances. If you get a state retirement pension or certain other benefits, or if you received the payment last year, you should automatically receive the money before Christmas each year. If you don't fit these criteria you'll need to make a claim.

The rules for eligibility have changed, so if you were 60 or over during the winters between 1997 and 2000, but did not qualify for a winter fuel payment under the criteria then in operation, you may now be able to make a back-dated claim for one or more of those years. For more information or to make a claim, call the Winter Fuel Payment Helpline on (08459) 151515.

If you receive Income Support (now also called the Minimum Income Guarantee) or other income-related benefits, you should automatically be paid **cold weather payments** when the average temperature is recorded as, or is forecast to be, 0°C or below over seven days in a row in your local area. This payment is currently £8.50 per week. (Age Concern★ suggests keeping the temperature in the room you use most at 21°C during cold weather.)

A large number of **grants and other schemes** are available to help with the costs of making your home more energy-efficient. The grants on offer vary across the UK and range from special low prices for low-energy light-bulbs to cash-back schemes for people installing condensing boilers, as well as help with the costs of draught-proofing, insulation or even installing central heating. Some of the grants are available to anyone, others only to those over 60 or people on a low income.

It's worth checking what's on offer – the EST★ has an excellent database with details of all grants and offers available from the government, the different energy companies and local authorities. You can contact the EST by phone for details (call your local EST Energy Efficiency Advice Centre★) or you can look up the EST website. You enter a few simple details such as your postcode and whether you are on any benefits and will get a list of all the grants available to you.

Water

Fitting a meter

If you use less water than the average household, a water meter may save you money. Ask your water company for advice on whether switching to a water meter would make sense in your particular case; it can give you details of its metered and unmetered tariffs and will probably have a leaflet with a 'ready reckoner' to help you estimate your water usage. Alternatively, if you've got access to the Internet, many water companies' websites (as well as sites such as *www.buy.co.uk*) have an online calculator which will do the sums for you.

Your water company will install a meter free of charge unless the location or pipework makes it impractical (for example, the pipework has to be moved or split to serve your property alone). If you subsequently change your mind, provided it's no more than a year since you had the meter installed, you have the right to go back to unmetered charging. However, this applies only to the household that had the meter installed. If you've bought a house that already has a water meter, you don't have this right, although your water company may have its own policy and will be able to give you more details.

If a meter cannot be fitted at your property, your water company should offer you an 'assessed charge' which should be a better reflection of how much water you actually use than the standard rateable charge.

Making water services more accessible

Water companies must make sure their services are accessible as possible – for example, bills should be made available in Braille, large type or audio tape, and all water companies now offer a password scheme for people concerned about personal security in the home. Contact the customer services number on your last bill to find out more, or get a copy of *Services for disabled or elderly customers: Guidance to companies* from Ofwat★.

If you have a meter, are on benefits and someone in your household has a medical condition that means you need to use extra water, you may qualify for a discount on your bill. Contact the customer services department of your water company to find out more.

Complaints about water companies

You can get leaflets from your water company setting out its guaranteed service standards, which include things like compensation for unplanned interruptions of water supply that meet set criteria.

In England and Wales water companies are regulated by Ofwat★ (the Office of Water Services). This includes independent regional consumer committees called WaterVoice. If you have a complaint which isn't resolved by discussion with your water company, contact the WaterVoice for your area (the address will be in the phone book). If you are not happy with the way WaterVoice handles the problem, the complaint will be passed on to Ofwat's Director General. You should refer problems about water quality to the Drinking Water Inspectorate (DWI)★.

In Scotland, the regulatory body is the Water Industry Commissioner for Scotland★. In Northern Ireland, the government provides water services and you should contact the Northern Ireland Water Service★, an agency within the Department for Regional Development.

Home phones

BT lost its monopoly on home phone services almost 20 years ago – but 70 per cent of us still use BT to make all our home calls. You may save money by switching company or by using another company to make some calls. Changing companies doesn't mean you have to change your number, although the new company may charge you for keeping an existing number.

Working out the best deal on phones is not straightforward. There's no single best-buy company and it can be hard to untangle the many different discount schemes and packages. This section is a guide to what's on offer to help you choose the service that suits you best.

Choosing a home phone company

There are several different types of phone company you can use for your calls.

- Traditional wire network phone companies – BT★ and Kingston Communications★ (in the Hull area only).
- Cable companies – NTL★ and Telewest★. These offer connection via a fibre optic network to over half the UK's homes. Check with them to see if they cover your area.
- Indirect operators can redirect some or all of your calls to another company, using your existing phone line and number (see opposite for more information).
- Companies offering new 'one bill' services use BT's network but bill customers for both line rental and calls – for example, Servista★.

Indirect operators

If you make a lot of overseas calls, it's worth considering using an indirect operator. They are increasingly offering competitive national and even local rates. To use an indirect operator, you'll either need to enter a code, dial a freephone number or use a special autodialler box which re-routes your calls. The company may charge you for the autodialler.

Alternatively you can opt for 'carrier pre-selection' whereby your indirect service provider organises for BT to divert your calls to its service at the exchange. If you opt for carrier pre-selection and you have a burglar or community alarm that uses this phone line, you must check with the service provider that it will carry these types of calls in an emergency (carrier pre-selection does not affect normal 999 emergency services calls).

Indirect operators bill you only for the calls you make with them and you continue to pay your existing phone company for line rental and any other calls. There's usually no minimum contract term and if you find you aren't saving money or that using the service is inconvenient, you can simply stop using it.

Comparing prices

A number of websites will compare tariffs for you, but as we went to press none had yet been awarded Oftel's Price Assurance Standard (PASS) mark. You can find details of the scheme, plus links to any websites that have since signed up to it, at *www.oftel.gov.uk*.

If you do not have Internet access, you will need to contact the phone companies you're interested in and ask for a copy of their tariffs. Reviewing old bills will give you a good idea of how you use the phone and you can compare rates with your current company. You should make sure you take discount schemes into account (see below).

Discount schemes

If you're a BT customer, the Friends and Family discount scheme is worth joining. It's free and gives you a 10 per cent discount on 10 numbers, including one international and one mobile number, and an extra 10 per cent off calls to one 'best friend' number. Call (0800) 800150 to register.

Two other discount schemes which may be relevant if you rarely use the phone are the Light User scheme and the In-Contact Plus scheme. Under the Light User scheme, if you spend less than the scheme threshold (currently £18.75 a quarter) on calls you get a rebate. The In-Contact Plus scheme is for people who want to receive incoming calls, but don't want to make many calls themselves. The quarterly line rental is cheaper than normal, but apart from calls to the Emergency Services or the Operator, you can't make outgoing calls unless you use a special pre-payment phone card (these calls cost 10p per minute). You are not eligible for either of these schemes if you use another fixed line or mobile phone service. You can find out more about the schemes and qualifying criteria by calling (0800) 800150.

Many other discounts are offered by telephone companies. You'll need to check the small print to make sure you know what's really being offered. Watch out for the following.

- Adverts often claim big savings on BT's standard rates. But these don't usually take into account BT's discount schemes. For instance if you're considering using an indirect operator for regular calls to just one international number, check the tariff against BT's Friends and Family scheme.
- Companies that round up call charges to the nearest minute rather than billing you by the second.
- Minimum charges for calls or connection fees can mount up if you tend to make a lot of short calls.

Choosing a phone handset

There are many different types of phone on the market – analogue or digital and corded or cord-free. Here are some points to bear in mind.

- If you have a cordless phone you can carry the handset around with you so you don't have to rush to the phone, and can hear it in different parts of the house.
- Some models of cordless phone come with more than one handset and can be used as an intercom system around the house – very useful if someone is in bed with flu, say.
- With cordless (and some corded) phones, the keypad is on the handset. This can be a nuisance when you're following instructions of the 'press the # key now' type.

- Don't rely on a cordless model as the only phone in your house as it may not work if there is a power cut.
- Phones are available with easily visible key-pads – these tend to be corded phones. They are widely available and the Royal National Institute of the Blind (RNIB)★ also stocks them.
- If you dislike fiddly buttons on phones, try them out in shops before you buy. With cordless models especially, some of the handsets are smaller than you might think.
- If you use a hearing aid, you may find that a digital phone causes interference. Ricability★ and the Royal National Institute for Deaf People (RNID)★ can give you further information on using a phone with a hearing aid.
- Some phones let you adjust the ringer volume or pitch. But check this out – the range of adjustment may be limited and may not make the phone easier to hear in practice.

Ricability★'s booklet *Stay in touch* is an excellent guide to phones for older people and people with a disability (including hearing difficulties). The RNID★ can also advise on a variety of devices to help you hear telephone conversations more clearly. These range from amplifiers to neckloops used in conjunction with a hearing aid.

Making home phone services more accessible

Industry regulations mean that fixed-line telephone companies must offer extra services to people with certain disabilities. This includes free directory enquiries for people unable to use the phone book, alternative formats for bills or literature and priority fault repair. Contact the customer services department of your phone company for full details. The booklet *Stay in touch* from Ricability★ is a good source of comprehensive, independent guidance.

If you have a disability or are chronically sick, you may be able to get some help with the cost of your telephone service from your local authority. Local authorities decide for themselves what help to give and what criteria people have to meet to be eligible. For further information contact the Social Services department of your local authority or get a copy of the Age Concern★ factsheet *Help with telephones*.

RNID Typetalk is a service which enables a person with hearing loss to communicate with a hearing person. The textphone user dials a special prefix before the number he or she wants to call and an operator joins the line. The operator reads out exactly what has been typed to the hearing person and will then type the reply into a textphone. If you use this service you should be able to get a rebate towards the cost of text transmission calls; contact RNID★ for further details.

Complaints about home and mobile phone companies

All telecommunications – home and mobile phones, faxes and the Internet – are currently covered by Oftel★, but from January 2004 a new regulator, Ofcom★, should be in place. This body will regulate the UK communications sectors, including televison, radio and broadcasting as well as telecommunications. Until then, Oftel's Consumer Representation Section can give you advice on taking your complaint further if you haven't been able to resolve it with your telephone company. If this is the case, your options might include contacting the new telecoms ombudsman, Otelo★. Otelo can only investigate complaints about companies which have signed up to its system (currently there are nine including BT, NTL and Vodaphone) and other criteria apply – contact it to find out more.

In Northern Ireland, the Northern Ireland Advisory Committee on Telecommunications (NIACT)★ handles complaints on behalf of Oftel.

Mobile phones

Ownership of mobile phones has increased dramatically in recent years. Many people value the peace of mind a mobile can give – it's easy to call for help if your car breaks down, for example. They're also great for keeping in touch while you're out and about or on holiday. But it's important to get the right tariff or they can be an expensive buy.

Choosing a payment method

There are three ways you can own a mobile phone. You can have a **pre-pay** phone where you pay up front for calls, a **contract,** where you pay monthly by direct debit for your calls and line rental, and a **no line-rental** deal, which is a sort of hybrid between contract and pre-pay where you pay in arrears for calls by direct debit but there's no contract and no line rental.

If you use your mobile for less than three minutes a day or simply want one for emergency use, then a pre-pay or no line-rental phone will probably be best for you. The up-front cost of the phone handset may be more expensive than with a contract, but the call charges will work out cheaper.

If you're going to use your mobile for more than about three minutes a day, a contract tariff will probably be the best value. Contract tariffs involve little or no initial outlay but do commit you to making 12 monthly payments for line rental and calls. Depending on the deal, you get a number of inclusive 'free' minutes each month before you start paying for calls.

Choosing a network

The four main networks at the time of writing are Orange*, O2* (formerly BT Cellnet), T-Mobile* (formerly One2One) and Vodafone*. Virgin Mobile* has its own billing system but uses T-Mobile's network.

All four networks claim to cover almost 100 per cent of the UK population but most mobile users experience loss of reception occasionally. The best thing to do is ask friends or neighbours whether they have any problems using mobiles locally. If you make a lot of calls to one particular person it may be cheaper if you're both on the same network.

Choosing a tariff

To compare tariffs you can either look for past reports in *Which?* magazine or, if you have access to the Internet, look at the price-comparison calculator on *www.switchwithwhich.co.uk* (you don't need to be a subscriber to *Which?* magazine to use this website).

You can also ask for advice in shops but bear in mind that in November 2000, *Which?* research found that most shops gave poor advice, with the exception of Carphone Warehouse. Before you go shopping think about how you will use the phone. When and how often will you use it? Who will you call and how long might an average call be? Will you want to use the phone abroad? You should expect to be asked these sorts of questions by the sales assistant. If he or she does not ask these questions, you are unlikely to get sound advice.

Making mobile phones more accessible

New conditions of service are being introduced in the summer of 2003 to ensure that mobile phone companies provide similar services to people with disabilities as those offered by home-phone companies. Contact the customer services department of your company to find out more – most networks publish guidance for older customers or those with disabilities detailing the services and products they provide.

All mobile phones sold these days are digital, so if you use a hearing aid, you may get interference when you use a mobile. You can buy a neckloop for some mobiles that gets around this problem. For more details or to buy a neckloop, contact RNID*.

For information on complaints about mobile phones see page 38.

If you can't pay your utility bill

The golden rule is – speak to the company as soon as possible. In almost every situation, you'll be able to sort out a way to pay the bill, perhaps in instalments over time. You can also contact your local Citizen's Advice Bureau* for advice. There are special regulations to protect older customers who have trouble paying utility bills.

- **Gas and electricity companies** are not allowed to disconnect people over 60 who can't pay bills during the winter months, so if you have trouble paying a bill, make sure you let the company know if everyone in your household meets this criteria. If you are on benefit and are in debt with your fuel bills, you may be able to use the Fuel Direct scheme where money is taken directly from your benefits to pay your bills. You can find out more about this scheme from your supplier or Social Security office.
- **Water companies** are not allowed to disconnect any householders for non-payment of their bill.

- **Home telephone companies** do not have the same regulations about disconnection as the other utility companies. However, they should only disconnect people as a last resort and must not disconnect a person with a disability which means they are housebound.

Urgent repairs

All the energy and water companies should give high priority to essential repair work for older people or people with disabilities (as should the telephone services if you have a disability or are housebound). Some mobile networks also offer this. So, if you need an urgent repair and fit the priority category, make sure the company knows about your circumstances.

Chapter 3

Safety and security in the home

Despite the impression you can get from the press, retired people are no more at risk from crime than anyone else. In fact, people aged over 60 are three times *less* likely to be affected by crime than the rest of the population, and most burglaries take place during the day when people are out at work. Some companies offer retired people a discount on home insurance, partly because they are actually less of a risk as they don't tend to leave their house unoccupied all day, every day. However, fear of crime can be almost as worrying as crime itself, so it's only sensible to make your home as secure as possible and to pay attention to your personal safety.

We give some starting points here. This chapter also gives advice on how to prevent accidents. Many of the recommendations are the sort of precautions that apply to everyone, but as accidents and falls can be more serious as we get older, it pays to take extra care.

Who to contact in an emergency

In an emergency, don't hesitate to dial 999 for help. The operator who takes your call will assess your case over the phone and will respond immediately if necessary. If the person doesn't think the problem warrants an emergency call-out, he or she may recommend that you contact your local police station or doctor for further advice.

The last time you want to be hunting round for a phone number is when you need it urgently. So it makes sense to keep a list of useful phone numbers to hand. This might include:

- the local police station
- your doctor and NHS Direct★
- neighbours, particularly those with keys to your house

- Transco ((0800) 111999) for suspected gas leaks
- your electricity, gas and water companies.

It's also helpful to have a list of useful tradespeople such as lock-smiths, plumbers and electricians – perhaps you already have details of people you've used before. If you've moved to a new area, it's a good idea to gather contact details before you need them in an emergency. Asking friends or neighbours for recommendations is a good way to find someone reliable. Alternatively you can contact Quality Mark*, the government-approved quality assurance scheme, to see if any members are in your area. This scheme is a national register of independently assessed tradespeople who work in almost all aspects of home maintenance. It offers a complaints process and a warranty of up to six years on all work. Always obtain two or three names and numbers – even when you need work done fast, it's wise to get several quotes.

Letting people into your home

Consider fitting a door viewer and chain so you know who's calling before you answer the door. Some officials, such as gas or electricity meter readers, may call on you unannounced. Always insist on seeing an identity card with a photograph first, even if the caller is in uniform. If in doubt, shut the door on the caller and ring his or her company to check identification. Use the phone number in the phone book or on a bill, not on an identity card. If you're still suspicious, ring the police. Most utility companies operate a scheme whereby you can agree a confidential password in advance that the caller will use whenever they call on you. Contact your company for details.

In general, don't let salespeople in but deal with them on the doorstep. If you do let someone into your house, stay with them and never let them wander around alone. Anyone with a legitimate reason to call on you should carry an ID card, and will willingly display it. Don't let anyone you don't know – male or female, adult or child – into your house, even if they claim it is an emergency.

A secure home

Most burglaries are opportunistic crimes. So you should aim to make your home as unattractive a target as possible. Take a hard look at your house from a burglar's point of view. Look for the weak spots. What would be the easiest way to break in?

Crime Prevention Officers (CPOs) are police officers who can give you free advice about home security tailored to your neighbourhood. In many areas, CPOs will also make home visits to give specific advice on how you could improve your security. Ring your local police station to find out how to get in touch with your CPO.

Locks and bolts

The locks on your back door should be as good as the locks on your front door. You may find you get a discount on your home insurance if you fit high-security door and window locks – in some areas it may be a condition of the policy. If so, make sure the locks you have comply with the policy standards and that you meet the requirements (for example, ensuring the locks are used every time you go out), otherwise an insurance claim may be rejected.

Door locks

There are two main types of door lock – cylinder rim locks, where the lock body is fitted to the surface of the door, and mortice locks that fit into a recess (the mortice) in the edge of the door. Both types can be deadlocked (so that the lock can't be forced by a burglar sliding a flexible tool between the latch and the door frame). Some simpler rimlocks don't offer this protection and shouldn't be used as the only lock on an exit door.

The most secure locks are kitemarked to BS 3621. Ideally, you should have an automatic deadlocking rimlock and a five-lever mortice deadlock. Be particularly careful if any door has glass panels: make sure that at least one lock is out of reach of the panes, and preferably fit laminated glass for extra security.

Fire safety

Remember that you may need to get out of the house quickly in case of fire. If you are indoors, keep keys to mortice locks and window locks handy and make sure everyone in the house knows where they are.

Other security measures for doors

Consider replacing weak doors that have plywood panels with solid doors. A good external door should be at least 44mm thick and should be hung on three heavy 100mm hinges. The standard to look for is BSI PAS24-1. Manufacturers that meet this standard can use the police-approved 'Secured by Design' logo, a distinctive blue-and-white chequered diamond. Your letterbox should be at least 400mm away from any locks, so a burglar can't reach the lock through the letterbox.

Several other items can give additional security and help you see who's calling. A door chain allows you to open the door slightly to check a caller's identification. Buy the sturdiest chain you can find and secure it with screws that are at least 30mm long. You can also buy metal door limiters that are, in effect, heavy-duty door chains.

You could fit a door viewer to your door to enable you to see callers before opening the door. Some give a clearer image than others, so have a look through them in the shop first. Closed circuit TV (CCTV) systems can give you a better view. Basic DIY systems cost from £30, more sophisticated ones allow you to talk to your caller via an intercom and cost from around £100. Security mortice bolts or surface-mounted sliding bolts will help to strengthen the top and bottom of the door, and hinge bolts (sometimes called dog bolts) will protect the hinged side of the door from being forced.

Discounts and shopping around

Some of the large do-it-yourself superstores offer discounts for the over-60s on certain days. But don't automatically assume this will give you the cheapest deal – it pays to shop around. When *Which?* checked the price of a shopping basket of home security products in March 1999, it found a wide range of prices. Even though two chains offered discounts to over-60s at that time, they were not the cheapest.

Window locks

Fit locks to all downstairs windows and any upstairs windows where a burglar might be able to gain access. Window locks differ in design far more than door locks and no single established standard covers them. The type of lock to use will depend on what your windows are made of and whether they are sash or casement windows. When *Which?* tested window locks in October 1998, it found that none of them held up against a determined attempt to break in for more than one minute. But window locks are fairly easy to fit and do help put off a casual thief – get the sort that show from the outside as an added visual deterrent.

The standard to look for with windows is BS 7950, which allows the window-manufacturer to use the police-approved 'Secured by Design' logo. If your windows don't already meet this standard, check with the company that installed or made the frames to see if their security can be improved. You generally can't add extra locks to UPVC frames once they're installed. French doors can be particularly vulnerable – if they have wood frames, make sure they have bolts at the top and bottom; mortice rack bolts are the best sort.

Spare keys

Be careful with your spare keys. Thieves know all the usual hiding places – like on a string tied to the inside of the letterbox, or under an outside doormat or flowerpot. When you go out, it's best not to leave any spare keys in an obvious place; otherwise, if someone did break in through a window, they could simply walk out of the door with their booty. Be especially careful with spare car keys – a bowl on the hall table is probably the worst place to leave them. A thief could be out of your house and off with your car within seconds.

If you move to a new house, you should make changing the locks one of your first jobs – you never know who's got sets of the old keys. And if you lose your door keys, change the locks as soon as possible.

If possible, find someone you trust who lives nearby and give them a set of keys in case you lock yourself out or need help while you are indoors. Don't label the keys with your full name and address – use a distinctive key ring or your first name instead.

Burglar alarms

A burglar alarm is a very effective deterrent but can be expensive. There are two main types.

Most **bell-only alarms** consist of a combination of sensors that guard the main doors and windows, plus a number of movement detectors. When the alarm is switched on, if any of its sensors detect an intrusion, the bell on the outside of the house (and the siren inside) will ring. A professionally installed bell-only alarm will cost from around £400 to £1,000, depending on the system. You can get bell-only alarms that you fit yourself costing around £50 to £200 from DIY stores. Some of these are wire-free, which makes them simpler to fit. If a bell-only alarm goes off, the police won't act unless they have some other indication of crime (for example, a call from you or a witness).

A **remote signalling alarm** works in a similar way, but when the alarm is triggered an alarm is sent to a 24-hour monitoring centre, which can call out the police if necessary. This type of alarm is more expensive – usually well over £1,500 plus an annual monitoring fee to the control centre of about £60 to £300 per year. However, the police will only respond at once if you have this type of alarm.

If you're having an alarm professionally installed, always get at least three quotes and check that the company is approved by the National Security Inspectorate, the Alarms Inspectorate and Security Council, Integrity 2000 or the Security Systems and Alarms Inspection Board. You should also make sure that the system conforms to BS 4737 or BS 6799. Be wary of systems that just claim to be 'BS compliant' without specifying these numbers, as this could refer to an electrical rather than a security standard.

If your insurance company has made an alarm a condition of the policy or is giving you a discount for having one, check that the type you choose meets with its approval and make sure you know about any conditions, such as always having to set it when you leave the house. If your alarm has just one box outside the front of your house, it's a good idea to install a second dummy box at the back as a low-cost visual deterrent.

Watch out for maintenance contracts: some may tie you to a contract for several years, with annual fees that rapidly increase. You don't have to have a maintenance contract with a bell-only alarm, but you will with a monitored alarm.

A watchful eye

Secure windows, doors and burglar alarms are important. A sense that the local community is keeping an eye-out is another powerful deterrent to crime. As most burglaries take place during the day, people at home during this time can do particularly valuable work in keeping an eye out for anyone acting suspiciously. If you see anything out of the ordinary, make a note of the person's description and contact the police. Don't be tempted to get involved in any situation yourself.

A Neighbourhood Watch scheme is a voluntary group of local residents working in liaison with the police to help prevent burglary and other crimes in the area. Your local Crime Prevention Officer (CPO) will be able to put you in touch with the Neighbourhood Watch Co-ordinator for your area. If there isn't a local Neighbourhood Watch scheme, the CPO will be able to give you information about setting one up.

Case history: June

After a number of neighbours had their cars broken into, June decided to look into setting up a Neighbourhood Watch group. She spoke to her local CPO and Neighbourhood Watch Co-ordinator. Along with a couple of neighbours she organised a meeting in a nearby church hall, inviting everyone who lived on her street. The meeting began with the CPO giving a talk about improving security in general, and then the Neighbourhood Watch Co-ordinator explained how the street could form its own group.

That was two years ago, and the group now has regular monthly meetings. June produces a regular newsletter with details of local crime figures and warnings of any scams going round the area. It took a while to get street signs erected to show the Neighbourhood Watch area, but most residents have got stickers in their windows. Most recently, the group arranged the loan of a property marking kit, so that people could mark their postcode on valuables.

When you go away

If you're going on holiday, move items such as the computer and video out of view of the windows, set a timer switch or two so lights come on in the evening, and lock away garden tools and ladders. Tell friends that you are going to be away and ask them to keep an eye on your home.

If you're going away for any length of time, the Royal Mail offers a Keepsafe service which will hold mail for just over two months so you don't have to worry about a give-away pile of post on your doormat. The cost of the service varies according to how long you want it for – currently it costs from £5.25 for up to 17 days to £15.75 for up to 66 days. For more information, pick up a leaflet from your local post office.

Check the terms of your home insurance policy, too – various types of cover, such as theft cover, may be withdrawn or limited if you go away on holiday for a long time (usually defined as over 30 days). You may also have to observe special conditions, such as draining the water system.

Storing valuables

If you have important documents, jewellery or other small valuables that you don't need at home, put them in a safety deposit box at a bank. Don't keep large amounts of cash at home. Photographs of any other valuable items, such as antiques, will help the police to trace them if they are stolen and could be useful for insurance claims. For televisions, videos and cameras, use an ultra-violet marker pen (available from stationers) to write your postcode and house number on each item.

Exterior lighting

As well as deterring theives, exterior lighting will be convenient when you're returning home in the dark. The most popular type of security lighting is movement-detecting or 'passive infra-red' (PIR) lighting, which switches on when it detects something crossing its beam. However, these lights (commonly 300W or 500W) generally use more power than is really needed, which wastes energy. They also tend to be set off easily by dogs or cats for example, which can annoy neighbours or cause unnecessary alarm. If you choose PIR lighting, 150W should be powerful enough for most gardens.

The Association of Chief Police Officers now recommends 'dusk to dawn' photoelectric cell lights which stay on all night instead. Recent research shows that a constant level of light is a better deterrent and if you use these lights with low-energy long-life compact fluorescent lamps, they can be cheaper to run than PIR lighting too. For more information about energy-efficient lighting see *The Which? Guide to the Energy-Saving Home*, from Which Books*.

Fitting most exterior lights involves drilling holes in an exterior wall and wiring up the light to the internal electrical circuit, so unless you're confident about your own skills this is a job for an electrician. The *Which? Book of Wiring and Lighting* explains how to tackle electrical projects for those who want to try DIY.

Garden security

You can use fencing, hedging and gates as an effective part of your home security. In the front garden, stick to low fences or hedges. Anything more than a metre high will provide a screen for someone breaking in. In the back garden, it's a good idea to put a trellis on top of a fence or wall. This will make it more difficult to climb over – especially if you grow a prickly climber up through it. Good thorny hedging plants which also look attractive include some of the beriberis, holly, hawthorn and the hedging rose, *Rosa rugosa*.

If you have some particularly valuable plants or garden ornaments, consider securing them with land anchors. But be realistic – you don't want to spoil the look of your garden by chaining everything down. It's worth marking valuable garden ornaments and tools with your postcode and house number, so if they're stolen and recovered by the police, they can be returned to you. You can etch your details on the base of ornaments so you don't spoil their appearance.

It's worth adding up the cost of replacing plants, containers, tools and furniture for insurance purposes – you may be surprised at the total. Read the small print in your insurance policy; the terms, conditions and payouts for garden items tend to vary widely and you may want to add some of your garden items on.

Pay particular attention to your garden shed. Besides the value of its contents, your shed may be a target for a thief looking for tools with which to break into your house. The vulnerable spots in most sheds are the door hinges, the locks and the windows. Hinges should be attached with non-returnable screws so the door can't be removed. Window locks or wire mesh fitted on the inside of the windows can be a good deterrent.

Victim Support schemes

Victim Support schemes offer free and confidential information and support to anyone who has been affected by crime, whether or not it has been reported and regardless of when it happened. This includes practical help and information on compensation and insurance. Victim Support also runs the Witness Service in the criminal courts to provide support and information to witnesses, victims and their families or friends. You can contact Victim Support through its national helpline on (0845) 3030900 or through your local police station. For information in Scotland call (0845) 6039213.

Extra help and advice

You may qualify for extra help with security measures. Some local authorities give discounts on security installations, particularly for older people whose homes have been repeatedly broken into. Some charities run similar schemes and Help the Aged★ has a free home security service, HandyVan, in some parts of the country for people on low incomes. To find out if there's a HandyVan scheme in your area call (01255) 473999. You can also contact your local CPO to find out if there are any other schemes in your area.

Preventing accidents at home

Falls are the most common type of accident in the home for older people. As we age taking a tumble becomes potentially more serious, as bone density decreases and fractures occur more easily. So it makes sense to take extra care and follow these simple precautions.

- Instead of balancing on a chair when reaching things from high cupboards or changing a lightbulb, get a proper step stool which is secure and can be kept conveniently to hand. Or better still, move things out of high cupboards so you don't have to reach at all.
- If your stairs are steep it might help to add an extra handrail to the inner wall.
- Replace any stair carpet that shows signs of fraying promptly and make sure the staircase is well lit.
- We need relatively high light levels as we grow older. Aim for similar lighting levels in all rooms.
- Having lamps as well as overhead lights means changing a bulb can wait until daylight (or until someone else can do it for you). But don't delay longer than necessary – keep a stock of spare bulbs in.
- Make sure that there are no rucked-up carpets or rugs, and that rugs have a non-slip backing.
- Run cables as close to the wall as possible – not across the room, and never under the carpet.
- In the bathroom, rubber mats and extra handrails in or near the bath are useful to prevent slipping.
- If you're using a ladder, place it at a safe angle to the wall and don't lean out from it when at the top. Have someone else on hand, preferably supporting the ladder at the bottom. Or consider whether it would be wiser to get someone else to do the job for you.
- Keep active; exercise improves balance and strength and may help prevent falls.

Electrical safety

Many electricity companies have telephone information lines which can help with queries about electrical safety or specific services for older people or people with disabilities. If you are worried about the wiring in your home, your electricity company may also offer a visual wiring check of the mains circuit – with some companies this is free, others may charge a small fee. Otherwise, employ a reliable electrician, but get at least two estimates first.

Electrical know-how

- Don't overload sockets – you shouldn't use more than one adapter per socket, and each socket should carry no more than 13 amps of current in total. Don't run more than one appliance that uses lots of current, such as a kettle or television, from one socket.
- Don't use any electrical appliances in the bathroom that have an ordinary three-pin plug. Any appliances used there should be specifically designed for the bathroom.
- At night, switch off and unplug all electrical appliances not designed to stay on.
- Danger signs include hot plugs and sockets, fuses that blow for no obvious reason, flickering lights and scorch marks on sockets or plugs. Get the problem checked out by a reliable electrician, or dispose of the product and buy a replacement.
- Don't let cables or plugs get wet, and keep liquids away from electrical appliances – it's dangerous to put a vase of flowers on top of the TV, for example. Make sure the kettle isn't leaking, and don't fill it up when it's plugged in.

Gas safety

If you think you have a gas leak or can smell gas, you should phone Transco on (0800) 111999 immediately.

The law on gas safety

If all the people living in your home are over 60, have a disability or are chronically sick then your gas company will carry out a free annual safety check. Contact your gas supplier for details. If you are a tenant, then by law your landlord must have any gas appliances checked for safety at least once a year, and get any faults repaired by a CORGI*-registered gas installer.

You need to have gas appliances serviced regularly, regardless of the gas safety check – boilers should be serviced every year to ensure they are working efficiently and safely.

Carbon monoxide

Carbon monoxide (CO) is a highly poisonous gas which can kill. Its most common source in the home is from gas fires, boilers and solid fuel appliances. Dangerous amounts of CO can build up as a result of poor installation, servicing or damage to an appliance, or where rooms are poorly ventilated.

The gas is difficult to recognise because it has no colour, no smell and no taste, and the flu-like symptoms it causes (headaches, sickness and dizziness) are easily misdiagnosed or ignored. Often appliances show no danger signs, but watch out for an orange or yellow flame (rather than a blue one), a pilot light that keeps going out, or scorching, soot marks or stains around the equipment. You can take several simple steps to minimise the risks:

- have your boiler and all your gas appliances serviced regularly by a CORGI-registered engineer, and make sure chimneys are swept
- take care not to block air vents or cover outside flues
- installing a CO detector in your home isn't a substitute for having your gas appliances regularly serviced, but it will give you added protection and peace of mind.

Choosing a CO detector

You can get battery-powered or mains-powered alarms and card detectors. The cards give a visual display if they detect carbon monoxide, but they don't draw your attention to a build-up of CO in your home in the way that an alarm does.

Mains-powered alarms avoid the problems of having to change batteries, but won't work in a power cut. Battery models are more flexible because they can be installed in places where it's inconvenient to provide a mains supply. You should choose an alarm that complies with BS 7860, or the equivalent North American standard UL 2034.

Fit the alarm according to the manufacturer's instructions. Generally, it should be situated on the ceiling or wall in rooms where there could be a source of CO – those containing a boiler, water heater or fire, for example. Many deaths occur when people are asleep, so it's vital to make sure the alarm is loud enough to wake you. If it isn't, fit a second one nearer to your bedroom.

Fire safety

Every house should be fitted with smoke alarms. They're cheap, easy to fit and could save your life. Many people just rely on one smoke alarm, but this isn't really enough for anything but a small flat or bungalow.

You can buy smoke alarms from DIY stores, hardware and electrical shops as well as supermarkets. They cost from just £5 and should be easy to fit, but if you find it difficult for any reason, ask a neighbour or a family member to do it for you. Your local fire station may also be able to help, so don't put off getting protected.

There are two types of smoke alarm: ionisation and optical. The ionisation type is good at detecting small, fast-burning fires. The optical type is better at detecting smouldering, slow-burning fires. If you need two or more alarms, it's best to have both types. You can also get combination alarms which detect both slow- and fast-burning fires. Whichever you choose, make sure it has the BS 5446 Part 1 kitemark.

Smoke alarms should be fitted in communal areas such as at the bottom of a staircase, in a hallway or an upstairs landing, preferably in the centre of the ceiling. Have at least one on each floor but don't fit them in the kitchen or bathroom – they may go off accidentally. Position the alarm according to the manufacturer's instructions. This will usually be at least 30cm from any wall or light fitting.

There are also smoke alarms for people who are hard of hearing. These have vibrating pads which go beneath your pillow or a flashing light and are available from the Royal National Institute for Deaf People (RNID)*.

Test your alarms every month, even if they have a self-test mechanism, and change the batteries every year. Some detectors on the market now have a ten-year battery life so will not need replacing as often.

Heaters and fires

If you use any electric, gas, paraffin or solid-fuel fires or heaters, make sure that they all have secure fireguards and keep them well away from any bedding, clothes or curtains or places where they could be knocked over. Never leave clothes drying in front of any fire or heater. Don't move any portable fire or heater when it is on or alight.

The popularity of candles as decorative items has soared over the last few years – and so have house fires caused by them. They can look lovely, but always use a proper holder for them and never leave a lighted candle unattended. Always make sure they are properly extinguished when you've finished using them.

Smoking in the home

If there is a smoker in the house, ensure that there are plenty of ashtrays around where they can't be knocked over easily. Never leave a burning cigarette in the ashtray – always stub it out properly and make sure the contents of any ashtray are cold before throwing them in the bin. Be wary of falling asleep while holding a cigarette – this is how many fires begin. Old foam-filled furniture in particular may be highly flammable. Smoking in bed is particularly dangerous and should be avoided.

Electric blankets

Some electric blankets can be left on all night, while others must be switched off before you get into bed. Whatever type you have, follow the instructions carefully, and make sure that the blanket is kept in good condition, stored without creasing when not in use, and serviced every few years. Never attempt to repair one yourself. If a blanket shows signs of damage or wear, return it to the manufacturer or replace it.

Dealing with fires

Everyone should have an escape plan of possible routes from their house in case of a fire. Make sure you never leave furniture or clutter blocking these routes. Your door and window keys should be kept somewhere accessible that everyone knows about. If a fire does break out, close internal doors to help prevent fire and smoke spreading quickly.

Be wary of tackling a fire, even if it seems small; the best idea is for everyone to get out of the house and then ring 999. If a fire is small and in its early stages, you might use a fire blanket in the kitchen, say, to smother flames such as those caused by a chip-pan fire – choose one that is kitemarked to BS 6575. Never throw water on to burning oil or fat. Fire extinguishers may be less helpful – they're more expensive, need servicing and if you use the wrong type of extinguisher on a fire, you will make the fire worse. You may also lose valuable time trying to deal with the fire yourself; possessions can always be replaced – your priority should be to get out of the house safely and as quickly as possible.

Further advice and information

The Community Fire Safety Officer at the Fire Brigade Headquarters for your area will be able to give you further advice on fire safety (find the number in the phone book). In some cases a firefighter may be able to visit your home to help you improve safety and advise or fit fire alarms. If you have Internet access, the National Community Fire Safety Office has a website with lots of detailed advice and information at *www.firekills.gov.uk*. Leaflets are also available from your local fire station.

Chapter 4

Your rights as a householder

A dispute with a neighbour, a problem with a builder or the local authority may become something more than a minor irritation once you are retired and at home at times of the day when you would previously have been out. It's always best to sort out matters in an amicable way if you can. However, it is helpful to know the legal position in case things get difficult. The Community Legal Service★ has a range of leaflets about common legal issues in England and Wales and a directory of community legal services.

As well as the information in this chapter, Which? Books★ also produces *160 Letters that Get Results*, which gives practical information on resolving common consumer problems.

Neighbours

Being good neighbours is not always easy, especially if you are living close together and have very different lifestyles. Legally speaking, you have certain rights and interests in relation to your property and, in turn, your neighbours have rights and interests of their own. At times, these rights may clash, causing tension or sometimes even a serious dispute.

Ways to resolve disputes

If a dispute arises between you and one of your neighbours, it's definitely worth trying to sort it out informally. You may have the right to involve the local authority or start legal action. But invoking these rights should be a last resort as it could escalate the dispute and sour the relationship between you and your neighbour. Try these suggestions to resolve a dispute amicably first.

- Meet informally to explain the problem. Sometimes your neighbours will be genuinely unaware that they are causing a problem and after realising that something is an issue they will be happy to do what they can to put it right.
- If the nuisance affects other people living nearby, talk to them too. Sometimes a neighbour might be quicker to accept there's a problem if he or she can see that it's not just you who's affected.
- If this fails to resolve the problem, start to keep a written record of incidents, recording times, dates and details of the problem.
- A mediation service might be able to resolve the situation (see overleaf for further details).

Case history: Frank

Frank lives in a ground-floor flat. Recently the flat above his was sold to a young couple who set about re-decorating. When he was chatting to them about the work he was dismayed to find they were planning to rip out the carpets and sand the floorboards. They'd already taken up the carpet and underlay in their sitting room – which was right above Frank's bedroom – and Frank was worried about the potential noise.

Frank went through his files and sure enough, he found there was a provision in the lease forbidding wooden or laminate flooring in the flats. 'They seemed a nice enough couple and I'm sure they just hadn't thought about the noise,' he says. Frank invited them into his flat to listen for themselves. 'With the carpet and underlay up, you could hear the TV almost as loudly as if you were in the room yourself and footsteps really reverberated. I mentioned the lease too, but casually, I didn't want them to think I was threatening to tell tales.' The couple hadn't read this part of the lease and were disappointed but accepted it and put down new carpets instead. 'I suppose if they hadn't, I would have gone to the management company, but I'm glad I didn't have to and we've stayed on good terms,' Frank concludes.

Mediation

There are free neighbourhood mediation services in many parts of the country; contact Mediation UK* for details of the service nearest to you.

Typically, if you contact a mediation service to ask for help with a neighbour dispute, trained mediators will visit you to find out more about the problem. The other party is then contacted to see if they are willing to take part. If so, they also receive a visit from the mediators.

If both parties agree to meet together with the mediators to try to work through a solution, the chances of a successful outcome are good. When the parties resolve their differences, they are asked to sign an agreement. This has no legal standing but helps to clarify what has been agreed and outlines individual responsibilities. Trying mediation does not affect your legal rights; you are still free to pursue a legal action, subject to any normal time limits that apply.

Contacting the local authority

In cases where neighbours may be breaching public health or pollution laws (including noise) contact the local authority environmental health department.

If you think there has been a breach of planning control, such as a neighbour carrying out building work without permission or using land for an unauthorised purpose, you should contact the planning department.

If your neighbour is a tenant, it may be worth contacting his or her landlord as many tenancy agreements include clauses about nuisance to neighbours and the landlord may be prepared to talk to the tenant about the problem. Local authorities have powers to deal with trouble-makers living in local authority housing. The law also covers other social landlords such as housing associations

Court action

In general, you should consider court action only as a last resort as it can be expensive, stressful, and if you have to continue living alongside your neighbours it is unlikely to promote a good relationship. You also need to bear in mind that behaviour that annoys you may not be a nuisance in the legal sense (see opposite), so you need to be sure you really have a case.

If you feel you have no option but to take court action, it's worth consulting a solicitor and/or your local Citizen's Advice Bureau (CAB)* first.

The legal meaning of nuisance

The law says that an occupier of property is not allowed to use it in such a way as to interfere with other people's reasonable enjoyment of their property. Loud music or barking dogs may fall into this legal category of 'nuisance', as might an offensive smell, or irritating smoke.

But just because you find something a nuisance doesn't mean the law is being broken. The law accepts that a fair amount of give and take is necessary in everyday living. For example, in a semi-detached property or flats a degree of noise penetration is unavoidable; you have to put up with what is reasonable. And you must react reasonably too, and not, say, turn up the volume on your television to drown the music from next-door's stereo.

Someone who is especially sensitive to a particular form of nuisance is not entitled to a legal remedy for behaviour that would not be a nuisance to others. For instance, if you like to have a nap in the afternoons but are disturbed by children regularly playing loudly in a neighbouring garden, you have no right to complain if other people going about their daily activities would find the noise level tolerable.

Common causes of disputes

Noise

If you are bothered by noisy neighbours, contact the environmental health department of your local authority. An environmental health officer (EHO) can advise and give an expert opinion on whether the problem constitutes a statutory nuisance. If the EHO considers there is a statutory nuisance and has been unable to resolve the matter through discussion, the local authority can serve a notice on the person causing the noise forbidding any further unreasonable noise. If the noise continues, your neighbours risk a fine of up to £2,000 plus a further £50 for each day the noise continues.

The Noise Act of 1996 gives local authorities additional powers to deal with loud noise from domestic premises between 11pm and 7am. Offenders are liable to a £100 fixed penalty, equipment such as a hi-fi can be confiscated and there is a maximum £1,000 fine for cases that come to court. Local authorities in England and Wales can use this law at their discretion to tackle noise problems.

In Scotland, the police may be willing to get involved if an informal approach to your neighbour has failed to reduce the noise nuisance.

Instead of contacting your local environmental health department, alternatively you can go direct to the magistrates' court (sheriff court in Scotland). You will need evidence and will have a better chance of success if you get statements from other neighbours or even a doctor's note saying the noise is affecting your health. If you win, your neighbours can be fined if they continue to be noisy. If you wish to pursue this route, contact the Justices' Clerk's Office at your local magistrates' court for further information on the procedure – look under 'Courts' in the phone book for the magistrates' court's details.

The National Society for Clean Air and Environmental Protection★ can offer general advice on noise and has a series of informative leaflets.

Gardens, hedges and bonfires

'Country smells'

With smells, it is important to take into account the type of neighbourhood. If you live in a rural area you must expect to put up with 'country smells' – up to a point, anyway. If, say, a neighbouring farmer chooses to put his manure heap next to your hedge when there are alternative sitings, it is reasonable to expect the farmer to change this.

In a similar way, if you live close to a factory or industrial site in an urban area, you must expect to put up with a degree of noise and possibly emissions. However, checks are in place to limit emissions into the atmosphere in the case of most industrial processes.

As a first step it may be worth contacting the environmental health department of your local authority.

Bonfires

If your neighbours are keen gardeners, they may be in the habit of lighting bonfires. In general, there are no restrictions on when bonfires can be lit, but check with your local authority for any by-laws. Whether the bonfires are a legal nuisance depends on whether the fires interfere with the use and enjoyment of your property, and whether they are more frequent than the ordinary person would consider reasonable.

If you can't sort out a dispute over bonfires amicably, you could try your local environmental health department – keep a detailed diary and get statements from others affected first. The authority can serve a notice requiring the fires to be either stopped (though this is unlikely) or to be lit less frequently. If your neighbours ignore the notice, the local authority could take them to the magistrates' court, which could impose a fine if they were found guilty. You can bypass the local authority and go straight to the court to ask for a 'nuisance order' if you wish – but remember that if you do you will need to prove your case, so make sure you have evidence in your support: a diary of events, other neighbours' statements and the like.

Overgrown gardens

Neighbours who let weeds overgrow their gardens can be a bane at times, but there is no law which says that people must be tidy. However, your local authority has powers to clear up areas within its control, if it considers a highly visible mess is ruining the 'amenity' and beauty of the neighbourhood – you may even be able to get the local authority to shift the rubbish if this is the case (these powers exist in England, Scotland and Wales). If the rubbish attracts vermin the council will certainly act. The council can serve a notice requiring the removal of the mess, and your neighbours could face a considerable fine if they do not comply.

Overhanging branches

If branches from a neighbour's tree overhang your property, you are entitled to cut them off at the point where they cross the boundary. Of course, it's best to have a friendly word with your neighbour first, to let them know you're planning to do this and allow them the chance to do the pruning themselves from their side of the fence. Strictly speaking, the branches and any fruit on them continue to be your neighbour's property, so you should give your neighbour an opportunity to collect them.

Make sure that the tree is not subject to a Tree Preservation Order first by checking with your local authority (in Northern Ireland, the Department of the Environment). If it is, you will need permission first. If you live in a Conservation Area, you should ask the local authority before you start lopping the tree; the authority has six weeks in which to decide whether or not to issue a Tree Preservation Order.

Hedges

High hedges – especially leylandii – can be the cause of problems between neighbours but there is currently little you can do about it if negotiation with your neighbour fails to work. However, the situation may be about to change for the better, as the government has said it will bring in new laws to tackle the problem. Hedgeline★ is an organisation that has campaigned for legislation on hedge nuisances. It can give advice and information about your situation and put you in touch with a local organiser; the annual subscription is £5 (less for people on a very low income).

Tree roots

Sometimes tree roots affect foundations and cause subsidence. Usually it is not the roots themselves that cause damage but the fact that they are absorbing water from the soil, which contracts, causing foundations to shift. If the tree roots are the cause of the damage, the person on whose land the tree is growing will be responsible for the damage, but it must be shown that he or she knew, or ought to have known, of the danger. You will probably be covered for this type of damage in your buildings insurance and it is far simpler to claim under the policy than to sue your neighbour.

Boundaries

Trespass

Unless your house deeds show a right of way across your property, each time your neighbours cross over it without your permission they are trespassing. If a friendly word does not stop this, you are perfectly entitled to bar their way. Note, however, that you are under a legal obligation to ensure that people who come on to your land – including trespassers – are reasonably safe.

If you are faced with repeated acts of trespassing you may apply to the county court to get an injunction (or an interdict from the sheriff court in Scotland). You will need advice from a solicitor before doing this.

If your property is damaged by trespassers you can claim compensation. The amount you claim will depend on the number of times your neighbours have trespassed on your garden, the distress and inconvenience it has caused, and what type of damage occurred. Keep a log of events and take photographs of any damage.

If the next-door neighbour's dog is plaguing you by coming into your garden, you must provide your own fencing to keep it out; as a general rule, pet owners do not have to erect fences to keep animals in. The position is different in relation to farm animals: unless the deeds of the property put the obligation to maintain a fence on you, the farmer must prevent livestock from trespassing, and pay for any damage if this happens.

Boundary in the wrong place

It sometimes emerges from an examination of the deeds that a boundary wall or fence has been erected in the wrong place. For instance, it may happen that your fence encloses a strip of land that appears on the deeds as belonging to your neighbour. However, if the true owner has not asserted their right to the land over a long period – usually 12 years – it becomes your property. You don't have to have lived at the property for the entire period: you can take advantage of your predecessor's uninterrupted possession of the land when calculating the relevant period.

Walls and fences

Walls and fences can lead to problems when neighbours aren't sure who is responsible for their upkeep. The basic rule is that the person who puts up a fence is the person who owns it (if you live on a housing estate where the builder erected all the fences you will have to look at the deeds, which may clarify the position).

As a fallback position, there is a legal presumption that where the fence has supporting posts every so often, the fence belongs to the person on whose side the supports are. The reason for this is that the landowner is assumed to put a fence as near the boundary as possible; if the supports protrude over the boundary the landowner will be trespassing on the neighbour's land.

If you are planning to construct a new wall on a boundary, or repair or excavate near an existing wall, you must give adjoining owners notice of your proposals. The Party Wall etc. Act 1996 provides a way of resolving difficulties if your proposals aren't accepted.

Repairs to a neighbour's fence
If your neighbour's fence is in danger of collapsing and, for instance, ruining your herbaceous border, you cannot automatically require him or her to mend the fence; however, in the case of many estates, where the deeds allocate ownership of a fence, the owner may be responsible for repairs. In any event, if damage actually occurs you can claim the cost of putting it right.

Access for repair work
If, say, the side wall of your neighbours' property is close to the boundary between the two properties, they may wish to place a ladder in your garden or on your path in order to paint the side of their house or repair guttering. You are not automatically bound to agree to this unless the deeds to your property specify that your neighbours are entitled to access for such purposes; without such a provision or your express authority they will commit an act of trespass in entering on to your land. However, in England and Wales, the Access to Neighbouring Land Act 1992 gives your neighbours the right to seek a court order permitting them to enter your land for the purpose of carrying out works that are reasonably necessary for the 'preservation' of their property.

Neighbourhood nuisances

If you feel that litter control is inadequate on roadways or other places to which the public has access in your area, take up the matter with your local authority. If you are still not satisfied, you may apply to the magistrates' court (sheriff court in Scotland), applying for a litter abatement order against whichever body has a duty to clear litter from the area concerned – the local authority, say, if it is a public road – giving it five days' notice of your intention to apply for the order before doing so. Similar provisions exist in Northern Ireland.

Landowners are responsible for removing fly-tipped material from their own land; depending on its nature, the local authority could agree to collect it but may charge a fee for doing so. Local authorities also have powers to remove abandoned vehicles from streets and to remove graffiti from public buildings, though they are not obliged to.

Different local authorities have different ways of dealing with these problems. To get through to the right department, check the local authority's entry in the phone book. Many have an advice line or a listing showing numbers to ring for different issues (for example, an abandoned vehicles hotline). If this doesn't help, ring the general switchboard, explain what you want to know and ask to be put through to the right department.

If graffiti on private buildings is a problem, it's worth contacting your local crime prevention officer (CPO) for advice; your local police station will be able to give you contact details for the CPO. You can find out more about CPOs on pages 43–4.

Getting work done on your home

Most of the problems people experience with building work relate to the **cost**, the **quality of work** and/or the **time** taken to complete it. *The Which? Guide to Getting the Best from your Builder* explains how to stay in control throughout the whole process; we outline some key points to bear mind here.

If you are going to have any major work carried out, have a proper written contract drawn up at the outset to help avoid problems later. The Royal Institute of British Architects★ (RIBA) publishes a standard contract called 'Small Works SW/99' (you can request this from architects). Various organisations, such as the Joint Contracts Tribunal (JCT)★, produce standard contracts for consumers having building or repair and maintenance work done on their homes. The JCT contracts can be used in all parts of the UK except Scotland, where the Scottish Building Contract Committee★ is due to publish similar contracts by mid-2003. If your builder offers his or her own contract for the work, read its small print very carefully before signing.

Use these safeguards to prevent problems occurring in the first place.

- Always get several quotes before choosing a company to carry out the work. Discuss the work you want done in detail with

each company and make sure you give them all the same information on which to base their quote.

- Ask friends or neighbours for recommendations of reliable
tradespeople, or if you can see someone locally is having similar work done, ask him or her about the company he or she is
using.

- To help consumers avoid the cowboys, the government has set
up a national register of independently assessed tradespeople.
The scheme is called Quality Mark★ and offers a complaints
process and includes a warranty of up to six years giving insurance cover to protect against loss of deposit and to cover the
costs of rectifying substandard work for contracts worth
between £50 and £50,000.

- When you get a quote, ask the company for references and take
these up.

- For large pieces of work, try not to pay the full amount up
front. If withholding the whole payment until the work is complete is not practical, you could pay a deposit and then pay in
instalments as the work progresses.

Cost of the work

You should try to reach a clear agreement about how much the
building work will cost in advance.

Quotation or estimate?

Many people are confused about the difference between these two
terms. There is no clear distinction legally, and the fact that one or
other is used need not be decisive. The critical question is whether
the price or charge given in the estimate is intended to fix the liability of the customer (making it a quotation), or a rough-and-ready, if
informed, guide to the price ultimately to be charged (making it an
estimate). Given the difficulty in determining this, it is wise to clarify at the outset whether the figure represents the limit of your liability or merely an informed forecast of the likely cost.

Where no price is specified

If you have not agreed a price – say, in an emergency when you have
been anxious to get the work done as soon as possible – the

contractor is entitled to a reasonable price for the job done. If you feel you are being overcharged, you are not bound to pay what the builder asks but can pay a smaller sum in settlement. To ascertain what a reasonable price for the job would be, obtain estimates for the work from other contractors, or contact a trade association for guidance.

Quality of the work

When a contractor agrees to do work for you, he or she is entering into a contract. Quite apart from the provisions expressly agreed in any contract, there are various implied obligations the contractor must fulfil, which are set out in the Supply of Goods and Services Act 1982 (these are common law obligations in Scotland).

Essentially, you are entitled to have the work carried out with reasonable skill and care, and within a reasonable time. If the contractor fails to meet any of these obligations, you have a claim for breach of contract. This means that you are legally entitled to have the work put right, free of charge. If the contractor does not put the work right, you should get two or three quotations for remedying the problem and send these to the first contractor. This shows you are serious and will, if necessary, call in another firm to carry out remedial work. If eventually you have to get another firm to put the work right, you are legally entitled to claim the cost of this firm's work from the original contractor. You may need evidence from an expert to substantiate your claim; you can get this from the firm that does the repairs by asking it for a written diagnosis of what was wrong.

The time factor

If it is important that you get the work done by a particular date, you should get the contractor's written agreement to this, and also state in writing that 'time is of the essence'. Doing this strengthens your legal position, because in the absence of an agreement of this sort, the law will not regard the time of completion as being of critical importance.

Where no date for completion is specified, the work must be completed within a reasonable time; if it is not, you can claim compensation for any additional expense and inconvenience you suffer as a result (the cost of meals out if you cannot use your kitchen, for example). If, on the other hand, a specific date for completion has been agreed, and you have made time of the essence, you have the option of ending the contract and getting in another contractor if the work is not completed in accordance with the time specified. Having done so, you are entitled to claim back any extra costs (and compensation for any substantial additional inconvenience) from the original contractor.

Personal injury

If you have an accident that isn't your own fault you may want an apology or an explanation of what happened, and feel obliged to make sure it doesn't happen to anyone else. You may be entitled to compensation for any injury or financial loss you've suffered as a result.

You can simply complain to the organisation concerned; in some cases there may be an official complaints procedure you can use. However, this may be time-consuming and the final result may be no more than an apology. If you want compensation, there are time limits for taking legal action (for cases involving negligence, court proceedings must be issued within three years of your first being aware that you have suffered an injury). You can get further information from leaflet 17 *Personal injury* from the Community Legal Service★, available in public libraries.

Proving negligence

If you are injured as a result of someone else's negligence (for instance you trip on a badly maintained, uneven pavement or slip on spilt food in a supermarket), you may have a claim. However you have to be able to show that the other party was negligent – or careless – in carrying out its duty.

In the case of tripping on a pavement, your case would be stronger if you could prove that it was in a state of disrepair and had not been maintained with reasonable skill and care by the local authority. As a rule of thumb, paving slabs should not protrude by more than 2.5cm above the general level of the pavement.

However, liability for compensation will depend on a consideration of all the circumstances.

It will often help when making a claim if you have photographs of the scene of the accident – for instance, a close-up shot demonstrating unevenness in a pavement. It is also a good idea if possible to get evidence from a witness who can support your claim; this person need not necessarily have seen the accident – but he or she can, for example, give evidence as to the state of the pavement, which may help. You should also make notes on what happened while the details are still fresh in your mind. If you have suffered injury, it is important to get a medical report from your doctor as soon as possible.

Do not be surprised if the organisation concerned (or its insurer) rejects your claim at first; more often than not you will have to persevere – remember, it is for you to prove your claim.

Professional advice

If your injuries are at all serious, or the circumstances complicated, you are likely to need help from a solicitor who deals with personal injury cases. In England and Wales, you can ring Accident Line★ (founded by the Law Society) to be put in touch with an Accident Line solicitor in the area. You can also contact the Association of Personal Injury Lawyers★, which will give you a list of personal injury lawyers in your area.

Solicitors and barristers frequently take on personal injury cases on a 'no win, no fee' or 'conditional fee' basis. This means that your solicitor gets no fee if the case is lost. This doesn't mean you don't have to pay anything if you lose – usually you will still have to pay the other side's costs and your expenses. You can (and should) pay an insurance premium to cover these costs.

If you win, you pay your solicitor's fee, which may also include a 'success fee' that means you are charged up to twice the solicitor's normal fee. But if you win, the courts will usually order your opponents to pay most of these costs. Your agreement with your solicitor should clarify what counts as a 'win', because cases may well be settled by negotiation without going to court. For more information see leaflet 12: *No win, no fee actions* from the Community Legal Service★, available in local libraries.

You may already have some form of legal expenses insurance. Check the small print on your household insurance policies as this may be included as an option. Depending on the type of injury you are claiming for, your car insurance, travel insurance or membership of a motoring organisation may also have relevant legal expenses insurance.

Claims assessors

You will probably have seen adverts on TV for claims assessors (sometimes known as claims managers) offering to help people who've suffered an accident make a claim for compensation. These often work on a 'no win, no fee' basis. The Citizen's Advice Bureau★ (CAB) advises that you should think carefully before choosing to use one as there may be some disadvantages, including:

- claims assessors are not usually solicitors and may not have a solicitor taking responsibility for the case. Therefore, they may not be able to claim compensation through the courts, which may mean you receive a smaller compensation award than you would get in court
- the fee you pay the claims assessor may include a substantial percentage of whatever compensation you receive.

If you're considering using a claims assessor, it's a good idea to get advice from your local CAB first.

Part 2

Enjoying your retirement

Chapter 5

Employment and voluntary work

Retirement does not necessarily mean stopping work altogether. You might choose to cut down on the amount of work you do gradually, or devote time to a hobby which becomes a small business. Or you might be looking for full-time work, perhaps after being made redundant or taking early retirement.

If your main motivation for considering getting another job is not financial – or you want to keep your hand in – voluntary work may be just what you're looking for. There are lots of opportunities for retired people to get involved in worthwhile and rewarding voluntary work, whether it's a regular commitment of a few hours a week or a full-time stint volunteering abroad for a development agency.

Carrying on working

In general, you can carry on working as long as you like, regardless of your age. This is straightforward if you run your own business. But if you are an employee and there is a normal retirement age for your job, your employer can dismiss you if you have reached or passed that age. This position is likely to change as a result of anti-age discrimination legislation to be implemented by the end of 2006.

In the meantime, if your current employer insists on you retiring, you can still look for a job elsewhere, although you may experience some difficulty. For more information on age discrimination and employment, contact the Department for Work and Pensions (DWP) Age Positive Team★. For information about pensions, tax and National Insurance if you carry on doing paid work, see the companion volume to this book: *The Which? Guide to Money in Retirement*, available from Which? Books★.

Finding employment

You'll be familiar with all the usual methods of finding work such as adverts in national or local papers, sending out CVs, word of mouth etc. Unfortunately, older people can sometimes face difficulties getting prospective employers to take their application seriously, so it's definitely worth networking and making the best of any contacts you already have to follow up any possible vacancies. You may consider getting some training or new qualifications to enhance your existing skills. Although some ageism exists, older people tend to be valued by employers for their maturity, stability and reliability, and you should be able to offer the benefit of your life experience in a new role. It is worth thinking about any unique selling points you have which are not related to your employment history at a job interview, such as an ability to get on with people.

If you are over 50 and have been claiming Income Support, Jobseeker's Allowance or certain other benefits for at least six months, your local Jobcentre can give you practical advice about finding employment under the New Deal 50 Plus scheme.

Employment agencies and specialist organisations can also give you advice and information about finding a job. Many of these are online or cover specific parts of the UK; you can find a useful list of links on the DWP Age Positive★ website. Two other very useful organisations which can give you advice and information if you're an older job-seeker are the Third Age Employment Network★ and the Third Age Challenge★.

You'll find information on obtaining qualifications and embarking on a new career in *The Which? Guide to Choosing a Career* and *The Which? Guide to Changing Careers*, both from Which? Books★.

Making money from existing skills or interests

It's not unusual for people who have taken early retirement to return to work in the same industry or even for the same employer either on a consultancy basis, on specific projects, or on a seasonal basis at busy times of the year. It's certainly worth talking to your employer about any opportunities for this sort of work.

You might have other skills that you can market on a freelance basis. For instance, parents are increasingly hiring tutors to give their primary and secondary school-aged children extra help, which provides work for many retired teachers. If you have computer skills, a range of opportunities may be available, including working as a licensed computer trainer for Hairnet* (see page 94 for more information about this company).

Case history: Roger

Roger is a retired maths teacher. After retiring he gave himself a six-month 'holiday' and then contacted a specialist agency for tutors, which has found him plenty of work giving GCSE students private tuition. He has enjoyed the experience of teaching on a one-to-one basis: 'It's been much less stressful than my experience in the classroom and I found I'd missed those light-bulb moments when a child who's been having trouble with maths suddenly gets the hang of it. The money's not bad either – £20 an hour – and I can choose how much work I want to do.'

You may have a hobby which could become financially reward-ing. If this applies to you, you should be clear with yourself about your intentions. Do you want to set up in business on a professional basis, or are you just trying to recoup the costs of something you enjoy anyway? Whatever your answer, you should check the going rate for the product or service you're providing. You may want to keep your business on a small scale, but you shouldn't be selling yourself cheap.

Don't forget to check whether any laws or regulations apply to your venture. This is particularly important if your work involves food; check with the environmental health department at your local authority about hygiene standards. If you make products such as handmade clothes or toys, ask your local Trading Standards office about regulations. You should also look into whether any special insurance will be required, and the implications if you employ other people.

The Which? Guide to Working from Home covers all the legal, practical and financial aspects of settting up a home business.

Case history: Pamela

Pamela has enjoyed china painting for some years, specialising in decorative personalised plates. Occasionally she rents a table at a craft fair to sell her products, but has found that she can also do a good business from attending local women's groups to give talks and demonstrations. This costs her nothing except her time and sometimes she even gets a speaker's fee. People attending often place orders there and then, or take one of her cards and contact her later in the year when they're looking for a birthday or Christmas present.

Starting your own business

You might be thinking of expanding a profitable hobby into a fully-fledged business. Or perhaps you've got a new business idea that you've been waiting to try out. A business started by someone in their early fifties is twice as likely to survive as a business set up by someone in their early twenties. But don't underestimate the amount of determination, hard work and energy required. Your local Business Link★ (Business Connect★ in Wales and Scottish Enterprise★ in Scotland) can supply helpful information and advice. The *Which? Guide to Starting Your Own Business* gives detailed advice on what's involved.

Volunteer work

There are many opportunities for interesting voluntary work that can be as rewarding for you as it is valuable to the community. But make sure you know how much commitment it involves and whether out-of-pocket expenses (such as travel or meals) are paid. As with choosing any form of employment, it is important to be discerning about which organisation you select.

If a particular cause is close to your heart, contact the relevant national organisation to be put in touch with the local volunteer co-ordinator if you don't already know the local group. If you're not sure what you want to do, it's worth considering what type of work best meets your skills and interests as well as the cause you want to support. There are three main categories of voluntary work: office duties, working with people and practical work.

Office and business skills

An extra pair of hands to help with everyday office tasks will be warmly welcomed by many charities, but there are also opportunities to contribute to committee work, organising, fundraising, accounting and personnel work. Reach★ is a charity which specialises in matching volunteers with technical, business, managerial or professional expertise with charities that need their help. There are no age restrictions and the average age of their volunteers is 52. You can make a regular weekly time commitment or work on one-off projects, and the work can even be done from home.

Positions at board level on national charities or public bodies are often advertised in the broadsheets. You could also go to an agency such as Charity and Fundraising Appointments★, which finds unpaid trustees as well as full-time paid executive staff for charities. You can find out about appointments for board members to all sorts of public bodies from hospitals and Primary Care Trusts to Boards of Visitors for prisons from the Public Appointments Unit★ which also publishes a list of upcoming public appointment opportunities. You can get this by post or view it online at *www.publicappts-vacs.gov. uk*. There is no age limit for most public appointments and about half the positions are paid.

Working with people

Working directly with a group of people can be very rewarding. Volunteer work of this nature could involve, say, hosting tea-parties for elderly people (Contact the Elderly★ is among groups that organise this sort of activity) or helping at a homeless shelter (contact Crisis★ or your area may have its own Cyrenian organisation or other similar local charity), or being a volunteer driver for a local hospital transport scheme. Other options are telephone work on an advice or support helpline or perhaps working in a Citizens Advice Bureau (CAB)★. Training is usually available for these sorts of positions.

You could work with the public in a more general way; for example, helping out at an arts centre, serving in a charity shop or being a volunteer guide at a National Trust★ property. The Age Concern★ ActivAge Unit has set up the Intergenerational Network, a scheme designed to bring different generations together. Under this scheme, older volunteers are trained to work in settings such as local schools, helping children with literacy skills, art work, cookery or computer skills.

Before you begin to work with children or other vulnerable people, the voluntary organisation involved will have to check that you do not have a past conviction which makes you unsuitable for the work.

Practical projects

Many charities are delighted to hear from anyone offering practical skills. Perhaps you could lend a helping hand with conservation or environmental work. The British Trust for Conservation Volunteers (BTCV)★ offers working holidays and also runs regular one-day conservation projects all over the UK, during the week and at weekends. You can help out at these regularly or just once in a while, whatever suits you. Tasks vary from tree planting to dry stone walling, footpath construction to creating wildlife habitats. The Royal Society for the Protection of Birds (RSPB)★ welcomes volunteers who can carry out bird surveys or make nest-boxes as well as help out at nature reserves. Alternatively, your local area may have its own wildlife trust or conservation group – your local library should have details.

Any technical or professional skills you have may come in handy. For example, the Society for the Protection of Ancient Buildings★ seeks retired architects, buildings surveyors and structural engineers who could give voluntary help on specific projects to repair old buildings. If you have some mechanical ability you could help Remap★, a charity that designs, makes and adapts equipment that is not available commercially to fit the needs of people with disabilities.

If you were a member of a profession, there may well be some sort of charity associated with your professional or trade body – contact the organisation to find out.

Some more ideas

It would be impossible to list all the charities that need help. Try your CAB or Volunteer Bureau for information about charities nearby. Your local library may have a copy of the *Voluntary Agencies Directory*, which gives contact details for national groups. Another good starting point is Community Service Volunteers★ which runs a Retired and Senior Volunteer Programme with local groups throughout the UK.

You may also consider helping out a local religious group or political party to which you are affiliated.

Case history: Margaret

Margaret lives on a large housing estate which is home to a thriving community centre. 'We call it the Village Hall – we're in a city, but that's how it functions. Lots of different groups meet here, from playgroups to bridge players. It's given the estate a wonderful villagey feel and really brought the community together.

At one of the events, she got chatting to the Chair of the community centre's management committee. 'He was bemoaning the fact that they hadn't been able to replace the Treasurer who was due to move soon. Apparently lots of voluntary organisations have this problem. People tend to think only retired bank-managers can do the job, so they don't volunteer. Well, listening to him I thought "I could do that", and he was delighted.'

Margaret didn't have any specialist knowledge but she took evening classes in book-keeping. The community centre offered to pay for this, but as Margaret is retired the fees were only a few pounds anyway. She's been Treasurer now for two years. 'It does take time – particularly at the year end when I have to make sure all the books balance. But the benefits of having a community centre like this on our door-step make the effort worthwhile – and it certainly keeps my brain working!'

Setting up your own community project

If you can see a need in your local community and want to provide some way of meeting it, there are a number of organisations you can approach for help.

Help the Aged★'s *Speaking up for our Age* project enables older people to set up and run forums which promote their views on issues that affect them at local, regional or national level. The forums aim to influence policy development in areas such as health, transport and local authority services. Help the Aged offers training, grants and advice but the actual running and management of the forum is done at grass-roots level by the volunteers.

If you are thinking of setting up a scheme that will benefit local people in some way, you may be eligible for a National Lottery grant awarded by the Community Fund★. You do not need to be a registered charity to apply, but your organisation must be established in the UK for charitable, philanthropic or benevolent purposes. The Community Fund determines whether an organisation matches this description on the basis of the words used in its constitutional document, rather than on the work it does or plans to do. For further information contact the Fund to get its *Guide to eligibility*.

Longer projects

Many organisations are looking for help on a more full-time basis than a few regular hours each week or month. Some of these qualify as 'working holidays', while others may seem more like plain hard work but can still be extremely satisfying.

Projects in the UK

The Council for British Archaeology★ can give you information on archaeological excavations requiring volunteers, normally for two weeks. The accommodation can be basic and while there's no formal age limit, you'll need to be fit as the work is likely to involve lifting and bending. But no training is necessary and if you like *Time Team* on TV, you may enjoy working on a dig.

The National Trust★ runs a programme of working holidays which mostly involve outdoor conservation work such as hedge laying, dry-stone walling, scrub clearance and footpath work. Some projects are aimed specifically at the over-fifties.

The British Trust for Conservation Volunteers (BTCV)★ also offers working holidays in the UK and abroad with similar aims to its one-day projects (see 'Practical projects' on page 80 for more details).

Volunteering overseas

The best-known overseas volunteer organisation is Voluntary Service Overseas (VSO)*, which organises placements that usually last for two years in some developing countries. You must be 68 or under and in good health when you take up the placement. Depending on the destination country, opportunities for volunteers aged over 60 are more limited.

Other organisations that place volunteers overseas in developing countries include Skillshare International* which works in Southern Africa, Tanzania, Uganda and India and has an upper age limit for most volunteers of 62 (although there is no upper age limit for health professionals). International Co-operation for Development* works with people in the Caribbean, Latin America, Africa and Yemen as part of the Catholic Institute for International Relations. Volunteers do not need to be Catholic and there is no upper age limit.

Short-term placements of between one week and four months can be found through the British Executive Service Overseas (BESO)*, which offers professional expertise to organisations in developing countries and economies in transition that cannot afford commercial consultants. There is no official upper age limit, but you must be fit to travel and your experience should be up-to-date.

The International Voluntary Service (IVS)* is a peace movement which runs volunteer projects in the UK, Europe, the USA, Australia and North Africa. These usually last between a fortnight and a month in the summer and include working with the local community and conservation and environmental work. Volunteers on the project will be from a mix of countries and of differing ages. There's no upper age limit but you need to be generally fit and prepared for fairly basic accommodation.

Chapter 6

Leisure and learning

Whether you want to expand your horizons with new activities or see retirement as an opportunity to spend more time on an existing interest, this chapter covers the sources you'll need to make the most of your free time.

Education and recreation tend to be cheaper once you are retired. You'll find that many organisations offer concessionary prices to older people, and local authorities generally offer discounts on adult education classes and leisure facilities. Some tourist attractions offer reduced admissions, and many organisations offer reduced subscriptions – for example, the National Trust cuts its rates for people who are over 60 and have been members for at least five years. You may be able to buy 'stand-by' tickets for theatres shortly before performances begin, and some theatres and cinemas allow older people to book discounted tickets in advance, especially for mid-week matinees. You'll even find that some restaurants offer reduced-price meals for older people – often at lunch time.

As well as giving you time to pursue a hobby on your own, an organised class or study programme can give you the stimulation of the company of people with similar interests. You can do as much or as little as you want. This could be the time to go on an afternoon 'introduction to computing' course or start work on a PhD.

Local classes

A number of organisations can help you find out more about opportunities and classes in your neighbourhood.

- **Learndirect*** is a government initiative designed to help people with training and adult learning, whether for work or for pleasure. Its database holds details of over half a million courses on almost any subject – you can search it yourself online, or speak to an advisor on the Learndirect Learning Advice Line. The scheme offers a number of advice centres throughout the country where you can get face-to-face advice and take part in computer courses covering a wide range of topics and levels of ability. You can also take part in these courses from home if you're connected to the Internet. You can find out more, and try out free taster sessions of some of the courses, on its website: *www.learndirect.co.uk*. A separate scheme for Scotland, Learndirect Scotland★, works in a very similar way.

- **The University of the Third Age★ (U3A)** is a learning co-operative for older people who are no longer in full-time employment. Local U3As provide members with a wide variety of educational opportunities at low cost by drawing on their own membership for tuition and expertise. Subjects can range from language studies and creative writing to archaeology and philosophy. No qualifications are required for membership and none are given. Try your local library for leaflets about U3A or contact the organisation direct for details of your nearest branch.
- **The Workers' Educational Association★ (WEA)** offers courses in subjects ranging from calligraphy to creative writing. There are no age barriers. You usually sign up for a term of classes – generally ten weeks – and residential courses are also available. Fees vary: ask about reductions for retired people. You should be able to get contact details for your local branch from the library or from the WEA head office.
- **Local authorities** run programmes of adult education classes. These usually offer reduced fees for retired people. Look in your local library for details of classes in your area.

Distance learning

You may get a greater choice of course via distance learning than is available to you locally, but check that the establishment with which you are enrolling is a reputable one. You can get a list of accredited colleges from the Open and Distance Learning Quality Council★.

The best-known distance learning organisation is the **Open University* (OU)**. With OU courses, as well as the study materials, you get support from a tutor by phone or email and at monthly tutorials held in your local area. You can study for a range of awards – from certificates and diplomas to research degrees in subjects ranging from art history to biology. There are no qualification requirements for entry to any of the undergraduate courses.

Studying for a Bachelor degree is likely to take three to six years and cost around £4,300 in total. You can do the degree in modules and if you decide it isn't for you, you can stop part-way through the degree or return to it in the future. You can pay in instalments and there is a student hardship fund.

Another option is to study a module from a degree course as a stand-alone course; these individual courses are likely to last a year and involve 8 to 15 hours a week. The OU has also introduced a selection of short courses (usually 12 weeks). Some are designed to prepare people for university study and others expand on primetime BBC/Open University TV series such as *The Life of Mammals* or *Leonardo*.

There are no qualification requirements for entry to any of the undergraduate courses. Degree courses cost around £4,300 in total and indidvidual courses from £200 to £450, while short courses start at £65. You can pay for degrees in instalments and there is a student hardship fund.

Two other large providers of distance learning courses are the **National Extension College*(NEC)** and the **Open College of the Arts***. These organisations also allow you to study at your own pace, and you don't need any special qualifications to take a course.

The NEC offers a large number of courses, whether you're aiming for a qualification, improving your skills or simply studying for interest. They range from GCSEs and 'A' Levels to courses in homeopathy, counselling, interior and garden design, book-keeping or creative writing. Courses range in price: most creative arts courses are around £200 while GCSEs and 'A' Levels are £275 and £325 respectively. The NEC has a monthly fee list with a different special offer each month giving good discounts on a particular course – for example, £80 off the price of a GCSE.

The Open College of the Arts is an educational charity. It offers subjects such as art and design, sculpture, textiles, music, video arts, photography and creative writing, mostly by correspondence. Completing a course may give you credits towards a degree. Course prices range from £300 to £470 and can be paid in instalments.

Case history: Hilary

Hilary's grandchildren live a long way away but they regularly ring her with news of what they've been doing at school – and then they ask how Grandma's been doing in the classroom too. Since she retired, Hilary has taken a whole host of courses from her local authority's adult education programme.

Each summer she gets the local authority listing for classes beginning in September and browses through to choose a new one. 'It just so happens that many of these have been ones leading to a qualification,' she says. 'I certainly didn't enjoy exams at school. But these courses have appealed the most and I do feel a sense of achievement. I've done a certificate in food hygiene and a GCSE in law. Last year I did a foundation course in art, and this year I've gone on from that to do an A-level in photography.' Another benefit is that the local authority subsidises the courses, so they're either free or very low-priced for pensioners.

Residential courses

Residential courses are a good way of combining a holiday with your study, and if you go on your own you should find plenty of like-minded companions among your fellow students. You'll find art and cookery courses advertised in the holiday pages of newspapers or magazines, and hobby magazines can be a good place to look for special-interest breaks. *Time to Learn,* published twice yearly by City and Guilds, contains details of residential short courses for adults. You can view it online at *www.timetolearn.org.uk* or buy it for £4.95 plus p&p from 020-7294 2850.

The Women's Institute's Denman College★ in Oxfordshire runs popular short-term residential courses. You don't have to be a

---

Choosing what to study

Browsing through a brochure of courses should give you lots of ideas. Here are some tips from people who've enjoyed taking up new interests when they've retired.

- Go to classes with a friend. You choose the first course and your friend chooses the next. This way you get to try things you might not have picked – and you get to share the travelling to classes, etc.
- The Internet can be a great help in tracking down obscure or special-interest groups. The amount of societies and groups listed on the Web is vast, and the Internet makes it easy to keep in touch with fellow enthusiasts spread across the UK – or even the globe.
- If you are considering taking adult education classes, try to go along to an open evening to meet the course tutors – this can give you a real indication of how well you'll get on with them.
- You can go on afternoon or one-day courses for many subjects, and these can be a good taster to see if you'd like to pursue further study.

---

member to attend and the courses typically cost around £300 for a three-night stay, including tuition. The college specialises in craft courses but also runs courses in subjects ranging from personal development to history.

Full-time study

If you're interested in formal studying for a degree or higher degree, contact your local university. Some have extra-mural departments for people who want to study part-time, but most universities are also very welcoming to mature students who want to join full-time. The extra experience mature students can bring to a degree course may mean that a lack of formal qualifications is not a bar to entry.

If you have not previously received a grant, your local authority will probably cover the cost of your tuition fees. Student loans are not available to people aged over 65, but it's worth asking the student welfare or student awards officer at your local college about any grants or bursaries that might be available.

Once you're a student, you may be able to get help with costs from an access fund or hardship fund from the college. Different universities have different systems but most allocate these funds according to need, and only students in the greatest financial difficulty are likely to benefit from these limited funds. Ask the student awards or welfare officer for more information.

Your local library

Whatever you decide to study, your local library may be able to help and will have details of courses available in the area. Local history is a particularly strong feature at many libraries, and they generally have information about the local history society. Your local library will also be part of the inter-library lending system, which means that you can get hold of practically any book in print (you may have to pay a small fee).

Most libraries subscribe to a range of newspapers and magazines that you can read while you're there. All local libraries stock large-print books and most also have tapes or CDs of talking books, and often videos or DVDs too.

Book services

The Royal National Institute of the Blind (RNIB)* offers a talking book service for people who cannot read standard type with the strongest possible glasses. The service costs £60 a year including the loan of a player. It also has a catalogue of audio-described videos for sale and rental. You can borrow a video for up to two weeks for £2.50 including post and packaging. Listening Books* provides a postal audio book library service to anyone with an illness or disability that makes it impossible for them to hold a book, turn pages or read it in the usual way. The library includes books for both pleasure and learning. Membership currently costs £50 per year to cover postage and the loan of the audiotapes.

Home study groups

You don't have to join an organised group – you can set one up for yourself. Book clubs have become more and more popular. One may be already running at your local library, but you can easily set one up with a few friends. The idea is that you choose a book, each member of the group reads it and then you meet to discuss it. Sometimes you take it in turns to choose which book is read – this can mean you get to try books you might not normally choose. Sometimes one person is nominated to lead the discussion (perhaps the person who chose that book), sometimes the discussion is more general. For classic works of fiction, the short study books designed for A-level students (e.g. the York notes series and Brodies notes series, widely available in bookshops) are inexpensive and can be a useful starting point.

This idea also works well with TV and radio programmes or films. With TV programmes, you could choose schools or further education programmes, documentaries or natural history programmes, drama series or even soaps. Many TV programmes now have back-up material for people who are interested in the topic; this will generally be advertised at the end of a programme. Websites for the TV channel or programme maker are also good sources of further information with the BBC Education site *www.bbc.co.uk/education* being particularly impressive. The Open University even has courses designed specifically around some programmes (see 'Distance Learning' on pages 85–7).

Reminiscence and scrap-booking

Reminiscence sessions have become recognised as a valuable way of preserving local and social history, as well as being an enjoyable activity for many people. They can also be a therapeutic activity for people with dementia.

Reminiscence covers a wide range of activities, from informal conversations to dramatisations or art based on the individual or collective memories of older people. It can be carried out at a series of group sessions, or alternatively material might be gathered into a book, leaflet, exhibition or display, using pictures, objects and written or taped memories. If you have a local museum, it may well be interested and able to help with setting up a local reminiscence project, as might a local history society (your local library will have details). You can get further information and advice from Age Exchange★. This organisation holds a database of reminiscence projects and runs training days for people who want to set up projects (concessionary fees are around £45).

The Age to Age project collects recollections of life in the twentieth century to be kept for posterity. It is run by the Dark Horse Venture★, which welcomes contributions in writing or on tape from individuals from all walks of life as well as from organised reminiscence projects or local history groups. Contact the organization for details on how to submit your contribution and for tips on topics to cover.

Scrap-booking is a craft activity that has become very popular in the USA. Essentially it is a way of organising photographs and other memorabilia, usually into themes such as holiday trips, children's schooldays or simply significant years and events in your life. Scrapbooks can be very elaborate, with heavily decorated pages, but regardless of the content the key thing is that labels are stuck into the albums, explaining who's who in the pictures and writing up memories of the occasion. You can include all sorts of souvenirs you may have kept from the past such as wedding invitations, children's drawings or local newspaper cuttings. People who enjoy the activity say it's wonderful to clear out drawers full of accumulated clutter and prune them into albums that you enjoy looking through – and it also means that in the future, the collections will tell a story to your descendants.

Other suggestions

The Dark Horse Venture★ encourages people over 55 to do things they have never tried before. You can pick activities from the fields of Giving and Sharing, Learning and Doing, Exploring and Exercising and Generations Working Together, and will be awarded a certificate when you complete the task you've set yourself. Contributing to the Age to Age scheme mentioned above is one of the possible activities.

The RNIB★ provides information and advice on leisure activities from knitting to yachting for people who are blind or have sight problems and also sells specially designed leisure equipment such as large-print crossword puzzles and specially adapted games.

Thrive★ is a horticultural charity that helps older people and those with disabilities to enjoy gardening. Their informative website is full of practical information on subjects from choosing tools to planning water features. If you don't have access to the Internet, contact the head office for a range of leaflets costing around £1.

TV licences

If you are aged 75 or over, you qualify for a free TV licence for your main residence. This can be the licence for your household if someone under 75 lives with you, provided it is in your name. You become eligible at the start of the month in which you turn 75. You have to apply for the free licence and can use the appropriate renewal form on licence renewal forms if you are already 75 or are going to reach 75 during the next year. Call (0870) 2416468 for more details or look at the website *www.tvlicensing.co.uk*

People who are registered blind can claim a 50 per cent discount on the cost of a licence. To apply, you will need to present your blind registration or confirmation on headed paper from your local authority when renewing your licence at a post office, or send it to TV Licensing if you're renewing by post. There are also discounts for older people living in care homes or sheltered housing, but strict criteria must be met. For more information contact your care home manager or warden or call TV Licensing★.

Chapter 7

Computers and the Internet

Older people are making good use of new technology. Over a third of over-55s use a home computer, with over 80 per cent of older computer users accessing their computer at least twice a week. As well as using a computer for things like household accounts, word-processing and games, more than two million older people also use the Internet. And the number of so-called 'silver surfers' is growing – Which? Online's 2002 Internet survey found that the number of Internet users aged 55 and above had increased by 40 per cent since 2001 – the largest increase in any age group.

The vast majority of home computer-owners use a PC rather than a Mac (Apple Macintosh), so the technical information in this chapter is aimed mainly at the former group, but the broader advice will be useful to Mac users as well.

Where to start

If you haven't got a computer yet, would like to see what the Internet can offer or simply feel you could be doing more with your computer, there are a number of places that can help.

Many local authorities run courses specially designed for older people, which are often subsidised or free. The government initiative Learndirect★ offers a range of computer training courses including introductory courses for the Internet, popular software packages including Microsoft and Lotus, and free 'taster' sessions.

In addition, many local libraries offer cheap or free access to PCs or the Internet – this facility is often linked with training sessions, some of which are specially aimed at older people. In some areas local authorities or other organisations run outreach projects to take lap-top computers into day centres, care homes and sheltered housing developments. For example, some local Age Concern★ groups have Age Resource desks which offer computer training.

Hairnet★ specialises in computer and Internet training for people aged over 50. They have a network of police-checked, licensed trainers spread across the UK who are all aged over 50 and can provide one-to-one training in your own home or at another suitable venue for £20 a hour.

What sort of computer do you need?

If you're thinking of buying a new computer, the first thing to do is work out what you want to be able to do with it. If you simply want to use the computer for basic word-processing, accounting, surfing the Internet and sending emails, then the sort of machine you're looking for will need the following:

- 1.7GHz processor (see the box opposite for fuller explanations of these terms)
- 128–256MB Ram
- 20–60Gb hard drive
- 56K modem
- CD drive
- 15-ins or preferably 17-ins monitor
- office software.

At current prices you should be able to get a PC like this for about £700, although prices change rapidly and higher-specification models tend to become available for lower prices.

Pay particular attention to the processor when choosing a system; think carefully about what you want the computer to be able to do now and how your computer usage might develop, and choose a processor that's fast enough for this. It's relatively easy to upgrade the memory later if you find you need to. However, if you want to download and store large files from the Internet or edit digital photgraphs then you'll need a PC with a hard drive of at least 60Gb.

Jargon buster

CD-ROM and DVD-ROM drives Both of these play and read CDs, and a DVD-Rom drive also plays DVDs. You use CDs and/or DVDs to install new software on your machine, and can also buy information sources (for example, an encyclopaedia) in CD or DVD format.

CD and/or DVD RW drive This allows you to save files to a CD or DVD, which can hold far more information than a floppy disk.

Hard drive This is rather like a filing cabinet, providing long-term storage for programs and documents. Capacity is measured in gigabytes (Gb). Most new PCs have at least 20Gb.

Modem This allows you to link your computer to the Web. Modems are measured in terms of transfer speed – the higher the number, the faster the modem can work. Almost all new computers bought today will come with a 56K modem (also known as V90 or V92 modems).

Processor This is the 'brain' of the computer, which enables the other components to function. Its speed is measured in gigahertz (GHz): most new PCs have at least 1 GHz.

RAM stands for random access memory and is where information is stored temporarily while in use. It's measured in megabytes (Mb). Most new PCs have at least 128Mb.

Where to buy

In November 2002, *Which?* explored the standard of sales advice offered to first-time computer buyers and found it was significantly variable, with no retailers giving good advice across the board. However, in a *Which?* survey of computer users in November the previous year, John Lewis came out top in terms of general satisfaction and after-sales service. Using independent computer shops and buying direct from the manufacturer were also found to be good options.

It's also worth talking to well-informed friends or relatives and reading computer magazines and retailer literature. You can consult a number of useful books including *The Which? Guide to Computers* and *Easy PC Projects* from Which? Books★. Consumers' Association★ also publishes *Computing Which?* magazine, which regularly examines the world of computers.

When you're looking at prices, make sure you compare like with like. Some retailers price monitors separately, don't include basic software in the price or don't include delivery in their quote. Ask for a printed statement of what's included to make sure there's no confusion.

You should also check out what after-sales support is on offer. All new computers come with a manufacturer's warranty of at least a year, and some retailers offer further free warranties. However, the type and cost of technical support offered by each manufacturer or retailer will vary – check the cost of price-per-minute calls to helplines in particular.

You may be considering paying for an extended warranty. This can give you extra peace of mind but it's expensive – typically around £200 for a two-year extension to the manufacturer's warranty. In November 2001 *Which?* found that most computers don't need any repairs within that time, and that problems which do occur tend to happen during the free first-year warranty period. If your computer does break down, *Computing Which?* research in July 2002 found computer repair services to be efficient and fairly cheap.

The wonderful world of the Web

The Internet can offer you a wealth of information, and using email is a wonderful way of keeping in touch with friends and relatives. Few people take the time to write letters any more and it's quick and easy to drop someone an informal email. You can type up your message without being connected to the Internet, so it's inexpensive too.

You might also use the Internet to research your family history, or to book flights, hotels or theatre tickets. Internet shopping can mean getting your everyday groceries delivered to your door. Or it can be a way to track down a recording of a hard-to-find piece of music. And however esoteric your interests are, you can almost guarantee that there's a chat site or forum out there where you can share your enthusiasms with like-minded individuals.

Getting online

Your computer

If you're buying a new PC, follow the recommendations above in 'What sort of computer do you need?'. If you've already got a computer, you'll need at least a 486 or Pentium processor and 32Mb of RAM (see 'jargon buster', on page 95 for an explanation of these terms).

You can check your computer's speed and memory (in both Windows 95 and Windows 98) by double-clicking on the 'my computer' icon on your desktop. Then double-click on the 'control panel' and 'systems' icons and this will bring up a window with your computer's details.

If your computer has less than 64Mb of memory, it's probably worth expanding it. This doesn't mean you have to buy a new computer. You can buy more memory in the form of cards which slot into your existing machine from as little as £20. However, there must be room on the 'motherboard' (a circuit board in the machine) for the extra memory and it must be compatible. Most retailers who sell memory will also install it for you. You can get more advice from *Which? Computer Troubleshooter*, published by Which? Books*.

Your modem

If your modem is slower than 56K you should upgrade to this level – this will cost from around £40. You can check your modem specification by double clicking on the 'my computer' icon on your desktop and then going into 'control panel' and 'modems'.

Choosing an Internet service provider

You can't connect your home computer directly to the Internet – you need to go through an Internet service provider (ISP). When you register with an ISP, it will usually give you a CD-ROM that you install on your computer. You then follow the on-screen instructions and are normally online within minutes.

Choosing an ISP

The most important factors in choosing an ISP are probably cost and speed. There are big differences between charges made by ISPs for connecting you to the Web, and the most suitable one for you will depend on how often you use the Internet.

> ## Case history: Hector and Flora
>
> Silver Surfer's Day has been set up to celebrate the contribution of older people to the Internet. It takes place in May and encompasses the Silver Surfer of the Year awards. In 2002, the award winners included Hector and Flora.
>
> Hector is an 86-year-old who describes the Internet as 'the best thing this age has produced'. He originally started using the Internet to keep in touch with his children and also finds it a good way to keep in touch with his local community, as he uses a wheelchair. He now manages an online community of almost 2,000 older people.
>
> Flora, who's 75, lives in a sheltered housing project and has encouraged other residents to learn about computers and the Internet. Flora enjoys using her computer to keep in touch with her sister, and using the web-cams that Flora installed means they can see each other as well as type messages. You can find out more about this year's champions and future plans at the website *www.silversurfersday.org*

Cost

If you use the Internet for less than ten hours a month, mostly in the evenings and at weekends, you'll probably be better off with a pay-as-you-go ISP. With this sort of deal you don't pay a monthly fee, you just pay for phone calls to the ISP (usually a local-rate number).

If you use the Internet for more than 11 hours a month, then a subscription ISP might be better value. Here you pay a monthly fee for 'unlimited' access to the Internet on a freephone number. (There may be some time restriction on the 'unlimited access' – check the small print.) Some ISPs charge you a subscription and add call charges on top.

Speed

Your online experience will be influenced by the speed of your ISP connection – slow or lost connections can bump up your phone bill and be frustrating. Check in *Which?* or computer magazines for reports testing the speed of different ISPs. You'll need a fairly recent copy as performance can vary greatly over time.

Top tips for smooth surfing

- Popular sites can get busy, so it can be faster to connect at quiet times. The early morning is good as it avoids both UK and US business hours.

- Make sure you've got the most up-to-date version of your Internet browser (the software that displays websites and allows surfing). You can download the latest versions of Internet Explorer and Netscape Navigator for free from *www.microsoft.com* or *www.netscape.com* respectively.

- If your Internet connection keeps cutting out, this could be due to interference on the phone line. Try unplugging any other phones or faxes you have. If that doesn't help, ask your phone company to check for a fault on your line. It's also worth checking the connection setting on your Internet browser. Your browser might disconnect you if you're online but not actively searching the Web for longer than a set period of time. Check the setting in Windows by looking in my computer/control panel/modems/properties/connecting, and raise the 'Disconnect if idle' setting to at least five minutes if this is not set up. Your ISP might disconnect you if you're not actively searching the Web, to reduce traffic. Check with your provider to see if this is the case, and consider switching provider if you're not satisfied.

- You can save time by opening a number of different web pages at once, and reading the first while the others are downloading in the background. You can do this by right-clicking on a link and selecting the 'open in new window' option. Don't overdo this though – if you try to open too many at once, your machine will slow down until you've closed them again.

If you're a heavy user of the Internet, you could consider a special high-speed connection such as ADSL or cable broadband. Broadband is widely advertised. It gives you a permanent Internet connection with unmetered access, and enables you to receive phone calls when you're online. However, all this comes at a price. Broadband packages are more expensive and at the time of writing it is not available in all parts of the country.

Extra services to consider which may affect your choice of ISP include:

- **Content** Some ISPs offer their own content which is only available to subscribers.
- **Email and web pages** Check how many separate email accounts are included. If you want to design your own web page, check that the ISP gives you space to do this.
- **Helplines** Some ISPs have premium-rate numbers for their helplines, some have freephone or local-cost ones.
- **Terms and conditions** As always, read these carefully; in particular check what notice you have to give if you want to change to another ISP, and whether there is a minimum contract term.

Online security

Shopping from the comfort of your computer desk can be very convenient, but many people have reservations about whether it is safe to use credit or debit cards to shop online. However, you are far more likely to have your credit-card details stolen and misused in the real world than online (it's far more common for fraudsters to steal card details from discarded credit-card slips dropped at cash tills in shops and supermarkets).

Follow these common-sense precautions to help ensure your online shopping trip is a safe one.

- Check the site is secure. When you are in a secure part of a site (e.g. when you give your credit-card details), a security symbol will appear on screen. This is usually a key or a closed padlock on the browser toolbar or the letter 's' in the Internet address after the 'http' prefix.
- Check whether the trader belongs to an online code of practice. Consumers' Association was involved in setting up a government-backed scheme called Trust UK which sets out minimum standards for online codes. Find out more on *www.trust.uk.org.uk*
- Look for 'real world' contact details. A phone number and postal address can reassure you that the company really does exist and is happy to be contacted by customers.

It's also worth remembering that anyone can set up a website, so just because you see some information published on a web page, it does not necessarily mean this is a reliable source. Use your common sense, particularly if you're looking for medical or legal information.

Your online shopping rights

If you buy goods over the Internet from a business based in the UK, you will have the same rights as if you buy from a shop (i.e. goods must be as described, fit for purpose and of satisfactory quality). Additionally, if you pay by credit card (rather than debit card) for goods costing over £100 and under £30,000, the credit-card company is liable as well as the retailer if there is a problem with the goods or service bought.

If you are buying goods from overseas, the law applicable to the contract could be that of the country you are buying from. It may be difficult and costly to enforce your buyer's rights against a non-UK trader. Remember that having 'uk' in a web address doesn't necessarily mean the site is based in the UK, so check the geographical contact details.

The Distance Selling Regulations give you extra protection when you buy most goods over the Internet from an EU country (they also apply to any other method where you don't have face-to-face contact with the seller). The regulations give you a right to a refund of all money taken through fraudulent use of your credit or other payment card. They also give you the right to a seven-day cooling-off period during which you can change your mind and cancel. However, it doesn't apply to everything you might buy – package holidays, financial services and food are three of the main things that are not covered. There are also a number of exclusions to the right to a cooling-off period including perishable goods (such as flowers), newspapers, magazines, audio or video recordings, and software if the seal has been broken.

Some good websites to try

Here are some of the most popular websites if you're new to the Internet, along with a few that you may not have heard of but which are well worth a surf. Note that sites alter all the time, and web addresses may disappear or change.

Information

- Even if you don't subscribe to *Which?* magazine, *www.switch withwhich.co.uk* gives you all the information you need to know to make sure you're getting the best deal on your bank account, energy company, mobile phone or holiday company.
- If you can't find a fact you're searching for try *www.ask-a-librarian.org.uk.* Here you can type in a factual question and forward it to the reference department of participating public libraries, and they'll email you an answer.
- You'll find everything you could ever want to know about 'netiquette' – the do's and don'ts of online communication – at *www.albion.com.*
- *www.consumer.gov.uk* gives a useful overview of consumer issues and links to other government and official sites.
- There are lots of route-planning sites which can help you find the fastest or shortest routes between two places. For example, *www.viamichelin.com* is Michelin's guide to driving in Europe. The route plans for France show hotels, restaurants and tourist attractions from Michelin's Red and Green Guides along the way.
- Age Concern (*www.ageconcern.org.uk*) and Help the Aged (*www.helptheaged.org.uk*) both have informative sites with advice and leaflets to download. Age Concern also have a chat site for the over-50s at *www.babyboomerbistro.org.uk.*
- All the national newspapers have websites carrying news and features; *www.wrx.zen.co.uk* has links to all the nationals and many local and regional papers.
- You can get information on local property prices, services and facilities from *www.upmystreet.co.uk*, and also check your ACORN profile here. ACORN stands for 'A classification of residential neighbourhoods'; click on 'full profile' to see full marketing data that describe the typical characteristics of people in your postcode area, from which newspaper they buy to where they go on holiday.

Shopping

- *www.amazon.co.uk* and *www.lastminute.com* are two of the biggest Internet retailers, and are deservedly popular for books and holidays respectively (though both also offer a wider range of goods and services).
- *www.ebay.co.uk* is a giant small-ads site where you can buy or sell just about anything. It can be a strangely addictive way to clear out your clutter or add to your collection.

Fun

- 'I don't feel fifty' is the full title of *www.idf50.co.uk*, a website with a lively mix of practical information and light relief. The friendly online community has a particularly active users forum.
- If you're a wine drinker, you're probably familiar with Malcolm Gluk's concept of superplonk – supermarket wine rated for quality and value for money. At *www.superplonk.com* you can enter the name of the supermarket or off-licence you're going to and how much you've got to spend, and get a list of recommendations.
- There are all sorts of sites where you can send someone a virtual greetings card or bunch of flowers. These are free and the recipient gets an email with a link to the web page where they can see a picture of whatever it is you have selected. Try *www.virtualflowers.com* – it sells real flowers, but also has a selection of over 80 'virtual' bouquets you can send for free.
- *www.friendsreunited.co.uk* has helped countless school, college and work friends get in touch with faces from the past. It's free to register and add your own details to the site, but if you want to get in touch with anyone listed, you'll need to subscribe to be able to send them an email through the site.
- If you're ever stuck for what to have for dinner, there are lots of sites where you can type in a particular ingredient and find recipes that use the item. One of the most popular UK cookery sites is Delia Smith's at *www.delia.co.uk*. The American site *www.epicurious.com* is also worth a look.

Chapter 8

Getting around

Retirement can give you the freedom to get out and about, travelling to visit friends or family. It can mean you've got the time to explore all those places, in this country or abroad, that you missed out on when 'free time' meant a few weeks' annual leave fitted around domestic responsibilities. This chapter covers the options to help you get the best deal on travelling around, whether as a car driver or using buses, trains and coaches. Even if public transport hasn't played a big part in your life to date, one of the great perks of being over 60 is free or reduced-price fares – the perfect incentive to really get to know your county or country.

You and your car

A typical new car costs almost £5,000 a year to run, including the cost of depreciation, which can take a big chunk out of anyone's budget. Retirement is a good time to consider whether you can cut the cost of your motoring. This may mean a major rethink. For example, if you and your partner have a car each, do you really need to be a two-car family? If your job meant lots of long motorway trips in the rush hour, are you likely to be doing the same kind of driving now you're retired?

It may work out cheapest not to have a car at all, and just rely on public transport and hire a car or use taxis when you need to. This will make environmental as well as financial sense, although you may be loath to give up the undeniable independence a car can bring.

Weighing up the costs

To calculate the true cost of your car you need to include the annual cost of:

- fuel
- servicing and repairs
- depreciation
- road tax
- insurance.

The sections below give more detail on how you can cut the costs of each of these factors.

Servicing and repairs

It's worth shopping around to get the best deal on servicing and repairs. You can choose either a franchised dealer or an independent garage. Independents tend to charge less than dealers, but if you've got an extended warranty on your car, check that you will not invalidate it if you get the car serviced by another garage. Using an independent garage should not affect the standard manufacturer's warranty.

Research by *Which?* magazine has consistently shown that the quality of garage servicing is often poor and that in general, franchised dealers are no better than independents. The best way to find a reliable garage is to take account of any recommendations friends can give you and use outlets you know offer a decent service. Some local Trading Standards departments run approved garage schemes, so check with your local office to see if there's one in your area.

Fuel

Significant differences can exist in fuel economy, even between similar-sized cars. All manufacturers publish reliable information about their cars' fuel consumption in their brochures and adverts and it's worth comparing this when choosing a car.

Top tips for economical driving

- Short journeys with lots of stopping and starting are the least efficient. So wherever practical, consider walking or using public transport for these journeys.
- Try to avoid lots of braking and subsequent acceleration – look ahead to see what's coming up on the road and adapt your driving accordingly.
- On the open road, a steady speed of between 50 and 60 miles per hour is usually the most efficient. Check your manual as the exact speed varies between cars, and obviously you will also need to adjust your speed to the road conditions.
- Using the air conditioning increases the fuel consumption, so only use it when you need it.
- Get your car serviced regularly to maintain engine efficiency.
- Check your tyres are at the correct pressure.

Depreciation

Depreciation hits you hardest if you buy a new car and replace it every two or three years. You lose thousands of pounds on the price of a new car in the first couple of years, but after that the decline slows. So it makes good financial sense to buy a second-hand car a couple of years old. See 'Buying a new car', on pages 108–9, for more tips on minimising depreciation.

Road tax

The introduction of graduated vehicle duty means that choosing a car in the right tax bracket can save you £80 or more a year. Cars registered before March 2001 are still taxed based on their engine size. You can get more information on car tax bands from leaflet V149/1 *Rates of Vehicle Excise Duty*, available from post offices or at *www.dvla.gov.uk*.

Car insurance

You'll probably find that your car insurance premiums decrease once you're over 50. However, premiums often start to rise again once you're over 70 and some companies will ask for a medical certificate after that age. What is required varies between companies;

sometimes it is a simple self-certification form (i.e. you declare yourself fit to drive), but sometimes you'll need to pay for a medical examination, usually from your GP.

You may find that some insurance companies hike up the premiums or refuse to insure you at all if you develop certain medical conditions. Not all companies have the same terms however, so if this happens, shop around for alternative cover. Contact one or two insurance brokers and some direct insurers (companies that sell direct to the public rather than through brokers, usually by phone).

If you've always had a company car, you may have problems getting a no-claims discount equivalent to your driving record when you take out your own policy. Getting a letter confirming your driving history from the fleet manager who organised your company car should help.

Changing your car

If you're changing your car, you will probably want to take the factors above into account. In addition, the *Which? Car Guide* (published each September with *Which?* magazine) includes independent car-crash test results, reliability ratings and drivers' opinions of most makes and models. *Which?* research shows that Japanese brands such as Mazda, Toyota and Honda have consistently scored very well for reliability over the years while Land Rover, Alfa Romeo, Citroen and Renault have been among the worst performers.

If you intend to keep your new car for a long time, then it's worth keeping an eye out for features that may make it easier to drive in future years.

- Automatic transmission and power steering are a must for many people as they get older, and can make a real difference to how easy a car is to drive. Both are widely available.
- Try getting in and out of any car you are seriously considering, to check you don't have to stoop or twist uncomfortably. Test this from both the pavement and road level.
- Automatic or electric controls may be useful – electric windows, door mirrors and electrically adjustable seats can be worth paying extra for.

- Are the locks and door handles easy to operate? Remote central locking and cars without an ignition key may suit you better.
- Some people prefer height-adjustable seats and steering wheels.
- Check how much movement and effort are needed to shift gears and how easy the handbrake is to operate.
- Look at the size and height of the boot opening, and test the amount of effort needed to open or close it. Remember that high sills mean more lifting.

Ricability★ offers a free guide *The ins and outs of choosing a car*, which gives more information if you are older or have a disability.

Buying a new car
Depreciation will hit you hardest if you buy a new car – but if you are tempted to get a new model, these tips will help you get the best deal for your money.

- Some cars hold their value better than others so it's worth factoring this into your decision. *Which?* found that models which are popular with fleet buyers in car rental companies tend to lose value quickly but that premium brands such as Audi hold their value better.
- Imported cars can offer big savings. Arranging the import yourself is likely to save the most money, but may take time and effort. Start by getting the DVLA's Personal Import Pack by calling (0870) 2400010. You can use an import agent, which should be less hassle, but make sure you're dealing with a reputable company. (Find out as much as you can about the company, and obtain testimonials from satisfied customers. In particular, make sure that your deposit and final payments are banked separately from the company's own accounts.)
- If you're buying in the UK, you might get a good deal on ex-demonstration models or models about to be replaced.
- Pre-registered cars can offer worthwhile savings. These are cars manufacturers or dealers register as sold to improve their sales figures, and may only have a few miles on the clock.
- It's vital that you test drive a car with the same specification as the car you're considering. Some features, especially power steering, can radically alter the way a car drives.

Buying a used car

Cars are getting more reliable all the time and their rust-resistance is improving too – so a second-hand car can be a wise buy.

Tips on buying second-hand

- If you're offered the opportunity to buy your company car when you retire, this can be a good option if it's the type of car you want.
- Cars are usually cheaper if you buy from a private seller rather than a dealer. However, you don't have the same legal comeback with a private sale. Cars sold privately must be correctly described, but if there's a problem, your only option is to sue. Buying from a dealer gives you full Sale of Goods Act rights so if it's not 'fit for purpose', 'as described' and of 'satisfactory quality', the dealer has a legal obligation to sort the problem out. A second-hand car from a dealer may also come with a warranty.
- As well as traditional car dealers, there are an increasing number of car supermarkets. These tend to be very large sites and often sell pre-registered cars. Prices are generally cheaper but you can't usually negotiate for extra discounts.
- If you want an expert opinion on the condition of the car, both the AA* and the RAC* offer expert inspection services. You don't have to be a member and the inspections cost around £100–£200. The Office of Fair Trading has a useful online guide to help you carry out simple checks yourself at *www.oft.gov.uk/consumer*.
- Check the registration document (V5) carefully. Make sure the Vehicle Identification Number and the engine number on the V5 match the ones on the car. If the car is over three years old, check the MOT certificates to ensure the mileage details and dates correspond.
- If you are at all suspicious about a car, contact AA Used Car Data Check* or the HPI Register*, which holds details of cars with finance payments outstanding, stolen cars and insurance write-offs. A check costs around £35.

Selling your old car privately will get you the best price, but it could be more convenient to trade it in part-exchange with a dealer. Check second-hand car price guides to assess how much you're paying for this convenience. *Parker's Car Price Guide* is one of the most comprehensive and is online at *www.parkers.co.uk*, or you could look in a car magazine.

Driving

Renewing your licence

There's no upper age limit for driving – you can carry on for as long as you can drive safely. However, if you develop a disability or medical condition that affects your driving, you are legally required to inform the Driver and Vehicle Licensing Agency★ (DVLA). Notifiable conditions include diabetes controlled by insulin or tablets, Parkinson's disease, a major or minor stroke, and any visual disability which affects both eyes (not including short or long sight or colour blindness). You can get a full list of the conditions from leaflet D100, *What you need to know about driving licences,* available from post offices, and the conditions are also listed on the DVLA's website at *www.dvla.gov.uk*. Check with your GP if you're uncertain whether your health might affect your driving.

Once you reach 70, you have to renew your licence and will need to keep doing this every three years (or more frequently if you have a notifiable medical condition – see above). You should automatically be sent an application form listing the relevant medical conditions. If you do declare a medical condition, the DVLA will probably ask you for more details and permission to contact your doctor. It may also ask you to have a medical examination.

If you've still got a paper licence, this will be replaced by one of the newer photocard licences for which you'll need to provide passport-sized pictures. You'll have to pay a fee each time you renew your licence (this is currently £6). If you have to renew it more frequently because of a medical condition, there is no charge for the interim renewals.

Safer driving

One of the reasons insurance premiums go down once you reach 50 is that insurers see you as less of a risk – mature, experienced drivers can be some of the safest on the road. However, when you've been driving for 40 or so years, it's easy to slip into bad habits. It can sometimes be difficult to be objective about your own driving, so listen to friends and family. And of course, if you develop medical conditions as outlined in 'Renewing your licence', opposite, you'll need to inform the DVLA.

If you want to brush up your driving skills, or get an honest assessment of your driving, a number of organisations can help. The Royal Society for the Prevention of Accidents (RoSPA)★ has two schemes. The Experienced Driver Assessment provides a report on your driving and tips on how to improve specific driving skills for £35 following an hour's drive in your own car with a trained assessor. The RoSPA also offers an advanced driving test which includes a full written report on your skills. This costs £45 and if you pass you'll be graded as a gold, silver or bronze driver.

Alternatively, you can take the Institute of Advanced Motorists (IAM)★ advanced driving test. The IAM offers a free assessment drive after which an IAM member will give you helpful, practical advice on any bad habits that may have built up and offer tips for improvement. If you wish, you can go on to take the advanced

---

Staying safe

As we age, our reaction times slow down, particularly when we're tired. To make driving as safe as possible, the IAM and RoSPA have these tips for older drivers.

- Plan longer drives carefully, choosing routes that will minimise stress and tiredness. Take a 20-minute break from driving every two hours, even if you don't feel tired. Some exercise and light refreshment during the break can help too.
- Keep up to date with changes in the Highway Code (you can buy a copy in any bookshop or large newsagent).
- Check with your pharmacist or GP on the side-effects of any medication you take (even non-prescription ones) to make sure it doesn't affect your concentration.
- Have regular eye tests to make sure your sight is up to standard.

driving test. This costs £45 including one year's membership of the IAM; or you can buy the 'skill for life package' which costs £85 and includes a driving course, the first year's membership of a local IAM group and an advanced driving manual as well as the test.

Case history: Laurie

Thirty years ago Laurie went to an evening lecture about advanced driving. He was fascinated, but has never found the time to follow it up until now. 'I'd been thinking that maybe my reactions had slowed down a bit. And after all, road conditions have changed hugely since I first started driving in 1952,' he says.

He contacted RoSPA to do its Experienced Driver Assessment, and was very impressed with the local instructor. 'He was first-class, very knowledgeable and helpful – there was no feeling that you were under examination or anything.' Laurie decided to go ahead and take the test and was awarded a gold pass. 'I feel much more confident about driving now, and I'll definitely be going for the re-test in three years' time. In fact I've found it so useful that now my wife's thinking of taking the course too.'

Driving for people with disabilities

Car adaptations and add-on features can enable people to carry on driving for years after it becomes difficult to use a conventionally equipped car. The range of controls is now so wide that almost anyone can drive, provided they meet DVLA requirements (see 'Renewing your licence' on page 110).

Just some of the adaptations available include extra-wide mirrors for people who find it painful to twist to look over their shoulder, and special grips called 'spinners' to help you hold and turn the steering wheel (these are around £25–£45 depending on design). Spinners with hand controls for acceleration and braking on an automatic car are the only adaptation required by many people with disabilities. These cost from £260 to over £400 depending on the type and options. At the top end of the scale, it's possible to replace all the driving controls of a car with a system specifically designed to meet the needs of the person driving it, although this will be very expensive.

Mobility Centres★ advise older people and those with disabilities on all aspects of outdoor mobility. They can carry out a specialist assessment of your ability to drive that takes into consideration any disability or medical conditions, and will explain the type of vehicle best suited to your needs, as well as advising you about any adaptations or equipment to make driving possible or easier. Fees for this service range from £40 to £130 (it is free for people in Scotland).

The charity Ricability★ produces a very useful guide to adapting a car entitled *Car controls*, as well as leaflets on *Getting a wheelchair into a car* and *People lifters*. These are all available from Ricability if you write enclosing the cost of postage, or you can download them from the organisation's website.

The Blue Badge parking scheme

The Blue Badge scheme (formerly known as the Orange Badge scheme) helps people with disabilities to park as close as possible to their destination. If you have a permanent disability that means you have great difficulty walking or have a disability that affects both your arms, you may be entitled to a blue badge. Alternatively if you receive the higher rate of the Mobility Component of the Disability Living Allowance or a Pensioners' Mobility Supplement, or are registered blind, you should also be eligible.

The badge is for the person rather than the vehicle, so it can be used if a friend or relative is driving you somewhere in his or her own car. Badge holders are exempt from some parking restrictions – for example, they can park for up to three hours on single and double yellow lines and can park free at parking meters – but the scheme doesn't apply in parts of central London (there are parking bays reserved for badge holders in these boroughs instead).

You can apply to the Social Services department of your local authority if you think you might qualify for a badge. You can also get a leaflet giving full details of the scheme from the Mobility and Inclusion Unit of the Department for Transport★.

Motability

If you get the higher-rate mobility component of the Disability Living Allowance or War Pensioner's Mobility Supplement, the Motability Scheme can help you put your benefit towards the cost of leasing a new car or buying a car, powered wheelchair or scooter on hire purchase. If money is a problem you can apply to Motability for a means-tested grant for an advance payment towards a Motability car, adaptations and driving lessons. For further information contact Motability★.

Tax exemptions

If you receive the higher-rate mobility component of the Disability Living Allowance or the War Pensioner's Mobility Supplement you usually don't have to pay road tax on your car. For more information see leaflet V188, *Exemption from vehicle excise duty for disabled people*, available from the DVLA★ and on its website *www.dvla.gov.uk*.

Wheelchair users don't usually pay VAT on the price of a car which has been designed or specially adapted for them. To qualify for this exemption you have to be a permanent wheelchair user and you must both buy and adapt the vehicle at the same time – you can't get a refund of VAT for adaptations made later. Adaptations which count towards the exemption include devices which make it possible for you to get in and out of a car, such as a swivel seat, and adaptations to enable a wheelchair to be carried in a car. For more details get a copy of VAT Information Sheet 07/01 *Motor vehicles adapted for disabled people* from the Customs and Excise National Advice Service on (0845) 0109000, or *www.hmce.gov.uk*

Public transport

Train travel

Discount fares

Generally, booking as far in advance as you can will save you money. A Senior Railcard currently costs £18 a year and is available to everyone over 60. It will give you a third off most fares in Great Britain (excluding peak-hour journeys within the south-east of England). This includes Cheap Day singles and returns, Saver and Supersaver returns and first-class tickets. It also includes discounts on some fares for rail and sea journeys to Northern Ireland, Eire and the Isle of Wight.

You can get an application form from any staffed station or rail-appointed travel agent, or you can buy one over the phone from your local train company (call National Rail Enquiries on (08457) 484950 to find out the number).

If you are making a long journey on a Saturday or Sunday and would appreciate the extra comfort of first class, it's worth knowing about Weekend First tickets. This enables holders of most tickets, including those bought with a Senior Railcard, to upgrade to first class, subject to availability on the train – you can't book these seats in advance. Almost all intercity train companies offer this for a flat fee (usually around £10).

Finding the best fare

Getting straightforward information on the best train fares is not easy. *Which?* research in May 2002 showed that the standard of advice from both staffed stations and the national rail enquiries line was unimpressive. When enquiring about train tickets, let the person dealing with your enquiry know whether you want the cheapest possible ticket or the shortest journey time. If you can be flexible about the time of day you travel and how long your journey takes, make this clear – it may help you to get the cheapest ticket.

A number of websites sell rail tickets and can help you plan a journey. If you have access to the Internet, these are probably the best way to find the cheapest route, even if you subsequently decide not to buy the ticket online. Two of the best-known sites are *www.thetrainline.co.uk* and *www.qjump.co.uk*

Accessibility

Since 1999, new trains have had to meet new standards of accessibility, and standards are improving as these trains come into service. Unfortunately, on the last few remaining slam-door trains, access is so poor that wheelchair users still have to travel in the guard's van.

All the train companies and Network Rail have agreed to a code of practice to provide assistance to travellers with disabilities. If you are likely to need help at your destination station, telephone the train company for your starting station in advance and they should be able to ensure that the help is in place when you arrive. You'll usually need to give at least 24 hours' notice.

A Disabled Person's Railcard gives similar discounts to the Senior Railcard but is cheaper (currently £14 a year) and allows you to take a companion with you at the same reduced rate. There are rigorous qualifying criteria; you can get full details from the leaflet *Rail travel for disabled passengers*, available from most staffed stations or at *www.disabledpersons-railcard.co.uk*.

Train travel abroad

If you've got a Senior Railcard, you can also buy a Rail Plus Card for £12 which currently gives you up to 25 per cent off most rail travel in Europe. You can buy the card at some staffed railway stations, or contact Rail Europe on (08705) 848848. It can send you an application form and give you further information about rail travel in Europe. Rail Europe also sells the French Railways Carte Senior for £30, which gives discounts of up to 50 per cent, subject to availability, on rail travel within France

Neither card can be used to buy Eurostar tickets, but Eurostar offers its own range of discounted fares for travellers aged 60 or over, with prices starting from £59 return. These tickets have no advance purchase conditions or overnight stay requirements. The company also offers reduced fares to wheelchairs users and people who are visually impaired, and their travel companions. You can book tickets at appointed travel agents, by ringing (08705) 186186, online at *www.eurostar.com*, or in person at Waterloo and Ashford International stations.

Coach travel

Coach fares are often cheaper than rail fares and while your journey may take longer, most coaches now have toilets and refreshments on board and you can usually reserve a seat. National Express Ltd★ is the best-known of the coach companies. It offers an Advantage 50 discount coach card, available to everyone over 50. This costs £9 for one year and gives you up to 30 per cent off nearly all standard fares (apart from special offers). The card can be used on all long-distance coach services in England and Wales and on some through services to Scotland. You can buy the card from any National Express coach station, by phone on (08705) 898989 or online at *www.nationalexpress.com*.

Accessibility

All new large coaches must be wheelchair accessible from January 2005, but it will take some time before all coaches in use are up to this standard. The steps on to coaches are usually higher than on buses and may be difficult for some people. If you will need help at the coach station, contact the coach operator in advance to see what assistance it can provide – National Express has an Additional Needs Helpline on 0121-423 8479.

Buses

Schemes for concessionary bus travel vary across the UK. In Scotland and Wales, everyone over 60 is entitled to free bus travel. In England, everyone aged over 60 is entitled to a pass giving them at least half-price bus travel. Variations include schemes that offer free travel, allow you to travel outside your local area or subsidise other means of public transport, while some impose time restrictions on when you can travel. Find out what the deal is in your area from your local authority. In Northern Ireland, bus travel is free after the age of 65.

Accessibility

New buses have had to be wheelchair accessible since 2000. But, as with other public transport, it will be some time before all buses in service reach this standard. Contact your local bus company for details of local facilities. If you need extra time to get to a seat before the bus moves off, let the driver know as you get on.

Air travel

For European travel, the low-cost airlines such as easyJet and Ryanair are proving very popular. These airlines take a deliberate 'no-frills' approach and can be a good-value way to fly. Tips to get the best prices for flights are as follows.

- Book early – at least a month before departure. Cheap tickets on all airlines tend to go quickly. You can sometimes get cheap tickets just before departure, especially on charter flights, but this isn't a reliable way to get on a flight.
- Don't automatically assume low-cost airlines will be cheapest. Prices for full-service scheduled flights or charter flights are worth checking out.

- In the past, if you wanted cheaper tickets on full-service scheduled airlines you had to go to a flight specialist (sometimes called a consolidator) such as Trailfinders. Nowadays the airlines are just as likely to sell the cheap seats themselves.
- Some of the low-cost airlines use small airports which may be further away from town than you expect. This isn't necessarily a problem, but it's a good idea to check where the airport is first if its name is unfamiliar to you.
- If being retired means you've got the freedom to travel in the middle of the week and avoid peak business and weekend break times, make the most of this and check the fares a day or so either side of your preferred travel dates.
- For long-haul flights, consider breaking the journey. This will give you a wider choice of airlines as well the chance to spend a few days in a new city. Talk to a flight specialist for the best deals on long or complicated journeys.

Avoiding deep vein thrombosis

Concern has increased about the risks of deep vein thrombosis (DVT) when flying. Experts believe that older people are generally more likely to suffer blood clots than younger ones, but more research needs to be done to investigate the specific risk of developing a clot after a long flight for passengers of all ages. While the picture is still unclear, it makes sense for everyone to follow these simple precautions.

- Don't sit still for the whole flight. Take the opportunity to move around in your seat and in the cabin.
- Rotate your ankles every half-hour or so.
- Drink less alcohol and caffeine and drink more water before and during the flight.

If you're concerned you might be at greater risk (for example, if you've had recent heart disease, leg surgery or are on HRT) then consult your GP. He or she may recommend that you take low-dose aspirin before flying or wear compression stockings ('flight socks').

Ferries

Some ferry companies offer discounts to Senior Railcard holders (see pages 114–16); others offer discounts to people above a certain age. As always, it's worth asking when you make a booking. You've got nothing to lose if they say no and you may get a better deal.

Transport if you have mobility problems

Taxi card and dial-a-ride schemes

If you are unable to use public transport and don't have a car, other schemes may help you get around.

Dial-a-ride is a scheme which provides door-to-door transport for people who can't use public transport. In most London boroughs and some other areas, taxi-card schemes offer low-cost taxi-fares. To find out if there is a scheme in your area, contact the Transport Planning Department of your local authority. If it can't help, check with the Community Transport Association★.

There may be other transport schemes run by volunteers or charities – your local Age Concern, Social Services department or Citizens Advice Bureau should be able to give you details.

Shopmobility

Shopmobility schemes are found in many shopping centres and offer temporary loans of powered wheelchairs, scooters and ordinary wheelchairs to help older people and those with disabilities to shop independently. You can also borrow this equipment if you have temporary mobility problems – after an operation, say – or if you simply find shopping on foot too tiring.

Low-speed scooters and buggies

There are special low-speed electric scooters, buggies and wheelchairs designed for people with disabilities. Some of these, with a maximum speed of 4 mph, can be driven on the pavement, while other models ('Class 3' types) can be driven at 8 mph on the road (but are still limited to 4 mph on the pavement). You don't need a driving licence for either type and you are not required to take out insurance, although it is advisable to do so. You can't use the vehicles in cycle lanes, operational bus lanes or motorways and it's not advisable to use them on dual carriageways with a speed limit of over 50 mph.

An investigation by *Which?* magazine in April 2002 found that some people buying these types of mobility aids felt let down by the advice they received from salespeople. If you have mobility problems, you can get good independent advice from the Disabled Living Foundation★, your nearest Disabled Living Centre and the Mobility Information Service★ (see Chapter 15 for more about these organisations).

Further information

Tripscope★ is a nationwide, telephone-based travel and transport information service for people with mobility difficulties. It offers assistance with travel queries in the UK and abroad, and can answer questions on the availability of suitable transport, equipment such as wheelchairs for hire, and accessible facilities.

Chapter 9
Holidays

The pick of the packages

Nowadays, packages for the over-50s include adventures to exotic worldwide locations as well as more restful holidays. Certain operators also run packages especially for the retired holidaymaker, such as British university and college stays, holidays for singles, cruises, religious tours, garden tours and walking tours.

Holiday Care* gives useful advice about holidays for older people, people with disabilities and those with limited mobility.

Holidays in Britain

Bed-and-breakfasting can be one of the cheapest types of holiday as well as the most varied. But don't rule out staying in hotels. Which Books* publishes both *The Good Bed and Breakfast Guide* and *The Which? Guide to Good Hotels*, with details of hundreds of establishments in each Guide.

Self-catering

You should be able to find holiday self-catering accommodation in pretty well any part of Britain you wish to visit. Several companies offer a range of accommodation, from the simple and comparatively inexpensive to luxury homes sleeping six to eight – a good option for a family holiday with grandchildren. Many have been checked by the relevant tourist authority and given an appropriate grading. A good place to look is in the classified columns of the Sunday papers, where you should find advertisements placed by companies and by cottage owners themselves. If you have Internet access this can also be a good resource for checking out potential accommodation.

Farm holidays

Farm holidays are increasingly popular; you can go as a paying guest in the farmhouse itself or rent a caravan or cottage. Bed-and-breakfast rates are usually good value, and some farms will provide an evening meal as well.

For a choice of over 1,100 farms that have all been inspected under the National Tourist Board accreditation schemes, contact Farmstay UK★. You can obtain a free copy of the Farmstay UK guide by either phoning or filling in the online request form.

Caravanning

Caravanning is an ideal way of touring without having to worry about what the accommodation at your destination will be like. The Camping and Caravanning Club (CCC)★ offers family membership for £27.50 plus a £5 joining fee (the latter waived if you join by direct debit or credit card), and members over the age of 55 qualify for a 20 per cent discount on some site fees.

The Club offers insurance and a foreign travel service, and each new member's pack contains a touring safety guide with advice for beginners. You can also obtain a listing of hire companies for caravans, motor caravans and extendable caravans – the advantage of the last type is that they are lightweight and have less wind drag, making them easier to transport. An annual guide called *Your Place in the Country* lists 93 full-facility club sites all over Britain, while the two-yearly *Big Sites Book* contains details of 4,000 sites, 1,200 of which are certificated – that is, they are small sites where only CCC members can go.

Holidays abroad

Independent holidays

The increased popularity of no-frills flights means that they are available from many regional airports around Britain as well as from London. For retired travellers they are a particular boon, as the cheapest fares tend to be during midweek. For the biggest savings, book online at least a month before departure. Websites that allow you to compare airfares include *www.kelkoo.co.uk*, *www.easyvalue.com* and *www.skyscanners.com*.

Some tour operators that traditionally offered all-in packages to European cities now produce 'accommodation only' brochures that allow you to book hotels without flights. This can often be cheaper than booking with the hotel direct – but it is always worth finding out. There are also numerous websites offering hotel bookings as well as discount flights. Some of the most popular travel websites include *www.lastminute.com*, *www.expedia.co.uk* and *www.travelocity.co.uk*.

Tips for getting the best deal

- Hotels, particularly in cities, often offer weekend deals to attract the leisure market.
- Pick your season – there are fewer bargains in the busy summer season or at Easter.

Self-catering

Self-catering abroad can be booked through most of the major holiday firms and can also be arranged privately. France offers a particularly wide choice in holiday homes, especially among gîtes – rural properties which range from converted barns to grander accommodation. The owner generally lives nearby and will usually help with advice on local services – but not necessarily in English. Various tour operators offer gîte holidays.

Timeshare

The activities of some salespeople have given timesharing a very bad name. The basic idea of timesharing is that you buy the use of a certain property, often abroad, for a certain period at a certain time of year. If you do not wish to use that time yourself you can lend it to friends, sub-let it or swap it for time at another timeshare property elsewhere and, if you have bought the timeshare in perpetuity, you simply leave it to someone in your will as you would any other property. Timeshare should not be regarded as an investment – resale prices can be as little as 40 per cent of the original price and you still have to pay for flights, food and maintenance fees, as well as exchange fees if you want to swap. Do your sums very carefully – you might be better off with package holidays.

Costs vary depending on location and period; for example, prices start from £1,500 for a one-bedroom apartment in Spain in high season. The second-hand value of most timeshares is far less than new, so consider buying from a reputable resale agency. But however you buy, do your homework and make sure you know the resort into which you are buying. The maintenance charges should be checked very carefully to see exactly what they represent and whether they are linked with a cost of living index. You should also make careful enquiries as to the resale value of the property, which may be a good deal lower than the initial purchase price; also note that it can be very difficult to resell a timeshare property. In some countries you might become liable for direct taxation as a timeshare owner, so this is another area to investigate.

Within the European Union (EU), timeshare resorts must conform to rules laid down by an EU directive on timeshare (this also applies to the European Economic Area – see page 19 – including Cyprus and Malta). The directive requires prospective purchasers to be given specified information, regulates the contents of the contract, and gives consumers the right to cancel within a minimum cooling-off period of ten days, during which no deposit may be demanded by the seller.

There is also the UK Timeshare Act 1992, which gives you a 14-day cooling-off period. The legal definition of timeshare covers only contracts of more than three years and minimum periods of a week. Share schemes and property bonds are not covered, nor are boats or cruises. Exploiting this, rogue companies have started to sell timeshare schemes of under 35 months – with the option to extend for more years – and 'time' on narrowboats and cruises.

Holiday or travel-club schemes where customers pay a hefty fee (which can be £10,000 or more) for holidays in different locations around the world, are not covered by legislation either. The pressure group Timeshare Consumers' Association warns that most of these holiday clubs are scams. For more information, see its website *www.timeshare.org.uk* or contact it on (01909) 591100.

Be particularly careful if you sign a contract outside the UK as you are unlikely to be protected by UK law. If you run into problems, you may have to go to a foreign court, which could cost you a lot of money and trouble.

You should resist the sort of presentations that are attached to offers of lavish prizes and free holidays, even in Britain, and avoid signing any contract until you have had it checked by a solicitor. Never produce your credit card to a sales person as identification – you could come under heavy pressure to use it to put down a deposit. The trick is to resist all blandishments, pressure and promises, and consider the purchase as coolly as you would with any other large item.

A checklist of points to consider when buying a timeshare, called *The Timeshare Guide*, can be obtained from the Department of Trade and Industry.★ Many timeshare companies belong or are affiliated to one of two exchange organisations: Interval International Ltd★ and RCI Europe Ltd,★ which give access to holiday resorts in nearly 100 countries and offer short breaks, cruises and coach tours. The Office of Fair Trading★ has produced a report on the industry which can be obtained free of charge by application in writing. The trade organisation for timeshare developers, exchange organisations, resale companies and so on is the Organisation for Timeshare in Europe★. This organisation offers a free advice and conciliation service to anybody who has dealings with its members.

Holiday peace of mind

No matter what sort of holiday you are planning, there are certain basic guidelines to follow in order to be prepared for all eventualities.

Money

Don't carry more cash with you than is covered by your insurance policy – usually around £150 – and don't be lulled by a holiday atmosphere into being more careless than you would be at home. Do not carry your wallet, passport or indeed anything else of value in your back pocket, and never leave your money on display. Carry a shoulder bag across your body, or preferably wear a money belt under your top layer of clothing. Leave jewellery at home or, if you must take it, stash it in the hotel safe or tuck it away in your rented accommodation.

If you are unfortunate enough to meet with a mugger, do not play the hero – hand over your money without argument. Pack a copy of your insurance policy in your hand luggage so that you can check the procedure if necessary, and keep a list of emergency phone numbers to ring in the event of theft.

Insurance

It is advisable to take out comprehensive insurance that is appropriate to your needs. Tour operators often insist on insurance as a condition of booking, but note that you do not have to take out the insurance package they offer; you may well be able to find a cheaper one elsewhere that will give you satisfactory cover. However, if you are travelling independently you may not be entitled to compensation for mishaps tour operators could be considered liable for. Note that many companies increase their premiums for people over 65, though you should be able to shop around for reasonable rates.

Read the small print carefully and ensure you will be covered for the following eventualities:

- loss of your deposit or cancellation of the entire holiday
- the cost of curtailing or cancelling your holiday in the event of serious illness or death in your family
- loss of money, baggage and personal effects
- the cost of emergency purchases if your baggage is delayed
- personal liability cover in case you cause injury to another person or damage to property
- compensation for any inconvenience caused by transport cancellations or delays

- medical treatment, hospitalisation, ambulance service, emergency dental treatment, special transport home, the cost of prolonging your stay and expenses for a companion who may have to stay with you.

In the personal liability and medical categories the sums become astronomical: allow £1,000,000 for the former and £2,000,000 for the latter.

Paying for at least part of your holiday by credit card could provide some medical cover while you are travelling (but not during your stay). This should not be considered as an alternative to medical insurance. If things go wrong, under the Consumer Credit Act you should be able to claim from the credit-card company as well as the tour operator (though you will get money only from one). But your holiday must cost more than £100 per person; the credit-card slip should be made out to the operator, not the travel agent; and note that debit cards, charge cards and most gold cards do not offer this protection.

Peace of mind while you are away

The Home Office has published a leaflet, *Peace of Mind While You're Away*, giving advice on preventing burglaries while you are on holiday. Free copies are available from police stations. See Chapter 3 for more on home security.

Health

For travellers abroad, the Department of Health★ issues a useful leaflet called *Health Advice for Travellers* (T5), which gives advice on precautions to take and how to cope in an emergency. This leaflet also contains form E111, which entitles you to free or reduced-cost emergency treatment in EU countries and a number of others that have reciprocal health care agreements with the UK. You must take this to a post office for processing. However, you should still take out insurance that will cover medical expenses (see opposite) as form E111 does not cover repatriation.

Get medical advice well in advance of your trip, as some courses of vaccinations need to be given over a few months. These are usually cheapest from a GP. Alternatively, try a specialist travel clinic, though these can be expensive. For further information, telephone helplines include the MASTA Travellers Healthline on (0906) 8224100 and the Public Health Advisory Service on (0900) 1600270. Good websites include *www.fco.gov.uk/knowbeforeyougo, www.who.int/ith/* and *www.fitfortravel.scot.nhs.uk.*

Do not forget to pack any medication that you take regularly in your hand luggage. Make sure that it is clearly labelled with both the trade name and generic name, and find out if there are any restrictions on taking it in or out of the UK or the country you are visiting. A back-up letter from your doctor may be useful.

In addition, take a simple first-aid kit with you. If you are going to a hot climate, use plenty of high-protection sun screen – and beware of ice-cream, seafood, salads, fruit (unless you can peel it yourself) and unbottled water (which also means ice). Avoid buffets laid out at room temperature – go for foods from the menu that have to be freshly cooked.

When travelling by air, wear loose-fitting clothes, drink plenty of liquid and remember that alcohol consumed in the air has much more effect than it does on the ground. Allow a couple of days for resting and acclimatisation when you arrive.

Complaints about holidays

The following information covers holidays arranged by a tour operator. Always try to get problems sorted out on the spot. Speak to the tour rep if there is one. Otherwise, try the manager of your accommodation and the tour operator's office locally or in the UK. Complete a complaint questionnaire while still in the resort. If you still aren't satisfied, take it up with the tour operator within 28 days of your return. Collect names and addresses of witnesses or people who have suffered similar problems, and take photographs or video footage if appropriate.

Write to the tour operator as soon as possible. Tell it what went wrong, how this reduced the value of your holiday, and state what sort of response you are expecting. If you are looking for compensation, put a figure on this. The amount will depend on your situation, but here are the three main elements to consider.

- The difference between what you paid for and what you got (for example, the cost of the three-star hotel you booked compared with the two-star hotel you were moved to). If only certain days of your holiday were affected, you should claim just for that proportion.

- Loss of enjoyment, disappointment, inconvenience etc. Take into account what your holiday cost and how much of it was affected.
- Out-of-pocket expenses (for example, the cost of eating out if you are not given an adequate means to cook on a 'self-catering' holiday).

Only in extreme cases are you likely to recover the full cost, but in many cases you should be awarded compensation for loss of enjoyment, plus reimbursement of extra costs incurred.

If you are not happy with the operator's response, write back stating why. If it makes an offer you think is too low, keep any cheque it sends (but do not cash it) and continue the correspondence until you get a more satisfactory outcome. If an exchange of letters does not get you what you want, consider other ways of settling the dispute.

The small claims procedure was designed to be a fairly quick, straightforward and cheap alternative to the full county court. It is kept informal and you can argue your case in person without having to use a lawyer. It can be used for claims up to £5,000 in England and Wales. The limit on small claims is £2,000 in Northern Ireland and £750 in Scotland, but the latter limit is currently under review. These limits apply to the total claim, not that of each individual – if, say, you were claiming for a ruined family holiday.

If your tour operator belongs to the Association of British Travel Agents (ABTA)★, you can use the independent arbitration scheme operated by the Chartered Institute of Arbitrators★. This relies totally on written evidence, although you can submit photographs and video evidence. You must apply within nine months of your return from holiday, and the decision is binding on both parties, so you can't go to the small claims court later if you do not like the decision. The Association of Independent Tour Operators (AITO)★ also has a scheme for settling customers' disputes with its members, run by an independent mediator.

You can also join Which? Legal Service★, which offers individual help and expert advice if something goes wrong with goods and services you've bought, including holidays.

Part 3

Your very good health

Chapter 10

You and the health service

We all want to stay as fit and healthy as possible throughout our retirement. Health is not just about the absence of illness – it's also about maintaining physical and mental well-being. This section of the book has chapters on fitness and healthy eating as well as medical conditions and health services.

When you think about health services you might think first of doctors, nurses and hospitals, but services which improve health are provided by a whole range of different professionals. This chapter explains how the system works along with tips for getting the best out of these services.

Setting standards for the care of older people

The government has set out a National Service Framework for services for older people in England. This states that NHS services 'will be provided regardless of age, on the basis of clinical need alone' and that 'Local Authority social care services will not use age in their eligibility criteria or policies, to restrict access to available services'. It also sets out targets for stroke, mental health and injuries from falls. The full document is now available only on the Internet at *www.doh.gov.uk*, but you can get a leaflet entitled *Standards in health and social services – what can I expect?* by writing to the Age Concern★ Policy Unit.

The National Health Service (NHS)

NHS services are often described as either primary care or secondary care. Primary care simply means general health care that is provided in the community or home setting by people such as GPs, district nurses, health visitors and dentists. Secondary care (sometimes known as 'acute care') means hospital and specialist services.

The current structure of the NHS in England means that the country is divided into primary care areas. Primary Care Trusts (PCTs) are responsible for the healthcare of people living in each area. You can find the address and contact details of your PCT in the phone book, or phone NHS Direct on (0845) 4647.

PCTs are responsible for ensuring the provision of local primary care services, such as GPs, dentists, pharmacies and community nurses. They commission secondary hospital and specialist care, and must also assess the health needs of their area and develop plans to ensure they are met (Health Improvement and Modernisation Plans).

In Wales, a new system was introduced in April 2003 and Local Health Boards now have a similar role to the PCTs in England. In Scotland the equivalent authority is the Health Board and in Northern Ireland it's currently called the Health and Social Services Board.

Medical appointments

Whether you're seeing your GP, a district nurse or a hospital consultant it's worth thinking in advance of any important points you want to discuss. Many people find it helpful to write these down and have a list with them at the consultation. Don't be afraid to be honest about your preferences and concerns and be as clear as you can about anything that is worrying you. It's the responsibility of the health professional to explain things clearly to you, including discussing options for your treatment with you. If you're unsure about anything, say so. You can always use your list of important points to make notes during the consultation. If you're concerned you might not take all the information in at once or may not feel able to ask questions, you can bring a friend or relative with you to the appointment who also knows and understands your concerns.

General practitioners

Your GP (General Practitioner or family doctor) is usually the first port of call for most health matters. GP practices vary greatly, with some offering health promotion clinics, complementary therapy or even minor surgery.

It's important that you have a good relationship with your GP as he or she will not only diagnose, treat and help you manage your health problems but will usually be the person who refers you on to other specialist medical services or for tests. If you don't get on as well as you'd like and can't sort out your differences, consider changing GP to one who suits you better.

If you want to change GP or if you've moved to a new area, it's a good idea to ask around for personal recommendations from friends and neighbours. You can also get a list of local GPs from your PCT or health board. This should include information such as the doctor's sex and date of qualification. You need to be reasonably local to the GP's practice to be in the catchment area – ask your PCT or health board if you're not sure about this. It's worth visiting practices you're interested in to get a copy of the practice leaflet. These vary, but should have more details about the services the practice offers and the way things like the appointments system work.

To register with a new GP, as long as you live in their catchment area and they are willing to accept you, all you need to do is turn up at the new practice and ask to be registered. Take your medical card with your NHS number on it if you have it. If you can't find a GP who will accept you, contact your PCT or health board as it has a duty to find you one (although there is a risk that you may be allocated to a GP whom you like less than your current one).

If you're away from home
If you're away from home, visiting relatives for instance, you can register with a GP as a temporary patient for up to three months. Even if they won't accept you as a temporary patient, any GP must still give you treatment that is immediately necessary.

Pharmacists

If you're over 60, you automatically qualify for free prescriptions. If you're under 60 you may be entitled to free prescriptions if you suffer from one of a number of specified conditions, if you receive a war pension or if you or your partner get one of a number of benefits including Income Support. Find out more from NHS

Special services for older people

- Everyone aged over 65 is entitled to free flu vaccinations. Vaccines are usually available from October and need to be repeated each year. Other vaccines, such as pneumococcus against pneumonia, or tetanus and polio boosters, may also be recommended.
- Everyone over 75 must be offered an annual health check-up. If you can't get to your GP's surgery, this can take place in your home. The check-up is likely to include assessing your mobility, hearing, diet and your mental and physical condition.
- According to the National Standards Framework for older people in England, everyone over 75 should normally have their medicines reviewed each year, and if you take four or more medicines you should have a review every six months.

Direct* or read leaflet HC11 *Are you entitled to help with health costs?*, available from main post offices or by phoning (08701) 555455.

If you don't get free prescriptions and are on regular medication, you may find it cheaper to get a pre-payment certificate which you use like a 'season ticket' to pay for prescriptions. Find out more by getting the application form FP95 from a pharmacist or by phoning (0845) 850 0030.

Dentists

Most dentists can choose to work privately or provide care under the NHS (this is currently called a national contract), although some are directly employed (community dentists) or have a contract with the Primary Care Trust to see patients on the NHS. Some dentists carry out both private and NHS work. You may also be referred by your GP or dentist to the dental department of a hospital for specialist treatment.

Finding a dentist

It should be up to you to choose whether to go to a private or NHS dentist. Some treatments are not available on the NHS – you will have to pay privately for cosmetic treatments such as white rather than amalgam fillings, for example. There is a fixed range of charges for NHS treatment and private care can be much more expensive.

However, it can be very difficult in some areas to find a dentist who will accept new NHS patients. If you have trouble finding one, try contacting your local Primary Care Trust or health board, or NHS Direct★.

In some parts of the country, Dental Access Services have opened. These provide routine as well as emergency dental care for people who are not registered with a dentist. However, they don't hold your dental records so you don't get continuity of care. To find out if there is a Dental Access Service near you, call NHS Direct★.

Registering for continuing dental care

It's best to join a NHS dentist's list by signing up for continuing care. This doesn't cost anything and means that you should be entitled to NHS treatment for all the dental care necessary to maintain the health of your teeth and gums. However, the dentist is still free to decide who should provide the care and what level of service to give. He or she can also decide at any time to stop providing NHS care.

Your registration with the NHS dentist lasts for 15 months from the time of your last visit, so it's important to 'sign-on' with your dentist for continuing care regularly. If you haven't been to see your NHS dentist in the last 15 months, you should contact the practice to check you're still on its list of NHS patients.

If you don't register for continuing care, a NHS dentist may accept you as an 'occasional patient' but you won't be entitled to the full range of NHS treatments.

Home visits

If you're registered with a NHS dentist for continuing care and your health or disability means it's impossible for you to get to the surgery, your dentist must visit you at home, without extra cost, provided you live within five miles of the surgery.

Alternatively, the Community Dental Service may also be able to provide treatment in your own home if you are unable to travel to a dentist. You can get contact details for your local Community Dental Service from NHS Direct*.

Paying for NHS dental treatment

In Wales, people over 60 can get free dental examinations but elsewhere, being over 60 does not in itself exempt you from NHS dental charges. Other exemptions or reductions in NHS charges are available only to older people who are on low incomes. People on Income Support (also called Minimum Income Guarantee) and their partners get free treatment as do some people who receive a war pension.

If you don't get Income Support but have a low income and limited savings, then you may be entitled to a reduction in the cost of treatment. For more information about this and the forms you need to apply, get the Department of Health leaflet HC11 *Are you entitled to help with health costs?* (see page 136).

Assuming you have to pay for NHS treatment, the most you will have to pay for any one course of treatment is currently £372. As a general guideline the current NHS patient charges range from £5.32 for a basic check-up to £14.60 or more for a large filling to £115.16 for a full set of plastic dentures.

Everyone who's registered with an NHS dentist for continuing care is entitled to the free replacement or repair of certain treatments (including fillings, root fillings and crowns) which have been carried out in the last year, as well as free repairs to dentures.

Paying for private dental treatment

You may have to pay a fee to register with the dentist privately. The charges for private treatment are often higher with no limit on the costs, so make sure the dentist gives you a costed treatment plan. Costs vary between practices, so it's worth ringing around a few dentists to get an idea of fees first.

You can simply pay as and when you're treated, or use one of several schemes to help spread the cost.

- Before joining a **capitation scheme**, the dentist assesses your dental health and this determines how much you pay each month. This covers most treatment, but you may have to pay separately for very costly work.

- You can pay regular premiums for **dental insurance**. When you receive treatment you claim on the policy. Depending on the policy, this might cover the whole cost or up to a specified sum. Most policies exclude dental problems you already have when you start the policy.
- **Credit schemes** give you a special credit card you use to pay. You make monthly payments and interest is added to the outstanding balance. Check the interest rate – if it's higher than your ordinary credit card, use that instead.

The cost of capitation schemes and dental insurance often increases with age.

Opticians

It's important to have your eyesight tested regularly (at least every two years). Tests are free for the over-60s and can help detect glaucoma and give early warning of conditions such as hypertension and diabetes. The risk of eye problems increases as you get older and conditions can be treated far more successfully if they are identified early. Any deterioration in your eyesight should always be checked – don't assume it's just 'old age'.

If you're under 60, eye tests are free if you're on Income Support, have diabetes or glaucoma or are at risk of glaucoma. You are also entitled to eye tests if you are registered blind or partially sighted, or if you need complex lenses. You may also be able to get help with the cost of glasses or contact lenses. You can find out more in leaflet HC11 *Are you entitled to help with health costs?* (see page 136).

Other primary care services

These services are often based at GP practices, and the NHS ones are all the responsibility of the Primary Care Trust or health board. You will sometimes need a referral from your GP or another healthcare professional to access these services, but you can self-refer yourself to some of them.

Care assistants and other domiciliary care A range of services exist to help elderly people or people with disabilities live more independently in the community. These may be provided by health services, social services or voluntary organisations. For more information see Chapter 14.

Chiropodists (now often called podiatrists) Chiropodists provide footcare which can be vital to maintain mobility. There can be long waiting lists so many people opt to see a chiropodist privately. You can contact the Society of Chiropodists and Podiatrists★ to get details of local practitioners. Members have to be registered with the Health Professions Council. If you are diabetic, you should have annual foot checks with a chiropodist on the NHS.

Community dieticians assess and advise on people's nutritional requirements and can help with conditions such as diabetes. You usually need to be referred by your GP or other health professional.

Community mental health nurses (previously known as community psychiatric nurses) assess the needs and provide support and counselling for people with mental health problems and their families. Referral systems vary according to local policies; you may be able to self-refer, or you may need a referral from your GP or other health professional.

Counsellors, psychotherapists and psychologists use talking and listening techniques to help people work out their problems. Some GP surgeries offer the services of a counsellor or may refer you to specialist services on the NHS. However, these services tend to be quite limited on the NHS and there may be long waiting lists. For information on finding a practitioner you can read *The Which? Guide to Counselling and Therapy*. Alternatively, see if your GP can recommend someone working in private practice or get a list from a reputable professional body such as the British Association for Counselling and Psychotherapy★, the United Kingdom Council for Psychotherapy★ or the British Psychological Society★.

District nurses are specially trained to care for people at home. They also work in GPs' surgeries, health centres and residential homes. You are most likely to be referred to a district nurse by your GP, although in some areas you can access them directly.

Occupational therapists (OTs) help patients regain strength and cope with the activities of daily living, including advice on equipment and aids. Your GP or other health professional can refer you to an NHS OT. OTs are also employed by Social Services departments to assess disability and recommend aids and equipment. These OTs can be contacted through Social Services departments.

Physiotherapists help keep people mobile and assist with rehabilitation after injury, surgery or stroke. They help treat conditions including severe respiratory disease, rheumatism, arthritis, muscular pain and incontinence. You can contact a physiotherapist through your GP (or you may be able to self-refer to a local hospital physiotherapy department). Physiotherapists also work in the private sector (you can find one through the Chartered Society of Physiotherapy★).

Practice nurses are based in GP surgeries or health centres and provide services such as breast awareness, cervical smears, management of diabetes and high blood pressure, and give advice on healthy lifestyles. You can usually self-refer to see the practice nurse.

Other **specialist nurses** can advise on specific topics such as incontinence. Health visitors mainly work with young families, but sometimes include older people in their remit. Macmillan nurses and Marie Curie nurses specialise in caring for people with cancer and their families. Ask your GP what specialist nurses work in your area.

Speech and language therapists work with patients with all types of speech and language problems and related eating and swallowing disorders, including the treatment of stroke patients. They can be accessed through your GP, other health professionals, Social Services or by self referral.

NHS Direct and NHS walk-in centres

NHS Direct★ is a 24-hour telephone advice and information service for England and Wales. It can be useful to call the service if, for instance, you're not sure whether you should call out a GP at night. It can also give you more information about particular conditions or details of local health services. In Scotland the NHS24 Helpline (0800) 224488 offers a similar service and should be expanded across Scotland in 2003.

NHS walk-in centres are run by nurses and provide treatment for minor illnesses and injuries in over 40 cities and towns in England. As the name suggests, you don't have to book an appointment. You can find out if there is a walk-in centre near you by calling NHS Direct★.

Complementary therapies

Complementary therapies are increasingly popular and some, such as acupuncture, are even offered by some GP practices. The law doesn't regulate most complementary therapies so anyone can legally advertise themselves as a reflexologist, say, even if they have no training or experience. The only complementary therapies with statutory regulation are osteopathy and chiropractic. Herbal medicine and acupuncture are likely to be next in line.

For professions not regulated by law, it's important to choose a practitioner who belongs to a reputable professional body. Some therapies have several different professional bodies, so it's worth contacting the different bodies to find out how they operate and what qualifications, training and experience they demand of their members; also whether they require members to have insurance cover to protect you if things go wrong. For more information, see *The Which? Guide to Complementary Therapies* from Which? Books★.

Hospital treatment

If you need to see a specialist, your GP will probably refer you to a hospital outpatient clinic, although larger GP practices are increasingly inviting specialists to come to the practice to see patients.

Waiting times

Waiting times vary. The Patient's Charter has been superceded by *Your Guide to the NHS* which states that waiting times for a first outpatient appointment should be no more than six months. The waiting time for inpatient treatment should be no longer than 18 months.

There are stricter standards for people with suspected cancer and people who have suspected angina for the first time and who need urgent referrals. In these cases the standard is that they should be seen by a specialist within two weeks.

The government pledged in 2003 that from summer 2004, people waiting more than six months for elective surgery will be offered the choice of at least one alternative hospital (usually four, either private or public).

Help with costs if you go into hospital

You may be able to claim for the cost of travelling to hospital for in-patient or outpatient treatment. You can claim your travel expenses for the cheapest form of transport if you are on Income Support or have an NHS Low Income Certificate HC2 for full help. If you have an HC3 certificate for limited help, you may be entitled to some help towards the costs. You can find out more from your Job Centre or by phoning (0800) 555777. If you need to accompany someone for medical reasons they may be able to claim your travel costs as part of their travel costs. For further information on travel costs for going to hospital, see leaflet HC11 available as described on page 136.

If you have difficulty travelling to hospital you may be entitled to go by the hospital car service. Ask your GP about this. NHS ambulance services provide free transport for those who are medically unfit to travel by other means. In many parts of the country there are Dial-a-Ride or other schemes which provide transport for people with disabilities – see page 119 for more information on this.

If you are visiting someone else in hospital, you may qualify for help with travel costs if you are on Income Support. Ask your benefit office if you can get any help.

Your pension in hospital

If you live in your own home your state pension is not affected until you have been in hospital for a year. If you live in a local authority care home and you are going into hospital for inpatient treatment on the NHS, your retirement pension may be reduced immediately.

Private treatment

The NHS covers medical and surgical treatments including emergencies, while most private treatment is for elective or non-emergency surgery such as hip replacements, varicose vein removal and hernias. These operations can be those with the longest waiting times, so going private may ensure faster treatment.

Private treatment can have some other advantages over the NHS, including choosing your own consultant and sometimes your hospital. The consultants who work in the private sector are usually the same consultants who work in the NHS (many have a part-time contract with the NHS which allows them to do private work). If you're a private patient you'll usually see the consultant, while in the NHS you may be treated by a more junior member of the consultant's team, under his or her supervision. The food, decor, privacy and visiting arrangements may all be better in private hospitals.

However, if you have complications you may be better off in an NHS hospital, as many private hospitals are smaller than NHS ones and don't have the same intensive care facilities. If you are considering private treatment, you should check the level of medical cover outside the usual working hours and ask about emergency and intensive care facilities. Using private facilities within NHS hospitals has the advantage that emergency facilities are on-hand if needed – and it's sometimes a cheaper option, although the surroundings may not be as plush as in a private hospital.

If you want the option of private treatment, you can either take out private medical insurance (PMI) or pay directly for treatment out of your income or savings. Don't assume that your private medical insurance will cover all your needs – read the small print carefully. PMI is designed to pay the bills for private treatment of 'acute' conditions – problems which can be cured. In general, policies do not cover the treatment of long-term illness which can't be cured (i.e. 'chronic' conditions), such as asthma, diabetes, mental health problems and multiple sclerosis.

Insurance or pay as you go?

You may have had cover through your work which you can extend into your retirement. However, as you get older PMI becomes increasingly expensive – a couple in their 60s may pay literally thousands of pounds a year for cover. Plus as you get older it becomes increasingly difficult to shop around for PMI because new policies usually exclude pre-existing medical conditions. So once you start to develop a health problem, there is a strong incentive to stick with your existing policy which covers the problem, rather than switch to a new policy which doesn't.

Of course, you don't need to have private medical insurance to have private treatment. You can simply pay out of your income or savings. This isn't cheap – prices may be in the region of £1,250 for removing a varicose vein, £2,000 for a cataract and £6,000-plus for a hip replacement – and more if there are complications. But increasingly, private hospitals are offering fixed-price surgery so you know up-front exactly how much you'll have to pay. And the premiums you'll save by not paying for insurance will soon build up into a reasonable pool of savings to dip into.

Organising self-pay private healthcare

Paying for private treatment when the need arises, rather than paying premiums for an insurance policy, is becoming increasingly popular. A number of hospitals now offer payment in instalments or credit schemes for people who can't afford to pay up-front (as always, if the scheme charges interest, check whether you could get a better deal from another financial institution).

You'll usually need a GP's letter of referral, and your GP can be a good source of advice to help you choose a consultant or hospital, particularly for local consultants where the GP is likely to know about their special interests. If you've got access to the Internet you can search *www.specialistinfo.com* or *www.drfoster.co.uk* for information about consultants by speciality and region. You can check a doctor's registration with the General Medical Council on its website *www.gmc-uk.org* or by phoning on 020-7915 3630.

You might also want to shop around for prices – when *Health Which?* investigated self-pay healthcare in 2001, it found large variations in prices in different areas of the country. But make sure you're comparing like with like. For instance, some quotes might include the cost of post-operative consultations, tests and x-rays while others might not. It is also worthwhile checking whether post-operative rehabilitation, such as physiotherapy, is included. Quotes you get from ringing around will usually only be a guide and you won't get a firm price until the consultant has examined you, which is charged for separately.

To get a quote from a consultant, contact his or her private secretary. You can ask the consultant's NHS office for the number. Alternatively you can contact a private hospital, rather than a particular consultant, and ask it to arrange your treatment. The big private hospital operators such as BUPA and Nuffield will all be

---

Case history: Anita

Anita needed a hip replacement and was dismayed when her GP told her she was likely to face a wait of over 12 months. She didn't have private medical insurance, but after reading an article about private healthcare decided to find out how much the operation would cost. She went back to her GP who recommended a local consultant and she rang his secretary.

'It wasn't as expensive as I thought it would be,' she says. 'I hadn't realised that you could just pay for an operation like that. I thought you had to be a member of an insurance scheme to be able to get private treatment. I know I'm lucky to be able to afford it, but compared with being not able to get around properly, it's worth spending some savings on this.'

---

happy to accommodate self-pay patients and many offer fixed-price costs to help avoid unexpected extras.

Choosing private medical insurance

If, despite the high premiums, you're keen to carry on with PMI, you can cut the cost by choosing a policy with more limited cover. There's no standard definition of different policy types, but PMI can broadly be divided into three categories, with the biggest differences being in the level of cover for outpatient care.

- **Comprehensive policies** are the most expensive. They cover a wide range of treatment, including all outpatient care, and have a wide choice of hospitals and clinics. Often there are extras such as cover abroad and for dental treatment.
- **Standard policies** provide cover for inpatient and day-patient care. Outpatient treatment might be covered only if linked to a spell as an inpatient. Often the choice of hospitals is restricted.
- **Budget policies** keep costs down by restricting cover: this means outpatient treatment may be very limited; there may be an overall cash limit on the amount you can claim each year, or on some items; cover may be available only if the NHS waiting list exceeds six weeks; and there may be a limited choice of hospitals.

Another way to reduce costs is to agree an 'excess' in the same way as you might for car insurance. This means you pay the first part of any claim yourself in return for a lower premium. Some companies offer schemes where you agree to pay a very large excess (between £1,000 and £5,000) of the first part of your claim and in return get big discounts on your premium, as a sort of half-way house between PMI and self-pay.

Complaints about health services

NHS patients

It's always best to try to resolve a complaint with the practitioner concerned, either in person or in writing. All GP surgeries and hospitals have a complaints procedure with a named person responsible for dealing with your complaints. If that doesn't help, contact the complaints manager at your local Primary Care Trust or health board. If you're still unhappy, the next step is to ask for an independent review. If this is granted, a panel will investigate your complaint. If you remain unsatisfied, you can take your case to the Health Service Ombudsman. Time limits apply to all stages of this system; you can get further advice on how to complain about health services from NHS Direct★.

In England and Scotland, you can also get help with making a complaint from your local Patient Advice and Liaison (PAL) service. In Wales, your local Community Health Council (CHC) can help. You can find contact details for your PAL or CHC in your phone book or from NHS Direct★.

If you have received NHS treatment in a private hospital or clinic, you can still use the NHS complaints procedure if you have a complaint about your care or treatment.

Private patients

Again, try to resolve the matter with the practitioner first. If this doesn't help the problem, you can complain to the National Care Standards Commission (NCSC)★, which has been responsible for regulating independent hospitals, clinics and solely private doctors since April 2002. However, private doctors and dentists who undertake any NHS care are not currently covered by the NCSC, nor are private patient units in NHS hospitals.

Independent hospitals are responsible for problems resulting from the premises, equipment or employees such as nurses and administrators. However, while they should investigate complaints about consultants working on their premises, the consultants usually work on a sub-contracted basis and the hospitals are not legally responsible for problems arising from the consultant's clinical care. Some independent hospitals also belong to the Independent Healthcare Association (IHA)★, which has its own complaints scheme including an independent review stage and the opportunity for independent, external adjudication or mediation (charges may be payable for this).

You may also be able to make a complaint to the practitioner's professional body, which should have a complaints procedure. However, many professional bodies will deal only with complaints that constitute serious misconduct. If you don't get a satisfactory response to your complaint, your only option may be to sue your consultant or practitioner.

Chapter 11

Healthy eating

Most people's eating habits are now very different to those of several decades ago. One of the main reasons, of course, is that a far greater variety of foods is available than ever before. Patterns of health and disease have also changed: people are living longer and are more likely to suffer from 'diseases of affluence', such as coronary heart disease, strokes, various cancers and diabetes.

Good nutrition is essential to help maintain health, reduce the risk of certain diseases and promote recovery from illness. Although there has been a welter of apparently conflicting advice in the media over the years on what you should or should not do, there is a consensus that the key factors for a healthy lifestyle, whatever your age, are to:

- eat a healthy balanced diet
- exercise regularly
- avoid smoking
- keep alcohol intake to a moderate level.

Government health experts recommend we should all:

- base our diet on starchy foods such as bread, potatoes, pasta, rice and other cereals
- eat plenty of fruit and vegetables
- eat moderate amounts of meat, fish, milk and dairy products
- eat fatty food and sugary foods and drinks sparingly.

The following sections contain suggestions to help you meet these recommendations. You don't have to change everything at once. Decide on priorities, make gradual alterations and experiment with different recipes and meals – remember that even small changes can help.

Breads, cereals, potatoes, rice and pasta

These are sometimes referred to as starchy foods or complex carbo-hydrates. Many people think of them as fattening foods to be avoided, especially if you are trying to lose weight. In fact, the recommendation is to eat more – this applies especially to older people, who tend to eat only small helpings of them. If you are dieting it is much better to cut down on fatty foods (see the section on page 156 on weight gain), which provide approximately twice as much energy (calories) as starchy ones.

Eating more breads, cereals and potatoes has a number of benefits. They contain a variety of vitamins and minerals (such as B vitamins, calcium and iron) and essential fatty acids (types of polyunsaturated fatty acids needed by the body in small amounts). In addition, wholemeal/wholegrain breads are a good source of fibre.

- Have thicker slices of bread and eat bread with your meals. Wholemeal bread has more fibre than white but if you don't like it stick to your favourite type – the important point is to eat more.
- Start the day with breakfast. Choose a low-sugar, high-fibre cereal, or try toast topped with sliced banana.
- As well as bread and potatoes, try different types of rice and pasta or use other cereals and grains.

Fruit, vegetables and salads

Fruit and vegetables provide vitamins and minerals, and are an especially important source of vitamin C. Research shows eating a sufficient amount of fruit and vegetables each day has very real health benefits – it could help prevent up to 20 per cent of deaths from heart disease and some cancers. Eating more fruit and vegetables also provides dietary fibre. Fruit and vegetables are ideal for filling up on between meals, especially if you are trying to lose weight.

- Aim to eat at least five portions of fruit and vegetables a day – either fresh, frozen, dried or canned.
- Start the day with a glass of fruit juice – choose a variety without added sugar.
- Choose fruit salads, stewed or baked fruit or fresh fruit and yogurt for dessert.
- Use less meat and add extra vegetables to stews, casseroles and soups.
- Don't overcook vegetables as this destroys some of their vitamins.
- Keep a supply of canned fruit and vegetables (but check the label to see if they have salt, sugar or syrup added).
- Keep a supply of frozen vegetables – they are quicker and more convenient to prepare than fresh ones. A survey for *Health Which?* magazine in June 1999 found that their vitamin C content was just as good and sometimes better than that of some fresh vegetables.

Meat, fish and dairy products

In the past everybody was encouraged to eat plenty of these foods because of their high protein content. These days, experts say we should eat 'moderate' amounts of meat, fish and dairy products. Foods high in protein do provide vitamins and minerals but they can also be high in fat and saturates (see pages 152–3), and we now know that high-fat diets are associated with an increased risk of heart disease and some cancers. Fat is also a concentrated source of energy (calories) that can lead to extra weight gain if it's not balanced with exercise.

At the moment in the UK our daily energy intake is about 38 per cent fat, with 15 per cent coming from saturated fat. The government target is no more than 35 per cent fat in total, with no more than 11 per cent coming from saturated fat. Eating more fruit, vegetables and starchy foods will mean that you have less room for high-fat and other foods anyway.

- Choose lean meat and remove any visible fat – preferably before you cook it. Poultry contains less fat than red meat, but remove the skin to reduce the level of fat further.
- White fish is low in fat – unless you fry it or add fatty sauces.
- Meat products like sausages, burgers and pâtés often contain large amounts of fat. Check the label.
- Milk and dairy products are an important source of calcium and vitamins; try using semi-skimmed or skimmed milk and low-fat yogurts and cheeses in place of full-fat ones – they contain just as much calcium.
- Try having a vegetarian meal at least twice a week based on beans or lentils. This will give you more fibre as well as being low in fat.

Fat, sugar, salt and fibre

Nutritionists agree that we all need to cut down on fat, sugar and salt and boost our fibre intake.

Fat

All types of fat contain the same amount of calories – about double that of carbohydrates or protein – and so should all be used sparingly. The difference between them lies in their chemical make-up. All fats are a mixture of different fatty acids, which give them different properties and effects.

Saturated fats

A high intake of saturated fat in the diet has been linked to an increased risk of heart disease. This is because diets high in saturated fat are associated with high cholesterol levels in the blood and thrombosis (or clotting). The main sources of saturated fats are meat, full-fat dairy products, biscuits, cakes, and butter or spreads. Although saturated fat intake in the British diet has fallen over the last 30 years, we still eat too much of it. Government advice is to keep saturated fat intake to a minimum – no more than 20g a day for women, and 30g a day for men.

Trans fats

Trans fat occurs naturally in butter, but can also be formed as a by-product of the spread manufacturing process. This happens when vegetable oils are heated to harden them (a process called hydrogenation). Artificially produced trans fat is thought to cause the same problems as saturated fat and be just as bad, if not worse for you. It is found mainly in margarines and spreads but can also be found in other processed foods such as pies, cakes, biscuits and pastry.

Polyunsaturated and monounsaturated fats

Both polyunsaturated fats and monounsaturated fats are thought to have health benefits, but the debate on whether one is better than the other is ongoing.

There are two types of polyunsaturates: omega-6 and omega-3. Sources of omega-6 include sunflower and corn oils, and sources of omega-3 include fish and rapeseed oil. Both have some beneficial effects, and replacing saturated fat in your diet with polyunsaturated fat has been found to reduce blood cholesterol levels. Omega-3 has also been found to reduce levels of another blood fat called triglyceride – high levels of this are associated with heart disease.

The major monounsaturated fatty acid in our diets is called oleic acid and it is found in olive oil, rapeseed oil, and some new varieties of sunflower and soybean oil. Studies have shown that if you replace saturated fat in your diet with monounsaturated fat, it can also help to reduce cholesterol levels.

- Cut down on total fat by limiting trans fats and saturates, using some polyunsaturates (margarines, oils, oily fish) and some monounsaturates such as olive oil.
- For everyday use, change to a reduced-fat spread or margarine which is low in saturates and high in polyunsaturates.
- Cut down on frying; try home-made oven chips, or try grilling or dry-frying in a non-stick pan. Use oil rather than a hard fat for cooking.
- Go easy on crisps, chocolate, mayonnaise, cakes, biscuits and pastries – all are high-fat foods.

Sugar

The problem with consuming lots of sweet foods is that they may fill you up without being very nutritious, and, of course, cause tooth decay. Sugar provides only calories, it has no vitamins, minerals, protein or fibre. Avoid sugar and sweet foods particularly if you have diabetes or are trying to lose weight.

Intense sweeteners such as aspartame, acesulfame-k and saccharin are much sweeter than sugar and are used in a variety of foods such as drinks and yogurts, or as a table-top sweetener. Although the government is satisfied that these sugar-substitutes are safe, they can help you lose weight only as part of a calorie-controlled diet, and it is probably a better idea to eat fewer processed foods containing these sweeteners and get used to eating fruit as a snack instead.

- Try to avoid adding sugar to foods – so cut out or cut down on sugar in drinks and don't sprinkle extra sugar on breakfast cereals.
- Use less sugar in recipes – try adding dried fruit if you need to sweeten something. This still contains sugar but you gain the benefits of eating more fruit.
- Check labels carefully – sucrose, dextrose, maltose, invert sugar syrup, glucose and caramel are all forms of sugar.
- Sugary foods are often high in fat as well (e.g. cakes, biscuits, chocolates).

Salt

Countries with high salt intakes such as the UK have higher average levels of blood pressure than countries with low salt intakes. Blood pressure increases with age, and high blood pressure is a risk factor for heart disease. If you are taking medication for high blood pressure you may have already been advised to eat less salt.

- Avoid adding salt to foods during cooking or at the table. Some salt is needed by the body but you can easily get this from salt naturally present in foods.
- Season foods with lemon juice, herbs and spices instead – you'll soon get used to the taste of less salty foods.
- Canned and processed foods are often very salty, so choose brands which have less or no extra salt added. More than half the salt we eat is added by manufacturers during food processing.
- Sometimes salt is labelled as sodium; to convert an amount of sodium to salt, multiply by 2.5.
- Salt substitutes still contain some salt (sodium chloride).

Fibre

Fibre is what gives seeds, fruits, roots, stems and leaves of plants their structure.

Some types of food naturally contain more fibre than others, but processing also affects the fibre content: refining cereals such as wheat (e.g. to make white flour) involves removing much of the fibre from the outer husk of the grain.

Dietary fibre (also known as roughage) combines with water to add bulk to the stools and greatly assists the passage of digestible materials and waste products through the intestines. It helps to prevent constipation and can reduce the risk of diverticular disease, and there is some evidence that it protects against bowel cancer.

Fibre can be broadly separated into two types: insoluble and soluble. All plant foods contain a mixture of both. These differ in some of their effects: insoluble fibre provides the most bulk, reducing the time taken for food to pass through the gut; and soluble fibre has been shown to have a modest effect of lowering blood cholesterol, especially if your cholesterol is already high. Whole-grain wheat and rye are rich sources of insoluble fibre. Oats, barley, beans and lentils, however, contain a significant proportion of soluble fibre. Fruit and vegetables contain roughly half and half of each.

Eating more fibre-rich foods also improves the overall balance of your diet – helping to reduce the amount of fat and increase the amount of starchy carbohydrate you eat. Eating more of these foods can also mean more nutrients: choosing wholegrain foods, fruits, pulses and vegetables will increase your intake of some vitamins, minerals and other substances thought to have positive health benefits.

Although raw bran is high in fibre, adding it to foods is to be discouraged because of its high phytate content. Phytate binds in the gut with certain minerals like calcium, zinc and iron from other foods so that their absorption is reduced. (Other wholemeal foods also contain some phytate but its effect is compensated for by their rich mineral content and the fact that processing reduces the amount of phytates present.)

- Choose wholemeal breads and cereals and have more beans, lentils, fruit, vegetables and salads.
- Eat a range of fibre-rich foods so that you benefit from both soluble and insoluble fibres.
- Increase your intake of fibre-rich foods gradually: unpleasant side effects such as wind decrease once your body gets used to having more fibre.
- Drink plenty of fluids, preferably water.

Dietary needs as we get older

Your energy (calorie) requirements as you get older will depend on your health and lifestyle. Some people may need to alter the quantities they eat due to changes in these; this does not necessarily mean that you have to eat less, as many people are more active in retirement than they were when working.

Weight gain

Keep an eye on your weight. If you notice you've gained or lost weight without trying, it's a good idea to see your doctor. Being overweight is associated with reduced mobility, diabetes and hypertension and puts extra strain on joints.

If you need to lose weight set yourself a realistic target, such as one or two pounds a week. Eat healthily, filling up with more fruit, vegetables, salads and starchy foods and cutting down on fatty and sugary ones, and increase your level of physical activity. Join a slimming group or ask your GP to refer you to a dietician if you need extra help. Unfortunately, there is no easy way to lose weight; the best way is to lose it gradually and get used to a healthy, sensible diet. See Chapter 12 for more on exercise, and remember to check with your GP if you're about to start exercising for the first time and have any health concerns.

Maintaining your weight

Some people lose their appetite and interest in food as they get older, perhaps as a result of illness, depression, bereavement or certain drug treatments, or because they are living alone. It is not just the amount that you eat that is important, but the type and variety as well. Poor food intake over a prolonged period can lead to weight loss, increased susceptibility to infections and illness and nutritional deficiencies. If you experience a sudden loss of appetite or unexplained weight loss, check with your GP.

- Have small regular meals and snacks, using a variety of different foods.
- If you don't feel like cooking, remember that cold meals and snacks can be just as nutritious.
- Choose milky drinks and fruit juices rather than tea, coffee and soft drinks.

If your appetite is very poor or you don't eat a variety of different foods you may need to take a vitamin supplement. Choose a multivitamin and mineral supplement. Very high doses of some vitamins can cause health problems, so stick to the recommended dosage and take one which provides amounts close to or just below the Recommended Daily Amount (RDA) – this information will be on the label.

Catering for one

Cooking and catering for one need not be expensive and time-consuming if you plan your meals and shopping in advance. If you have a freezer, buying and cooking larger quantities is often cheaper than buying small amounts; some foods can be divided into individual portions and frozen, or you could join up with friends or neighbours and buy larger quantities to share. Look out for special offers and buy produce in season.

You may not feel like bothering to cook just for yourself. Quick and/or easy meals like sandwiches, beans or scrambled eggs on toast, jacket potatoes and salads can be just as nutritious as a full meal, but try to make sure you include a variety of foods. Experiment with new recipes and try different foods – there are a number of cookery books concentrating on meals for one including Delia Smith's *One is Fun*.

Stocking up

It is a good idea to keep various storecupboard foods in case you are ill or unable to get to the shops. Useful items include UHT milk, long-life fruit juices, canned fruit and vegetables, dried fruit, canned fish, meat, beans, rice puddings and custards, crackers, breakfast cereals, oats, rice and pasta. If you have a freezer keep some bread, meat, fish, frozen fruit and vegetables and individual portions of meals. Make a regular check on stocks to make sure they stay within their shelf life.

Most milkmen will deliver a range of foods as well as milk to your doorstep, and if you have Internet access many supermarkets now offer home delivery for online shoppers. Local authority Social Service departments and voluntary agencies often run luncheon clubs, day centres and pop-in clubs – your local Social Services department should be able to provide you with details of these. If you are unable to cope with cooking you may be able to get Meals on Wheels delivered to your home.

Cooking skills and equipment

Retirement may prove a good time to improve or master new culinary skills. There are plenty of cookery classes available, aimed at men as well as women. Your local library should have information about adult education classes in the area.

If a disability means that you have difficulty cooking or preparing foods, a range of special equipment and appliances is available to make things easier. Details are available from the Disabled Living Foundation*.

Vitamins and minerals

Vitamin requirements for older people are generally similar to those for all adults. For most people there is no need to take vitamin supplements; a healthy, varied diet should provide all the vitamins you need.

The vitamin content of fruit and vegetables decreases during storage and cooking (especially vitamins A, C and some B vitamins). To conserve the vitamins as much as possible don't soak vegetables and avoid overcooking them – boil them lightly in a small amount of water and use a saucepan with a lid, or stir-fry, microwave or steam them. Don't add baking soda.

Calcium

Bones become weaker as you get older, partly because less calcium is deposited and partly because more is lost from the bones. This loss of bone density (osteoporosis) is a major problem because it means that bones are more likely to fracture following a fall, for example. Although the role of dietary calcium in the development and prevention of osteoporosis is uncertain, it is known that calcium is important.

Make sure you are eating enough calcium-rich foods. These include milk, yogurt, cheese, sardines, whitebait, spinach, parsnips, baked beans, almonds, white bread and dried figs.

Most people get all the calcium they need from their diet, but if your appetite is poor or you don't eat any dairy produce, a calcium supplement may be appropriate. Take one which gives at least 500mg per day (there is no advantage in taking extra-high doses). If you are already taking a multivitamin and mineral supplement, check the label to see if it contains any calcium and, if so, how much.

159

Vitamin D

Vitamin D is involved in the regulation of calcium absorption and is obtained from exposure to sunlight and a few dietary sources (fatty fish, margarine, eggs, liver, evaporated milk, skimmed milk powder and some breakfast cereals which have extra vitamin D added). Try to get outside during the day – walking or gardening are good ways of doing this. Remember to use sunscreen if you are going out for long periods during the summer. If you are housebound or unable to follow this advice you may need a vitamin D supplement and should consult your doctor.

Cod liver oil was often taken in the past as it is a particularly good source of vitamins A and D. Most people's diets now provide enough of these vitamins without the need for supplements. Both vitamins can be toxic in excess, so if you want to take cod liver oil, stick to the recommended dosage and don't take other vitamin supplements which contain either vitamin A or D.

Fluid and alcohol

Drink at least six to eight cups of non-alcoholic drinks a day. It is important to have enough fluid, even if you don't actually feel thirsty. Tea and coffee are diuretic (they increase the production of urine) so are not good sources of fluid. Water is best but you could also include milk, fruit juice, cordials or herbal teas.

As far as alcohol is concerned, there is evidence that a low amount of alcohol can have health benefits to men over 40 and women who have reached the menopause by reducing the risk of heart disease. The benefits can be gained by having one to two units of alcohol a day. There is no increased benefit in having more. Also, to reduce the negative health effects associated with alcohol (such as an increased risk of some cancers and high blood pressure), women should drink no more than two to three units of alcohol per day and men should drink no more than three to four units. A 'unit' is the same as a half pint of normal strength beer, a pub measure of spirits or a small glass of wine. If you're taking any medication, check with your pharmacist or GP that it's safe to drink alcohol with it.

Food labels and food safety

Food labels

Food labels can be confusing and misleading. Here are some points to watch out for:

- 'Use by' dates are found on highly perishable foods; don't eat food which is past its 'use by' date unless it has been cooked or frozen prior to the 'use by' date to extend its life.
- 'Best before' means that foods will be at peak quality until this date – after this they are still safe to eat (if stored according to instructions) but their quality may deteriorate.
- Ingredients are listed in order of weight, so that the main ingredient will be listed first.
- Watch out for health claims on foods, like 'Healthy' and 'Good for you'. There are no regulations controlling the use of these sorts of claims.
- Check foods with claims like 'low-fat', 'high-fibre', 'sugar-free'. There are no statutory definitions for these claims, so you need to check what the product actually contains. Food Standards Agency guidelines say that reduced-fat foods should contain at least 25 per cent less fat than the standard version, and low-fat foods should contain less than 3g of fat per 100g.

Storing foods safely

Store foods safely to minimise the risk of illness due to food contamination. Make sure that your fridge and freezer are the correct temperatures: between 0°C and 5°C and -18°C respectively. Keep foods covered. Cooked foods should be stored on higher shelves in the fridge and raw ones on the lower shelves so that the raw food (such as poultry) cannot drip and contaminate food that is not going to be cooked again before it is eaten. Store eggs in the fridge.

Food preparation

Follow the basic rules.

- Wash your hands before and in between handling raw and cooked food.

- Clean work surfaces before you start and continue to clean as you go.
- Don't use the same knife or chopping board for raw and cooked foods.
- Don't eat raw eggs or products containing uncooked eggs.
- Make sure that meat (including burgers) and poultry are properly cooked: when you prick the thickest part of the meat the juices should run clear.
- Left-over cooked food should be chilled quickly, covered, and then refrigerated or frozen.
- Reheat foods once only and heat thoroughly.
- Keep pets away from food and food preparation areas.

Chapter 12

Keeping fit and active

Mind the fitness gap

What does retirement mean to you? More freedom, more activity –
travelling, gardening, visiting new places, getting on with all those
things you meant to do but couldn't because you were working? Or
does it mean getting older? An inevitable deterioration? Being
unable to cope with everyday tasks which require strength, not
being able to keep up like you used to?

Some changes in our physical abilities are inevitable as we grow
older – but others come about simply because we become less
active. This can become a vicious circle, and experts talk about the
'fitness gap' between the inevitable changes due to ageing and
changes caused by lack of physical activity – put bluntly, it's use it or
lose it. Every individual has a different level of fitness, but it's
important to try to narrow this 'fitness gap' as much as possible so
you can enjoy an active retirement.

If you're considering skipping this chapter because you think you
are too old, too unfit or too unhealthy to consider exercise – don't.
Research shows that it's never too late to start – the benefits of
exercise can be enormous, and you don't have to suffer to feel them.

What is fitness?

Strength and endurance, stamina and flexibility are all part of being
fit. Together these things give you the ability to lift and carry, keep
up a fast pace while walking uphill, or reach something on the top
shelf of a cupboard.

Much of what we call ageing is nothing more than the results of being inactive, and losing these aspects of fitness. If muscles are not used they shrink, and become less powerful, making it harder for you to do things you could do easily when you were younger. Weaker muscles mean you are more likely to fall, and because bones also get weaker as you age, you are more likely to break something if you do.

Changes in your metabolic rate may mean you put on weight when you get older, but, more importantly, the proportion of muscle and bone to fat may change, so that there is more fat. Dieting may mean you lose fat, but unless you exercise you could lose muscle and bone as well.

Stamina

This is what we need to walk or run, and keep it up over any distance. Most unfit people can manage to run a short distance – to catch a bus, for example. But muscles need oxygen to keep working, or they will get painful and you will get tired. Unless you've got stamina your body will not be able to get oxygen to your muscles quickly enough.

Aerobic exercise (designed to increase the amount of oxygen to the blood) improves the way your body uses oxygen. People who have not been exercising aerobically will find they get tired more easily as they get older, but aerobic training can help. Aerobic exercise includes walking, jogging, swimming, dancing, climbing stairs, gardening and cycling. In order to reap the benefits you need to puff a little, and work up some sweat, but not to the extent that you are completely out of breath – you should still be able to carry on a conversation.

Strength and endurance

Strength is what you need to lift – including lifting your own body weight from a chair, for example. Endurance is what you need to carry what you have lifted. Strength or resistance training will make your muscles become bigger and more powerful. You don't have to lift heavy weights to do this – even squeezing a tennis ball regularly can help improve your arm muscles so that you will always find it easy to pull a plug out of a socket. Swimming and gardening are good starting exercises for building up strength (though be careful of your back when digging). This sort of training also helps to strengthen bones. Strength can help protect against back pain and against falling.

Suppleness

Suppleness means that you can move all your limbs through a full range of movement without difficulty. If you are flexible you will find it easier to bend your knees to pick something off the floor, and to stretch your arms above your head to reach something off a shelf. Swimming is a good way to get all your joints moving, while keeping them supported, but daily stretching exercises will also help.

The benefits of exercise

Apart from ensuring that you can keep fit enough to live an independent and active life, exercise can have a positive, preventive effect on many of the conditions associated with growing older. These benefits are summarised below. As outlined in the box 'Safety first' on page 168, remember to check with your doctor before taking up exercise for the first time or if you have a particular medical condition.

The Health Development Agency has two sets of recommendations for physical activity. At least 30 minutes of moderate-intensity activity on at least five days a week will achieve health benefits. At least 20 minutes of vigorous, intensive activity on three or more days a week will maximise aerobic fitness and help reduce mortality. The more activity that you do, the greater the health benefits.

Coronary heart disease (CHD)

If you're physically inactive, you are more likely to suffer from coronary heart disease. Exercise can prevent the onset of the disease. What is more, if you keep up the exercise you continue to benefit for as long as you persevere with the activity. This is a result of improvements in the way your cardiovascular system works (see 'Stamina', opposite), and a strengthening of your heart muscle. Exercise can also keep down the build-up of harmful cholesterol in your arteries.

As exercise can also help control your weight, it can also help reduce the likelihood of you suffering heart problems related to obesity. If you have had a heart attack, this doesn't mean you should avoid exercise: research shows that exercise can have a protective effect. Ask your doctor about rehabilitation exercise programmes (and see under 'Heart attack' on pages 194–5). The British Heart Foundation National Centre for Physical Activity and Health★ can also give you useful information about the benefits of exercise to help prevent heart disease and other medical conditions. The Centre is set up primarily to give information to health professionals but can give some useful information and contact details for local organisations to the general public.

High blood pressure

Exercise can have a similar effect to beta-blocking drugs, although it does not work in exactly the same way. Exercise has an acute blood pressure-lowering effect which means for a short while after exercise your blood pressure is lower than it would normally be at rest.

If you already have high blood pressure you should speak to your doctor before exercising – certain exercises might not be suitable for you; for example, heavy resistance and strength exercises.

Respiratory diseases

People with respiratory diseases such as asthma, bronchitis or emphysema often think that their condition means they cannot exercise. It is true that the amount of exercise that can be done is limited, but as exercise can improve these conditions it should not be avoided altogether. The amount of exercise you are capable of gradually increases, with the benefit that your capacity for everyday tasks increases too. Asthma attacks can be brought on by exercise in some cases, but warming up gently and using an inhaler can avoid this. Swimming in an indoor pool is less likely to provoke an attack because the air breathed is warm and moist.

Back pain

The less physically fit you are, the more likely you are to suffer from back pain. If the muscles in your back are weak, you are more likely to hurt yourself when you attempt to put stress on them – by lifting something heavy, for example. Strengthening stomach and back muscles helps prevent injury.

If you already have back pain, exercise can help reduce and manage it – ask your doctor or physiotherapist for advice.

Arthritis

If you have arthritis, exercise can help by producing increased movement in your joints and keeping your muscles strong. In general, people with arthritis should exercise every day to help prevent joints becoming stiff and painful. Exercise cannot 'wear out' your joints although you may find that resting is helpful if your joints are particularly inflamed and swollen; speak to your doctor or physiotherapist for advice.

Osteoporosis

Bones get weaker progressively after adolescence, as they lose their mineral content. For women this happens even faster after the menopause. Weaker bones are more susceptible to fracture – older people are more likely to break bones if they fall. One of the reasons for the loss of minerals is physical inactivity. Exercise can help make bones stronger, even after the menopause. Men also benefit, as exercise has been shown to protect against hip fractures. The best type of exercises to do are weight-bearing ones such as running or dancing, but even regular walking can have a good effect.

Exercise makes you feel good

Exercise can make you look and feel better about yourself. View it as part of your life, not a daily chore. It's a good way to increase your social life, to spend time in the fresh air and to make sure that you can enjoy life to the full for years to come. Most people who take regular exercise claim they feel better for it, and there is evidence to back this up. When you exercise, substances called endorphins released into the brain may help give a sense of well-being, so exercise can help you combat stress, anxiety, tension and aggression. It can also help you fight depression and tiredness, and make you sleep better.

Oxygen flow to the brain also increases when you exercise, improving mental alertness. Research has shown that there is a relationship between aerobic exercise and brain functions such as memory and problem solving.

Case history: Joyce

Forty years behind a desk had left Joyce feeling unfit. She hadn't played any sport since she was a teenager, and living in a rural area she relied on the car as the most practical way of getting around. While walking wasn't very practical for everyday errands, she decided it was a good way to get fit and enjoy the beautiful countryside around her. She joined a walking group run by her local University of the Third Age. 'It's more fun going in a group – and sometimes we have a guided walk with an expert who knows about the local wildlife. I started off with easy walks, but now I've started going on the more challenging hill walks too. My husband and I are even going on a walking holiday this year, where our baggage is transported from place to place while we spend most of the day walking.'

Getting started

Safety first

You should check with your doctor before starting exercise for the first time, or if you know you have a particular condition. This is especially important if you want to take up any weight-bearing exercise to improve your strength, or exercise involving strenuous aerobic activity. Some GP practices even offer a 'prescription for health' where they prescribe a form of exercise – for example, a course of exercise classes for a particular condition at a local leisure centre.

One of the most important things you can do to get your body moving and used to exercise is to walk more. If you walk, as briskly as you can, for half an hour a day, you are well on the way to improving your stamina and your strength – particularly that all-important strength in your legs which will help protect against falls (swing your arms too, to help work your upper body). Walking can easily become a part of your everyday routine if you walk rather than drive to the newsagent's, or get off the bus a few stops early or take the stairs instead of the lift. Once you have got into the swing of walking you might want to join a walking or rambling club.

Don't try to do too much, too soon, as that might easily result in injuries or strains. Before you start exercising always do some warm-up exercises to loosen up your joints – this is particularly important because as you get older muscles get stiffer, and tendons and ligaments get weaker. Even before you do some gardening it's a good idea to warm up. A little gentle marching on the spot, or walking up and down the stairs a few times, will get your cardiovascular system working. In the same way, you should always end an exercise session by warming down – a gradual tapering off of activity.

Where to go

Your local authority leisure centre is an obvious place to start. Many have special programmes and discounts for older people, for example concessions for swimming at off-peak times. Your local University of the Third Age★ (U3A) will probably also have some physical activities in its programme of events, with walking and gardening groups being particularly popular. If your U3A does not already offer a fitness or activity group that appeals to you, you could always offer to start one up yourself (see page 85 for more on the U3A).

Exercise includes sports such as bowling, dancing and golf. If you have, or used to have, an interest in any sport, there may well be a local club of like-minded people. Many local associations will have 'veterans' or the rather more flatteringly titled 'masters' groups of people who already take part in the activity. Sport England★ will also be able to put you in touch with its own regional offices and national associations of various sports which will have more local infor-mation.

Joining a class

There are also many books, videos and audio tapes for sale giving instructions on particular types of exercise, especially yoga, keep-fit and other body-toning exercises. Some are targeted specifically at older people. These may be useful to help you exercise at home but the quality of these tapes vary and without an instructor to watch you, it can be hard to know whether you're doing the exercises correctly. Plus, of course, it means you miss out on the social aspect of going to classes.

Before you take part in an organised exercise class, a good instructor will probably ask you to fill in a PARQ (Physical Activity Readiness Questionnaire). This is a short list of questions designed to identify anyone who should check with their doctor before exercising, including questions about any heart condition, dizziness or joint problems you might have. A good instructor should also pay close attention to how everyone in the class performs each exercise, correcting people as necessary.

Joining a gym can give you access to plush facilities – but usually at quite a price. Your local leisure centre will probably have a much less expensive gym. It might be worth trying this out first to make sure it's something you will enjoy and use regularly before committing yourself to a lengthy membership at a private gym.

What to do

A target to aim for is five occasions of moderate activity, lasting at least 30 minutes, each week, but you can take your time in working up to this. Any moderate physical activity is better than none, and as frequent exercise brings the most health benefits, you will need to get into the habit. Start by aiming to exercise at least once a week. At least 20 minutes of vigorous activity on three or more days a week will maximise aerobic fitness.

Try to improve all aspects of fitness – stamina, strength and endurance, and suppleness. Table 1 lists different forms of exercise, comparing their effectiveness in each of these areas.

Table 2 divides activities into light, moderate and vigorous. You should aim to be reasonably fit before you do the more vigorous ones. To make yourself aware of how much you are achieving when you start exercising, make a chart of how you are doing. Monitor how far or fast you walk, and how long you can continue for without feeling tired, for example.

Table 1

Activity	Stamina	Suppleness	Strength	Comment
Aerobics	***	***	**	A lot depends on the teacher; can be pricey
Badminton	**	**	**	Most sports centres have courts
Circuit training	***	***	***	A lot depends on the quality of the routine/class
Climbing stairs	**	*	**	You don't need a gym
Cricket	*	**	*	Sociable; find a club
Cycling (hard)	***	*	**	Wear a helmet
Dancing (ballroom)	*	**	*	Good for co-ordination
Dancing (line or disco)	**	**	*	Not just for the young
Digging the garden	*	*	***	Mind your back
Golf	*	**	*	Start by taking lessons
Jogging	***	*	*	Use grass, not road; wear proper shoes
Rope-skipping	***	**	*	Not just for boxers
Rounders	**	*	**	Or try soft-ball
Rowing	***	*	**	Mind your back
Soccer	**	**	**	Keep on running
Squash	***	***	**	Wait till you're fit
Swimming (hard)	***	***	***	Best all round
Tennis	**	**	**	Find all-weather courts
Walking/rambling	**	*	*	Hill walks can score ** for strength
Weight training	*	**	***	Make sure you're properly supervised
Yoga	*	***	*	Start in a class

KEY
*** very good
** some effect
* little or no effect

Your skill and how hard you play will also affect the rating

Table 2

Light activities	Moderate activities	Vigorous activities
long walks (2 miles plus) at an average or slow pace; lighter DIY (e.g. decorating), table tennis, golf, social dancing and 'exercises' if *not* out of breath or sweaty; bowls, fishing, darts and snooker	long walks (2 miles plus) at a brisk or fast place; football, swimming, tennis, aerobics and cycling if *not* out of breath or sweaty; table tennis, golf, social dancing and exercises if out of breath or sweaty; heavy DIY actvities (e.g. mixing cement); heavy gardening (e.g. digging); heavy housework (e.g. spring cleaning)	hill walking (at a brisk pace); squash, running; football, tennis, aerobics and cycling if out of breath or sweaty

Accessibility

Having a disability doesn't mean you can't benefit from exercise. The Disabled Living Centres★ can advise on equipment that might be helpful and your physiotherapist may also suggest specific exercise programmes. The Royal National Institute of the Blind (RNIB)★ can offer advice on sport for people with sight problems, including a factsheet on bowls. Disability Sport England★ is a charity which coordinates national and regional sports events for people with all types of disability. They are a good source of further information and advice.

Chapter 13

Common health problems

Getting older can bring health challenges. Our bodies are like cars; older models can be highly reliable and serviceable, but they do require a bit of maintenance and the occasional spare part.

Stay physically active

As you grow older, you will notice a slight loss of flexibility and muscle strength, as well as a reduction in endurance (stamina). However, taking regular physical exercise should help maintain the heart, lungs, muscles and circulation in the best possible condition, making it easier to perform normal daily activities like shopping and housework without becoming unduly breathless or tired. This exercise routine will also keep balance and coordination in good working order, reducing the chance of a fall indoors or out.

Exercise is most likely to become a regular part of your life if you choose an activity you enjoy and are good at. Gardening, doing your own housework and playing with young grandchildren all involve useful activity. Simple exercise, such as walking two miles a day, helps to stave off falls, heart disease, stiffness and even depression. Swimming is excellent for maintaining stamina, strength and agility, while fast walking and cycling provide ideal aerobic exercise for your heart and lungs. Start gradually, get expert instruction if embarking on a new sport, and stop if you feel dizzy, short of breath or get chest pain.

If you are housebound, have specific disabilities or are recovering from a major operation or illness, you may benefit from physiotherapy which can be organised by your GP.

Staying mentally agile

At all stages of our life, the old maxim 'use it or lose it' applies. To prevent memory loss and intellectual decline, we need to use our brains. Learning new facts and attempting to try to recapture stored information is healthy exercise for the brain. Doing crosswords with a friend, signing up for courses or learning a new language can be sociable and intellectually stimulating projects.

One in 20 people between the ages of 70 and 80 suffers from dementia, which is a progressive loss of memory causing decline of intellectual and social function. But mixing up grandchildren's names or forgetting where we put our glasses is probably not a sign of anything more serious than natural forgetfulness.

A positive old age

Getting older can be a mixed blessing. For many of us, there is the joy of seeing a new generation growing up, and the chance to enjoy the fruits of a working life. But ill health, loneliness, poor living conditions and lack of money can make this a challenging time. It is possible to seek help and companionship to improve your quality of life. GP surgeries, social workers at day centres, the Citizen's Advice Bureau and organisations such as Help the Aged* are valuable sources of advice.

Common health problems

Some of the most frequent health problems that we face as we get older include mobility problems due to wear and tear of joints, failing hearing and eyesight, urinary problems and womb prolapse. However, improvements in hearing aids, cataract operations, prostate and gynaecological surgery and hip and knee replacements mean that these common health problems can readily be alleviated.

The four commonest cancers arise in the lung, colon, prostate or breast. A diagnosis of cancer is not necessarily a death sentence by any means; generally the older you are when you get cancer, the slower-growing it is and the less likely that your life will be shortened by it. However, most of us will eventually die to heart disease, stroke or cancer.

Infections such as pneumonia can prove dangerous or even fatal, especially if we are already weakened by other disease. Diabetes and high blood pressure significantly increase our risk of heart disease and stroke, and treating these conditions adequately reduces that risk. It may seem pointless to start taking blood pressure pills for the first time in your 70s, but it will reduce your risk of having a potentially debilitating stroke.

Maintaining your health

There is a lot you can do to enhance your chances of enjoying a healthy retirement. The single biggest favour you can do yourself is to stop smoking if you're a smoker. Every cigarette causes some narrowing of blood vessels in the heart, brain and limbs, increasing the risk of heart disease, stroke and gangrene. Every cigarette is also packed full of carcinogens (chemicals that promote cancer). It's never too late to stop; the health benefits of quitting start immediately and there's never been more support available on the NHS with smoking cessation clinics, nicotine replacement therapy such as patches, and drugs to reduce craving, for example bupropion (Zyban).

As we age it takes longer to recover from falls and accidents, so it makes sense to try to avoid obvious pitfalls such as loose carpet round the home. Fitting bath and stair rails and using a stick or mobility aid if and when you need to, may stop you falling.

Dizziness on standing up is a common problem, usually due to blood not getting to the brain efficiently. Standing up slowly and taking care not to look down when descending stairs may help. Medication can cause dizziness, and it's worth discussing your tablets with your GP to see whether they can be stopped or changed.

Immunisation against flu and pneumonia – in the form of an annual flu jab and pneumococcus jab every five to ten years – is an excellent precaution to take. An annual blood pressure check and a urine or blood test for diabetes are also a good idea. If you have diabetes, high blood pressure or other signs of heart disease such as angina, your cholesterol levels will need to be kept as low as possible which usually requires medication. If you have no signs of these conditions, you may not be at any increased risk from a slightly high cholesterol level.

Our dietary needs change as we get older. We need fewer calories and many of us prefer to eat little and often rather than to have large, heavy meals. Calcium-rich foods such as dairy products are important to maintain bone health, as bones tend to become more brittle and prone to breaking as we get older.

Lifestyle factors

Doctors and scientists who have studied the effects of ageing on health and fitness have yet to agree on the exact nature of the biological processes involved. One theory is a progressive decline in the body's immune system so that it is no longer able to defend itself as efficiently against bacteria, viruses and the growth of cancer cells. Alternative mechanisms include the gradual build-up of toxins inside the body; or the wearing down of the templates that control the copying of different types of cell, allowing errors to occur during tissue regeneration.

What is agreed is the influence of lifestyle factors such as smoking, poor diet, lack of exercise, excessive alcohol consumption and over-exposure to strong sunlight – all of which are known to accelerate the degeneration caused by ageing of body organs and tissues, including the skin, bones, nervous system and circulation.

Although genetic inheritance also influences the ageing process in a way that is obviously beyond your control, adopting a healthy lifestyle can significantly reduce your risk of developing many of the diseases that are more common in older people. The importance of lifestyle is discussed in more detail under each of those health problems where it represents a significant underlying cause.

IMPORTANT NOTE

It is important to seek medical help for any persistent, recurrent or unexplained symptom. Unfortunately, many elderly people suffer their symptoms in silence, blaming their aches and pains, blurred vision, deafness, dizziness, falls – to name just a few of the more common complaints – on getting older.

Do not regard any troublesome symptom as being a normal part of ageing. Often the cause is a particular disease, treatment of which may relieve that symptom, making life a lot more fulfilling.

Health problems A-Z

Angina

Angina is a transient pain or tightness which occurs in the chest and sometimes spreads to the neck, jaw or arms. Typically, the pain comes on suddenly during exercise, although it may be brought on by stress, extremes of temperature, or eating a large meal.

Descriptions of angina vary from a mild discomfort to a heavy, crushing pain, and sometimes it is mistaken for indigestion or acid reflux. Other symptoms that often accompany an angina attack include sweating, nausea, dizziness and breathing difficulty. The pain usually eases with rest; if symptoms persist this may be due to a heart attack, where the heart muscle is permanently damaged.

Angina is caused by a lack of oxygen and nutrients reaching the heart muscle, usually because the coronary arteries which encircle and supply blood to the heart have become clogged up with fatty deposits – a condition known as atherosclerosis. This narrowing of the coronary arteries prevents the normal increase in blood flow that should occur when extra demands are placed on the heart, such as during exercise. Atherosclerosis tends to increase in severity with age, which is why angina is more common in elderly people. Women are protected from atherosclerosis by their oestrogen hormones until the menopause, when there is a sudden decline in oestrogen production.

Treatment of angina includes drugs to widen the coronary arteries (nitrates, calcium channel blockers) and drugs to reduce the heart's demands for oxygen by slowing the heart rate (beta blockers). Surgical procedures such as angioplasty (insertion of a catheter with an inflatable balloon tip into the narrowed arteries to flatten the fatty deposits) or bypass grafting (attachment of a blood vessel to divert blood flow around the blockage) are successful in relieving symptoms in many people.

Self-help measures for angina sufferers include stopping smoking to help increase blood flow through the coronary arteries; exercising regularly but only until the symptoms come on; relaxation measures to reduce stress; avoiding exercise on hot or very cold days, or soon after a meal; and losing excess weight to put less strain on the heart.

Anxiety

The main causes of anxiety in older people are worries about health, money, or loss of independence. While anxiety is a perfectly normal reaction to any problem or fear that cannot readily be resolved, it can become a disorder in its own right if it is preventing the individual from thinking clearly or rationally, sleeping properly, or carrying out everyday activities.

Many elderly people live alone and because there is no one to share their worries with on a regular basis, they are more vulnerable to a build-up of anxiety. Therefore, the first step is to find someone to talk things through with, perhaps a friend, a relative, a neighbour, a religious leader or your doctor or health visitor.

If there are persistent or recurrent symptoms related to anxiety, such as difficulty falling asleep, loss of appetite, a feeling of suffocation, constant trembling, or a sense of impending doom, it is important to seek professional help. A variety of measures can relieve anxiety, including relaxation exercises, regular physical activities, meditation or counselling. The National Association for Mental Health (MIND)* may be able to offer advice.

Tranquillisers can also be very effective in the short term, but these do not help the individual to overcome the underlying reasons for the anxiety. Also, if they are taken regularly for longer than a couple of weeks, there is a risk of addiction, memory loss and confusion.

Arteriosclerosis

Hardening of the arteries – arteriosclerosis – is a group of disorders which cause a progressive thickening and loss of elasticity of the artery walls. The most common of these disorders is atherosclerosis, a condition where the arteries become clogged by a build-up of fatty deposits.

The risk of atherosclerosis increases with age, but there are a number of lifestyle factors which speed up the development of fatty deposits inside the arteries. These contributory factors include tobacco smoking, high cholesterol levels in the blood and high blood pressure.

Common disorders which may be caused by atherosclerosis (discussed under their own separate headings) are angina, heart attack, dementia, stroke and transient ischaemic attacks.

Back pain

The most common cause of back pain in elderly people is osteoarthritis of the spine. In this condition, wear and tear of the joints between the vertebrae (spinal bones) leads to narrowing of the spaces between the joints and overgrowth of bone around them.

As a result of this joint degeneration, the spine becomes painful, stiff and often tender over specific areas. Movements such as bending over or getting out of bed can prove difficult, mainly because of the stiffness that develops in the lower spine.

A sudden attack of severe back pain in someone over the age of 60 is occasionally due to collapse of one or more vertebrae that have been weakened by osteoporosis. In this condition, which mainly affects women after the menopause, the bones lose their normal density and become more fragile. The spine has to carry a considerable load as it is the main supporting column of the body; it is therefore not surprising that vertebrae affected by osteoporosis sometimes compress and crumble.

Anyone with persistent back pain should be careful over their choice of painkillers: they all have their potential side effects which are more likely to develop the older you are and the longer you take them. Codeine and dihydrocodeine are very effective pain relievers, but often cause constipation; aspirin and other anti-inflammatory drugs may cause indigestion, peptic ulcers and a variety of other adverse effects that you should discuss with your doctor; paracetamol is a relatively safe painkiller, but should never be taken in excess because of the risk of liver damage.

For those people with osteoarthritis of the spine, there are a number of important self-help measures in addition to medication. These include exercises to strengthen the supporting abdominal and spinal muscles – swimming is a particularly good activity in this respect; a heating pad to relax any painful muscle spasm; a corset to act as a lumbar support; a firm mattress or a board under the mattress to provide support at night; and a resolve to lose any excess weight if you can to reduce the load on your spine. The BackCare Association* may be able to offer further advice.

It is not a good idea to rest your back all the time. Prolonged sitting or lying will only make the discomfort and stiffness due to osteoarthritis worse. Ask your doctor, nurse or health visitor which exercises you can safely do to keep your spine mobile and the supporting muscles firm.

Finally, see your doctor as soon as possible if your back pain is getting worse, or if you develop symptoms of pressure on a spinal nerve, such as weakness, numbness, pins and needles, or problems with bladder or bowel control.

Bereavement

Bereavement, which is a natural reaction to the death of someone you loved or were close to, is a traumatic experience whatever your age. However, because older people are more likely to suffer the loss of their partner or a close friend, bereavement is a relevant issue in any discussion of health problems after retirement.

Although bereavement itself is not a disease, it can cause a variety of symptoms that may be mistaken for the onset of mental illness and, because it is such a stressful life event, it is important to take precautions to prevent any long-term effect on health and well-being. Symptoms that may occur as the result of bereavement include numbing of emotions, outbursts of grief, feelings of hostility even towards the individual who has died, seeing or hearing the dead person, and guilt about not having done more for the person when he or she was alive. Realising that all these responses are perfectly normal will help in the recovery process as you slowly come to terms with what has happened.

To protect your own health, try not to bottle up your emotions; keep busy to avoid brooding, but don't take on too much; look to friends and family for comfort and support but don't allow them to overburden you with their grief; and even if you don't feel like it, eat at least one proper meal each day and take some exercise.

For those people who are unable to cope or who become severely depressed or agitated, their GP may prescribe antidepressants or a short course of tranquillisers. A number of organisations offer practical help and advice to the bereaved, including Cruse Bereavement Care*, the National Association of Widows*, and Age Concern*, all of which have branches all over the UK.

Blindness

Blindness may be the result of a variety of disorders; in elderly people the most common causes are damage to the retina due to diabetes (diabetic retinopathy), cataracts (opacities developing in the internal lens of the eye), untreated glaucoma (abnormal build-up of pressure inside the eye), stroke (where the haemorrhage or blood clot damages the part of the brain which responds to visual information) or degeneration of the central part of the retina (macular degeneration).

It is important to consult a doctor as soon as possible in the event of any loss of vision or persistent visual disturbance, such as seeing coloured haloes around lights. However, because loss of vision is usually a gradual process which may pass unnoticed, regular eye checks are essential. These are free for those over 60. Anyone with a close relative who has suffered from glaucoma should mention it to the optician because this eye condition can be inherited; in any case, pressure checks are a routine part of an eye test for an elderly person.

Treatment of sight problems will obviously depend upon the underlying cause, for example surgical removal of a cataract which can be replaced by an artificial lens, or laser therapy to seal damaged blood vessels on the retina in someone with diabetic retinopathy.

Anyone who is left with a permanent severe defect in their vision should ask the GP to register them as blind or partially sighted, which will entitle them to a range of visual aids as well as certain benefits from the Benefits Agency. The Royal National Institute for the Blind (RNIB)* can also offer advice.

Bronchitis

A productive cough that brings up sputum (also referred to as phlegm or mucus) may be due to an attack of bronchitis. This condition, which may come on after a cold or flu, is due to inflammation of the bronchi (the main airways inside the lungs). As a result of the inflammation, the normal production of mucus in the bronchi is increased; it often becomes discoloured due to the infecting viruses or bacteria, and the white blood cells that are fighting them.

For an acute attack of bronchitis, the doctor may prescribe a course of antibiotics to deal with any bacterial infection present. To relieve the cough, take an expectorant to make the sputum easier to shift, and a cough suppressant if you are troubled by a dry cough.

Also, use a steam vaporiser because a moist atmosphere will be less irritating to the airways, and drink plenty of fluids to help thin the mucus.

Chronic bronchitis is mainly a disease of smokers and those who have been exposed to high levels of air pollution. It is defined as a productive cough on most days for three months or more every year. Tobacco smoke and air pollutants have an irritant effect on the bronchi, increasing the production of thick, sticky mucus which clogs up these airways. In addition to the productive cough, there is likely to be wheezing, tightness in the chest and breathing difficulty on exertion.

The problem is mainly due to an increase in the size and activity of the mucus-producing glands and a greater susceptibility to chest infections. Just stopping smoking should improve the situation although the longer the individual has smoked, the more severe the lung damage is likely to be.

Measures to deal with a sudden flare-up of symptoms in chronic bronchitis are as described for acute attacks. In addition, the doctor may prescribe a bronchodilator, usually as an inhaler, to try to open up the obstructed airways, but these do not work as well in chronic bronchitis as they do in asthma.

Anyone with the tendency to develop bronchitis as a complication of a cold or flu should visit the GP for treatment as soon as the symptoms emerge in order to reduce the chance of a bad attack. Because older people are more vulnerable to respiratory complications with flu, vaccination each autumn against flu is routinely recommended for everyone over the age of 65. Vaccination against pneumococcus, the bacteria responsible for many cases of pneumonia, is also advisable.

Cancer

Cancer is not just one disease; there are many different types, each of which starts by involving a specific organ or tissue in the body. If you develop any of the symptoms listed in the box opposite, arrange a visit to your doctor straight away – early diagnosis means that treatment is more likely to be successful.

Unfortunately, many people are scared to report symptoms they think might be due to cancer. This is ill-advised for two main reasons: their symptoms will often be due to a harmless or non-cancerous condition which will not only respond to treatment, but also allay their fears; and in those few cases where the diagnosis is cancer, any delay in treatment reduces the chance of a successful cure.

CANCER WARNING SYMPTOMS

Any of the following symptoms may be an early-warning signal for cancer:

- Changes in a mole on the skin.
- A new lump or bump.
- An unexplained ulcer on the tongue, mouth or vulva lasting longer than one month.
- Persistent change from normal bowel habit.
- Unexplained weight loss.
- Vaginal bleeding after the menopause.
- Hoarseness lasting longer than six weeks.
- Coughing or vomiting up blood, or a cough lasting longer than six weeks.

There have been a number of advances in the treatment of cancer, with improved surgical techniques and a wider variety of powerful anti-cancer drugs available. In addition, doctors are now better able to control the complications that sometimes accompany cancer, such as pain, nausea, constipation, cough or difficulty swallowing.

The cancer screening tests offered to women on a regular basis – cervical smear and mammography (breast X-ray) – are usually only recommended up until the age of 65. However, if any woman has passed this age without having had either of these checks, she should ask her doctor whether the screening test is still advisable. You can also continue having breast screening for as long as you want – ask your GP. Cancers of the cervix and breast may not cause any obvious symptoms until they have reached an advanced stage.

The British Association of Cancer United Patients (BACUP)* can give further information on general and specific queries to do with cancer.

Colds and flu

For most people, catching a cold or a dose of flu is no more than a temporary inconvenience. These viral infections may cause a variety of familiar symptoms, including sore throat, fever, dry cough, aches and pains, runny nose, weakness and swollen glands. The main difference between a cold and flu is that the latter typically makes you feel too ill to do anything other than stay in bed, and lasts a few days longer.

Traditional cold and flu remedies, like paracetamol or aspirin to relieve discomfort and bring down a temperature, plenty of fluids to replace those lost with the increase in sweating, and inhalations to ease nasal congestion, are helpful whatever your age.

However, for older people, flu is potentially a lot more serious. Complications such as pneumonia and pleurisy are more likely to develop, and if there is any long-term heart or lung disorder, or if you are diabetic or debilitated, the risks are even greater.

It is therefore advisable for all people over the age of 65 to ask the doctor about receiving an annual flu jab, which is designed to provide immunity against the influenza viruses expected to be around that year. This immunisation is normally given in September or October.

In addition, if cold or flu symptoms do start, it is important to visit the doctor if any complications seem to be developing, such as a productive cough, chest pain, breathlessness or wheezing.

Constipation

Everyone has their own characteristic bowel habit, and for some a bowel movement only once or twice a week is perfectly normal. The proper definition of constipation is either having to strain to open the bowels, or a decrease in the usual frequency of bowel movements.

Although constipation may affect people of any age, it becomes more common with advancing years. One reason for this is the tendency for older people to eat fewer high-fibre foods; another is the influence of physical activity on bowel function – those who take less exercise as they get older are more prone to constipation.

A number of drugs can also cause constipation including iron pills, painkillers and cough medicines that contain codeine, and certain antacids, all of which are commonly taken by older people. In addition, a significant number take a laxative routinely, in the mistaken belief that they need to have a daily bowel movement, and this can lead, paradoxically, to a lazy bowel.

Self-help measures to relieve constipation include taking more exercise – even a gentle stroll can help; eating more fibre-rich foods such as fresh fruit and vegetables, beans and pulses, wholegrain bread and cereal; and drinking six or more glasses of water or soft drink each day. If these remedies fail to help, seek medical help.

Deafness

Deafness can be a serious problem because it acts as a barrier to normal conversation, isolating and depressing the sufferer as a result. However, for many elderly people, it may be possible to improve their hearing significantly, so deafness should not be treated as a normal part of getting old.

The first step is to overcome any embarrassment and admit to the GP that you actually have a hearing problem. Sometimes the cause is simply a build-up in ear wax, and hearing can be restored to a satisfactory level by having the ear canals syringed with warm water. This is usually performed by the GP or practice nurse.

Your GP may need to refer you to an ear, nose and throat clinic or hearing aid centre for a full assessment of your hearing, and to see whether a hearing aid might help. However, be warned that in some parts of the country there are long waiting lists for this service on the NHS. Also, however sophisticated the hearing aid, it will only be able to amplify those sound frequencies you have difficulty detecting; it will not give you perfect hearing.

Other measures to help you communicate include asking people to speak slowly and clearly, and to avoid shouting at you, which only distorts the words being spoken. Keep any background noise like the television or radio to a minimum. It may be worthwhile taking a lip-reading class to acquire the basic skills. Further advice may be obtained from the Royal National Institute for Deaf People (RNID)*, the British Deaf Association*, and the Council for the Advancement of Communication for Deaf People*.

Finally, there has been a lot of adverse publicity about the sale of hearing aids through advertisements in magazines or newspapers. This is because they can be very expensive, and they may not work properly for you if they haven't been designed to suit your particular pattern of hearing loss.

Dementia

Dementia is not a specific type of illness: it is a general term for grossly impaired mental function which may result in loss of short- and long-term memory, altered personality, disorientation and confusion, disruption of speech and comprehension, erratic moods and behaviour, wandering, and an inability to carry out simple everyday activities like washing and dressing.

The most common cause of dementia is Alzheimer's disease, which accounts for about 75 per cent of cases in people over the age of 65. Another common reason for loss of normal mental function is a stroke or series of minor strokes that may not necessarily have caused any physical disability such as paralysis. Parkinson's disease and long-term alcohol abuse may also lead to forms of dementia.

Dementia is not a normal part of ageing and anyone who develops symptoms of mental deterioration should be seen by his or her GP for a thorough evaluation. Referral to a specialist known as a psychogeriatrician may be arranged. Occasionally, these symptoms are the result of a disorder which can be treated successfully, for example certain types of anaemia, an infection or even depression, in which case normal mental function can usually be restored.

Unfortunately, however, there is no cure at present for conditions such as Alzheimer's disease. Research into Alzheimer's has suggested several possible causes, for example the excessive build-up of a protein in the brain, which is actually being produced to stimulate nerve cell regeneration as part of a natural mechanism designed to compensate for the effects of ageing. Other theories put forward have included the toxic effects of an accumulation of aluminium inside the brain; or an abnormal response to a viral infection.

New drugs are available which may improve memory and intellectual ability in some sufferers, though availability on the NHS is limited and results may be disappointing.

For anyone who has to care for someone who is suffering from dementia, here are a few useful self-help measures that may make life a little easier:

- Establish a daily routine with a fixed schedule of events.
- Make sure that clothes are easy to put on.

- Keep doors and windows locked if the sufferer is likely to wander.
- Do not move objects to new places in the home.
- Help the person keep a diary and a daily checklist of tasks.
- Be patient in the event of stubbornness or aggression, and remember that this is due to the condition.
- Claim benefits from the Benefits Agency such as attendance allowance.
- Arrange with your GP temporary care in hospital or a nursing home so that you can take a well-earned break.
- Contact the Alzheimer's Society★ for support and advice.

There is more about Alzheimer's disease on pages 223–4.

Dental problems

With a daily routine of brushing and flossing and a bit of luck, most people should be able to keep their natural teeth into old age. However, older people have to take extra care of their teeth as the gums tend to recede with age, exposing the neck of the tooth, which has no protective enamel.

Ask your dentist or dental hygienist to check your brushing technique if you are unsure, or use a disclosing tablet, which shows how effectively the teeth have been cleaned by colouring any plaque left behind. Dental floss can be useful in removing particles of food lodged between the teeth, but take care not to cut into the gums.

If there are large spaces between some of the teeth, try using a toothbrush with a single pointed bristle so that all the tooth and gum surfaces can be reached. Toothpicks should be used cautiously because of the risk of damaging the gums.

Around one quarter of adults in the UK have lost their teeth, usually because of gum disease that was not treated soon enough. It is also important to take good care of dentures, cleaning them regularly to reduce the risk of a mouth or gum infection.

For older people who still have some or all of their natural teeth, a dental check-up is recommended at least once a year. Dentures should be checked every three years, and sooner if they are no longer fitting properly or causing soreness in the mouth. Because the gums shrink after the natural teeth are lost and the shape of the mouth may also change, it is often necessary to adjust the structure of the denture or make a new one.

Before having any dental treatment, check that the dentist will provide this under the NHS. Your local Primary Care Trust or Health Board can supply a list of NHS dentists in the area. Even under the NHS, you still have to pay a proportion of the charges, so ask the dentist to provide an estimate of the likely bill.

Depression

Although older people are more prone to depression, sometimes as a response to a chronic illness such as Parkinson's disease or osteoarthritis or as a side effect of medication, symptoms of depression should not be accepted as an inevitable part of getting older. Also, it is important not to allow a serious bout of depression to continue without seeking help from the doctor. Depression will not usually disappear on its own and in severe cases there may be a risk of suicide. Treatment with antidepressants is usually very effective.

Warning symptoms of a depression that should be treated if they persist include waking in the early hours of the morning, generalised aches and pain, a sense of despair, being unable to concentrate, and not feeling like eating anything. Confusion, agitation, extreme apathy and drinking more alcohol than usual can each be the result of depression. Often a friend or relative may have to persuade the depressed person to go to the doctor. Any threat of ending it all should be taken seriously and the doctor called out if necessary.

To ward off depression, it is important to avoid becoming isolated. After retirement, build new social contacts, for example by taking a daytime or evening class, joining a club or getting involved in voluntary work. You might like to contact the Fellowship of Depressives Anonymous★ for further information.

Diabetes (maturity onset)

Maturity onset diabetes is the form of diabetes that typically only comes on after the age of 40 and usually does not require insulin injections to keep the condition under control. Unlike the juvenile type of diabetes, where the pancreas stops producing insulin altogether, in the maturity onset or type 2 form the pancreas does release some insulin into the bloodstream, but not enough to prevent a build-up of sugar in the circulation.

Many elderly people with maturity onset diabetes become aware of it only as the result of a routine blood or urine test, which reveals abnormally high blood levels of sugar, or the presence of sugar in the urine.

WARNING SYMPTOMS OF DIABETES

- Excessive thirst; frequent urination.
- Fatigue and weakness.
- Numbness or tingling in the feet and hands.
- Blurred vision.
- Impotence in men.

Symptoms to watch out for are listed above. In some sufferers, all that may be needed is a diet with fewer refined carbohydrate (sugary) foods and more high-fibre, unrefined carbohydrate (starchy) foods to help slow down the absorption of sugar into the bloodstream, along with cutting down on fatty foods, particularly saturated fats, to help lose any excess weight.

If these measures are not enough, the doctor can prescribe tablets to keep blood sugar levels normal. In rare cases, insulin injections may be required. Regular check-ups either by the GP or hospital diabetic clinic are advisable to detect the onset of any complications such as eye, nerve or skin damage. Most diabetics monitor the sugar level in their blood or urine using a simple testing kit at home in order to ensure that their condition is not going out of control.

The British Diabetic Association★ can offer further information.

Emphysema

Emphysema is a serious lung disease which involves extensive damage to some of the millions of tiny air sacs (alveoli) that make up the lung tissues. As a result of the walls of these alveoli ballooning and bursting, with clusters of alveoli merging to form fewer, larger air sacs, the surface area of the lungs (through which gases pass to and from the bloodstream) is reduced. The lungs also become less elastic, making it more difficult to breathe, particularly to breathe out.

Symptoms of emphysema include a wheezy cough and breathlessness. Because less oxygen reaches the bloodstream, the skin may develop a bluish tinge. There may also be signs of heart failure, with swelling of the ankles, if the heart is unable to cope with the additional workload resulting from blood no longer flowing freely through the lung circulation.

Emphysema is most commonly caused by heavy smoking, as chemicals inhaled within the tobacco smoke having a toxic effect on the alveoli. Another contributory factor may be air pollution, and a few people develop emphysema because of an inherited defect in a lung enzyme.

Drugs to widen the airways, usually in the form of an inhaler, and steroids to reduce lung inflammation, may be helpful for some sufferers. In severe cases, oxygen may have to be provided in the home.

In addition to giving up smoking and avoiding smoky or polluted atmospheres, which will only make the lung damage worse, an annual flu jab is essential to reduce the risk of a flu-related chest infection. Prompt antibiotic therapy for any chest infection is also essential before it makes the breathing difficulties far worse.

Eye problems

A normal change in the eyes that occurs due to ageing is a gradual loss of elasticity in the internal lens, which leads to a tendency to get more long-sighted. This condition, known as presbyopia, causes difficulty with near vision. As a result, small print may appear blurred when held at normal reading distance, but can be brought into focus by reading the page at arm's length or, if you are normally short-sighted, by taking your glasses off.

Presbyopia is easily corrected with a pair of reading glasses; it is best to have your eyes checked by an optician to establish the appropriate lens prescription for each eye. Although reading glasses can now be bought over the counter using a do-it-yourself eye chart, the advantage of seeing an optician is to have other more serious eye problems picked up before they cause any permanent damage and loss of vision. If you are short-sighted you may need two sets of lenses – one for reading and one for distance.

A routine eye test is recommended every two years, and sooner if any loss or disturbance of normal vision occurs. Reading glasses usually have to be changed several times, as the lenses become increasingly rigid, until all the focusing has to be done by the spectacle lenses.

There may be a charge for the eye test unless the person is receiving Income Support or belongs to one of the priority groups, which include anyone over the age of 60, people with glaucoma themselves (or whose close relative has this condition), diabetics and anyone registered blind or partially sighted.

Apart from presbyopia, the three most common eye problems in elderly people are cataracts, glaucoma and macular degeneration. A cataract is usually easily remedied by surgery; glaucoma can be treated successfully with eye drops, tablets or surgery, but any damage that has already been caused by the excessive pressure inside the eye ball cannot be corrected.

Although macular degeneration, a condition where the central part of the retina wears out, is not treatable, much can be done to reduce the difficulties resulting from the progressive loss of vision it causes (see 'Blindness').

Falls

About one third of elderly people are thought to suffer one or more falls each year, half of which are due to an accident such as tripping, while many of the remainder occur with no obvious cause. Because older people, particularly women, are vulnerable to osteoporosis – a condition which weakens the bones (see pages 203–4) – these falls may cause a fracture, usually of the femur, wrist or spine.

To prevent accidental falls, there are a number of preventive measures (see overleaf). If falls happen out of the blue, or are preceded by dizziness, weakness or some other warning symptom, a check-up from the doctor is essential.

Many of the medical conditions which can cause recurrent falls may be successfully treated, for example anaemia, heart irregularity or vertigo. The doctor can give advice on the easiest way to get up off the floor after a fall. For anyone who lives alone and does not have frequent visitors, it is a good idea to wear a portable alarm trigger so that help can be summoned if the fall has immobilised them (see page 228).

PREVENTIVE MEASURES AGAINST FALLS

- Do not wear loose slippers or long trailing clothing.
- Electric leads should run under the carpet, or around the edge of the room.
- Keep the living areas free from obstacles.
- Remove loose mats or rugs.
- Make sure that floors are not slippery or highly polished.
- Stairs and corridors should be properly lit. Fit two-way switching on stairs.
- Secure loose stair carpets.
- Fit a handrail at each side of the stairs, and add grab-rails in the bathroom.

Foot problems

Older people are more likely than younger ones to develop calluses and corns on their feet. A callus is a thickening of the outer layers of skin due to pressure or irritation; a corn is a callus found on or between the toes. The reason for the greater susceptibility to these skin changes among elderly people is the higher incidence of foot deformities such as bunions, hammer toes and arthritic joints in this age group. As a result, they often find it difficult to buy shoes that fit comfortably without creating areas of friction when they stand or walk.

All corns or calluses should be covered with tape or a non-medicated corn pad for protection. Try to eliminate the cause of the pressure, for example by changing to a different pair of shoes. Soak thickened areas of skin in warm water to soften them, and then gently rub them with a pumice stone. Do not use non-prescription medicated corn pads, and never attempt to trim calluses yourself.

See a chiropodist (or podiatrist) if a corn or callus becomes painful, tender or inflamed. For people who suffer from persistent or recurrent calluses or corns as a result of a foot deformity, which can be structural or postural, the chiropodist may construct a specially moulded insole. Occasionally, an orthopaedic surgeon may have to perform some type of corrective surgery. The chiropodist can also deal with bunions.

Anyone with diabetes or a poor circulation should have chiropody treatment routinely every few months because they are extremely vulnerable to infection of the skin if it becomes irritated or damaged.

Chiropody services are free for people over the age of 60; however, in some parts of the UK there may be a long delay due to a shortage of state-registered chiropodists. If you are seeking private treatment, make sure the chiropodist is state registered, shown by the letters SRCh after his or her name. The Society of Chiropodists and Podiatrists★ can supply names of state-registered chiropodists in your area.

Gout

Gout is a type of arthritis that characteristically attacks one joint at a time, usually the joint at the base of the big toe. It develops as a result of the deposition of uric acid crystals inside the joint, which cause it to become temporarily inflamed, and so extremely painful and swollen with redness of the overlying skin.

Treatment of an attack involves large doses of an anti-inflammatory drug and sometimes colchicine to suppress the inflammation rapidly. If the cause is abnormally high levels of uric acid in the blood and attacks are recurrent, the doctor may prescribe a drug which reduces the production of uric acid in the body or a drug to increase the amount of uric acid passed in the urine.

Occasionally, uric acid crystallises as white deposits under the skin (tophi), which may then ulcerate and have to be removed surgically.

Gout sufferers are advised to reduce their alcohol consumption and their dietary intake of purine, which is converted in the body to uric acid. Foods to avoid because they are high in purine include offal (liver, kidney, heart), game, anchovies, mackerel, herring, scallops, sardines, whitebait and mussels. Foods to eat only in moderation because they contain a fair amount of purine include meat, poultry, fish not mentioned above, peas, green beans, lentils, spinach, mushrooms, asparagus and cauliflower. The Arthritis Research Campaign★ produces a free leaflet on the condition.

Haemorrhoids (see Piles)

Hair loss

Gradual, mild thinning of the hair on top of the head is a normal part of ageing; unless the individual has inherited the condition known as male-pattern baldness, some hair should remain covering most of the scalp. Hair loss affects about 50 per cent of men by the age of 50.

In male-pattern baldness, which may also affect a few women after the menopause, hair is lost initially from the temples and crown to be replaced by very fine, downy hair. As the affected area of scalp widens, the normal hair line recedes.

There are many other causes of excessive hair loss which may occur whatever your age. Your doctor should be able to tell whether there is some underlying treatable condition by examining the scalp and skin on other parts of the body.

For hair loss that is causing distress or embarrassment, there are a variety of possible measures including wigs, toupees or a hair transplant. Application of a solution of the drug minoxidil (which was originally introduced to treat high blood pressure) may induce regrowth of fine hair in some people, but the results are not impressive.

Heart attack

A heart attack, also known as a coronary thrombosis or myocardial infarction, is a serious condition in which part of the heart muscle dies after interruption of its normal blood supply. In most cases, a heart attack is caused by the formation of a blood clot in one of the coronary arteries which encircle the heart. The clot develops in a section of the artery that is already narrowed by fatty deposits (see 'Arteriosclerosis').

Symptoms of a heart attack may include pain across the centre of the chest, pain spreading into the neck, jaw, shoulders or arms, sweating, nausea, vomiting, palpitations and breathlessness. Risk factors for a heart attack are divided into unavoidable ones, such as getting older, a family history of heart attacks, diabetes and high blood pressure, as well as avoidable ones, such as smoking, drinking too much alcohol, eating foods high in saturated fats and cholesterol, and being overweight.

Anyone suspected of having a heart attack should get urgent medical help. A new type of medication is available which, injected into the circulation, can quickly dissolve the blood clots that cause most heart attacks. These clot-busting drugs can halt a heart attack and minimise the muscle damage as long as they are injected within a few hours of the onset of symptoms.

After a heart attack, assuming there have not been any serious complications, ask the doctor to recommend an appropriate exercise programme. Taking regular exercise after an attack can reduce the chance of a recurrence.

Hernia

An abdominal hernia is the abnormal protrusion of an internal organ, usually part of the intestine, through a gap or weakness in the abdominal muscle wall. This type of hernia is more common in elderly people because the abdominal muscles tend to lose some of their strength and tone, partly because older people tend to be less active and because they tend to put on weight around the abdomen later in life.

If you notice a bulge on the abdominal wall or in the groin see your doctor. The main risk from an abdominal hernia is obstruction of the intestine or its blood supply as a result of the protruding loop becoming compressed, which in turn can lead to potentially fatal complications such as peritonitis or gangrene.

Surgical repair is recommended in most cases to prevent these complications recurring. The operation is usually relatively easy for the surgeon to perform, keeping the patient in hospital for a few days at the most. Before returning to normal activities, particularly doing any carrying or lifting, it is essential to follow a supervised programme of exercises to stretch and strengthen the abdominal muscles – otherwise the risk of recurrence is much greater.

For those people who are not fit enough to have an operation, a surgical truss or corset may be provided to prevent the hernia from bulging through the muscle wall. To be effective, it must be possible to ease the hernia gently back inside the abdomen; the truss should be put on before getting out of bed and then worn all day.

If a hernia suddenly becomes painful, tender, swollen or inflamed, seek medical attention at once, as these are signs that the intestine is under pressure.

High blood pressure

Blood pressure is the force that pushes blood around the circulation; it is generated by the pumping action of the heart and the natural elasticity of the artery walls. It is when this pressure is too high, a condition known as hypertension, that problems can arise.

Blood pressure tends to increase steadily with age because the arteries in older people are less elastic and often narrowed by fatty deposits (see 'Arteriosclerosis'). An excessively high blood pressure at any age usually occurs without any obvious cause, although in a few cases there is an underlying medical reason, for example kidney damage, a blood vessel disease or a hormone disorder.

Most people with dangerously high blood pressure experience no warning symptoms, which is why doctors like to check everyone's blood pressure regularly. The measurement of blood pressure comes as two figures: the higher one is the reading at the moment the heart beats, the lower one is when the heart is relaxed. For people over the age of 60, the ideal blood pressure is 140/90 or less.

If the upper reading is much higher than 140, or the lower reading is 100 or more, your GP will encourage you to take such steps as losing excess weight, taking regular gentle exercise, cutting down on salt and stopping smoking. Relaxation or meditation can also help.

If despite all this the blood pressure remains high, medication is usually recommended. This is because untreated hypertension causes damage to arteries, particularly in the heart, brain, kidneys and eyes, resulting in a greater risk of heart attack, stroke, kidney failure and blindness.

Hypothermia

Hypothermia is a potentially fatal condition in which the body's internal temperature falls to below 35°C/95°F. Elderly people are more vulnerable to hypothermia because as the body ages it becomes less sensitive to the cold. Not only are older people less likely to feel cold when their body temperature drops, but they are also less efficient at generating body heat, for example through shivering.

A number of medical problems that are more common among older people, such as immobility due to arthritis or an underactive thyroid gland, also increase the risk of hypothermia. Death due to hypothermia may occur as a direct result of a low body temperature, which can interfere with normal breathing and the heartbeat; or it may be an indirect cause, through making a heart or chest complaint worse or reducing resistance to infections such as pneumonia.

All elderly people should take steps to protect themselves against the cold, for example by living in one warm room if it is too difficult or expensive to heat the whole house, eating and drinking properly, wrapping up in several thin layers of clothing, doing regular arm and leg exercises, if possible, and getting the windows and doors properly insulated.

Help the Aged* runs the National Winter Warmth Campaign, which gives more advice on how to avoid hypothermia.

It is also essential for anyone who cares for an elderly person to be aware of the warning symptoms of hypothermia, which include pale cold skin, puffiness of the face, increasing drowsiness and confusion, slurring of the speech and shallow breathing. First-aid measures while waiting for medical help are to wrap the person in a warm blanket and if he or she is conscious to give a warm drink. However, it is dangerous to give alcohol, rub the skin, apply a hot water bottle or put the person into a hot bath.

Incontinence

Incontinence of either urine or faeces is not a normal part of growing old. Although it is an embarrassing problem that most elderly people would rather not talk about, incontinence is often curable and so it is important to visit your doctor for advice and treatment.

In older men, incontinence of urine is usually the result of an enlarged prostate gland (see 'Prostate enlargement') and takes the form of dribbling after passing urine, or not being able to get to a toilet in time. Treatment involves a surgical operation, but drugs are being developed that may help by shrinking the prostate, thereby taking pressure off the bladder and urethra.

In older women, incontinence of urine may be due to urinary infection, which should respond to antibiotics; or to a weakness of the pelvic muscles, usually as a result of stretching during childbirth. Pelvic muscle weakness typically causes 'stress incontinence', where a small amount of urine leaks out during coughing, sneezing or laughing.

If the pelvic muscles do not respond to an exercise programme, or if in addition to the muscle weakness there is a prolapse of the uterus which is stretching the neck of the bladder, surgical repair will usually be recommended. For anyone not well enough to have this operation, a plastic ring pessary inserted inside the vagina to hold the uterus in place may be sufficient to relieve the urinary symptoms.

Incontinence of faeces in elderly people is often due to prolonged constipation, the faeces having become compacted inside the rectum and lower colon and the resulting irritation of the bowel wall leading to the formation of a small amount of diarrhoea, which leaks out without warning. Treatment of the constipation, which may in such extreme cases require an enema, should relieve the problem.

In many parts of the UK, there are continence advisers – specially trained nurses – who can explain the practical measures, and give advice on the best aids available, to make it easier to cope with incontinence that cannot be cured. Ask your doctor, health visitor or district nurse whether there is a local continence adviser; if not, one of them should be able to offer support and provide information.

There is also the Continence Foundation* where you can get advice from health professionals with a special interest and expertise in bladder and bowel control.

Indigestion

When someone complains of indigestion he or she may be suffering from any of a wide variety of symptoms including heartburn, belching, a bloating discomfort, wind, abdominal pain or nausea. The most common reasons for all these digestive symptoms are bad eating habits, such as eating or drinking too much, eating too quickly, not relaxing for long enough after a meal, or eating too soon before going to bed.

If you develop abdominal discomfort or heartburn, you may subconsciously swallow air to try to relieve it, resulting in belching and bloating – flatulence – which makes your symptoms feel much worse.

For an acute attack of indigestion in whatever form, take a dose of antacid. Your pharmacist will be able to recommend one from the dozens of different brands on the market. The antacid should relieve indigestion within an hour or so; however, if the symptoms persist or suddenly get worse, for example an abdominal pain lasting more than four hours, see your doctor.

Recurrent attacks of indigestion should also be investigated by the GP; they may be caused by a peptic ulcer, acid reflux due to a hiatus hernia, irritable bowel syndrome or, rarely, stomach cancer. A physical examination and a few tests can exclude any serious condition; your doctor can then prescribe appropriate medication.

Insomnia

People often seem to need less sleep as they get older. This should not be regarded as a problem as long as the reduced amount of sleep is not causing tiredness, anxiety or distress. Insomnia is not just being unable to sleep for as long as you want, but sleep may be very fitful, causing the person to wake feeling tired and out of sorts; he or she may take a long time to fall asleep, or wake up in the early hours of the morning and be unable to fall asleep again.

If you are having trouble sleeping in one of the above ways, adopt the following measures to try to alleviate the problem:

- Take some exercise during the day, preferably outdoors.
- Stay up until you feel sleepy.
- Have a milky bedtime drink, but avoid tea and coffee which contain stimulants.
- Don't eat a large meal late in the evening.
- Make sure your bedroom is not too cold or hot.
- Get up at the same time each morning, regardless of how well you have slept.

It is also worth noting that many older people sleep better having had a short nap during the day.

See your doctor if insomnia persists despite these measures. Sometimes the underlying cause is depression, in which case antidepressants will usually help stop the early morning waking that is a characteristic of depression. Sleeping pills which contain a sedative may be prescribed as a short-term measure, but regular use can lead to addiction and unpleasant withdrawal symptoms if you stop taking them suddenly.

Leg ulcers

Leg ulcers are a common problem in elderly people, especially women. Most of them occur in association with varicose veins, because the pooling of blood that occurs in the leg veins in this condition causes the surrounding skin tissues to become unhealthy and vulnerable to relatively minor trauma.

A few leg ulcers are due to disease of the arteries, which interferes with the normal supply of oxygen and nutrients to the skin tissues, again making them unhealthy and at risk of gangrene as well as ulceration. Diabetics are particularly susceptible to leg ulcers, not only because they are more likely to develop arterial disease but also because this disease can damage the nerves in the legs so that minor injuries to the skin may not be noticed.

Ulcers as a result of varicose veins are usually treated with compression bandages and elevation of the ulcerated leg to help reduce blood pooling and allow the skin to heal naturally. Arterial ulcers are cleaned and dressed, antibiotics are prescribed to treat any infection, and drugs may be given to try to improve the circulation, but compression bandages must not be applied because they will make the problem worse by causing further constriction of the arteries.

To reduce the risk of developing a leg ulcer, take regular exercise, don't smoke, eat a healthy balanced diet, lose excess weight if you can, take good care of your skin, protect your legs from accidental knocks and if you suffer from varicose veins consider wearing compression hosiery.

Medication problems

The main problem for elderly people with regard to their medication is that they may be taking several drugs at the same time.

This can be confusing, particularly if doses are being taken at different times of the day and some of the drugs are taken more frequently than others.

Make a chart with each of the drugs and the times of the doses written on it, leaving a space to tick off each time a dose is taken. It is helpful to write what the drug has been prescribed for on the container, for example 'pain', 'dizziness', 'blood pressure'.

Do not put all the drugs for one day in the same bottle, as this can lead to dangerous mistakes over which drug is for which condition.

If you are taking several medications, make sure you tell the doctor about all of them before any new drug is prescribed. Some drugs can be dangerous when taken in combination. For the same reason, check with the pharmacist before starting any new over-the-counter medication.

When a condition such as arthritis makes it difficult to take the childproof tops off the bottles, ask the pharmacist to provide alternative containers; but this makes it even more important to keep all medications out of the reach of children.

Any unexpected symptoms that you think might be a side effect of a drug should be reported at once to the doctor, but do not stop the drug abruptly without checking that it is safe to do so. If a drug does not seem to be working, make another appointment with the doctor.

Anyone on long-term medication should ideally have a check-up every three months, and certainly at least every six months, to make sure the treatment is still necessary and not causing any hidden complications.

Menopause

The menopause is a normal stage in a woman's life that occurs around the age of 50. While the menopause can be said to be complete once the menstrual periods have stopped, the processes leading up to this point begin several years earlier and the symptoms associated with the menopause may continue for several years afterwards.

Hormonal changes are the cause of the various processes and symptoms that occur with the menopause. As the amount of oestrogen being made in the ovaries gradually decreases, ovulation (egg release) may cease completely and the menstrual cycle becomes irregular.

A wide variety of symptoms, both physical and emotional, may be experienced including hot flushes, night sweats, palpitations, vaginal dryness, mood swings, depression and forgetfulness. The reduction in oestrogen levels also accelerates the process of osteoporosis, which makes a woman more susceptible to angina and heart attacks and makes the bones become more fragile. There is also a tendency to put on weight, particularly around the abdomen.

Hormone replacement therapy (HRT) can help relieve most of the menopausal symptoms, as well as providing additional protection against osteoporosis. A woman may wish to discuss with her GP or at the well-woman clinic whether HRT might be suitable for her.

In addition to HRT, other measures that can help minimise some of the unwanted effects of the menopause include regular exercise to tone up the muscles, a sensible diet to avoid gaining weight, using moisturising cream or an emollient to counteract dry skin and stopping smoking, which is a major risk factor for both osteoporosis and coronary heart disease.

Finally, if menstrual bleeding occurs after the menopause, it is essential to have this checked by a doctor, as post-menopausal bleeding can be a warning symptom of cancer.

Obesity

Energy requirements, in the form of calories provided by our food, gradually decrease with age, partly because the body requires less energy for cell processes at rest, partly because older people tend to take less physical exercise during the day and therefore burn up fewer calories overall.

However, most elderly people do not adjust their calorie intake to match these changes. As a result the excess calories are laid down as fatty tissue, causing a steady increase in weight that can progress to obesity. In addition to the undesirable effect of being overweight from the point of view of appearance, obesity is bad for long-term health because it increases the risk of developing high blood pressure, diabetes, osteoarthritis and even cancer.

To avoid obesity, you should follow a diet which restricts high-calorie foods such as biscuits, cakes, chocolate, sweets and cuts down on fatty foods like butter, full-fat cheese and fried meals, while continuing to eat foods high in vitamins, minerals and fibre.

The ideal daily diet should include fresh fruit and vegetables, wholegrain bread and cereals and lean meats such as poultry. To ensure you get sufficient calcium without too many calories, choose low-fat milk, cheeses and yoghurts. For more on healthy eating, see Chapter 11.

Osteoarthritis

Wear and tear of the cartilage surfaces inside a joint, resulting in pain, stiffness and swelling, is the cause of the most common form of arthritis, known as osteoarthritis. This wearing out of the joint tends to occur gradually with advancing years, so that most people in their 60s have osteoarthritis in at least some of their joints.

The joints most commonly affected are those that have taken the most punishment over the years, like the hips, the knees and the joints at the base of the neck and lower back. Factors which increase the risk of osteoarthritis include being overweight, overuse of a joint playing a particular sport, or a serious or recurrent injury to a joint when younger.

There is no cure for osteoarthritis but symptoms can usually be controlled with painkillers or anti-inflammatory drugs taken by mouth or applied to the affected joints as a gel. Exercises to strengthen the muscles around an arthritic joint, under the guidance of a doctor or physiotherapist, can also help by protecting the joint against further damage. The Arthritis Research Campaign★ produces a leaflet on the subject.

In severe cases, where the arthritic joint has become very painful or stiff, it may be necessary to be referred to the hospital for a joint-replacement operation.

Osteoporosis

In osteoporosis, the bones become brittle and fragile as the result of a gradual loss of minerals, including calcium, from their internal structure. Affected bones are more likely to break as a consequence of relatively minor trauma, such as falling over in the street.

As part of the normal ageing process, almost everyone experiences a reduction in their bone density. After the age of 35, the amount of new bone being formed to replace the continuous degeneration of old bone is reduced and the body also becomes less efficient at absorbing calcium from digested food and storing it in the bones.

The gradual decline in bone mass speeds up in women after the menopause because of the loss of the protective effect of oestrogen. Other factors that may accelerate the onset of osteoporosis include inactivity such as prolonged bed rest, smoking and drinking too much alcohol.

To avoid osteoporosis, it is important to build up strong bones earlier in life by taking regular exercise, particularly activities that put stress on the bones; by eating adequate amounts of calcium, especially during pregnancy and breastfeeding, when calcium requirements go up, by not smoking, and drinking alcohol only in moderation. Hormone replacement therapy taken for at least 12 to 18 months during the menopause can also protect against osteoporosis.

Even when osteoporosis is already established, it is still worth increasing calcium and vitamin D intake and following a gentle exercise programme. Particular care must be taken to avoid any accidental falls by making the home extra safe (see 'Falls') and not going outdoors in icy weather, if possible.

In severe cases, a drug may be prescribed to try to halt the continuing loss of minerals from the bones. However, as yet, no medication is available that can restore the bone strength to normal, which is why prevention of this disease is so important.

More information can be obtained from the National Osteoporosis Society.*

Parkinson's disease

Parkinson's disease affects the part of the brain which controls all body movements. The exact cause is unknown, but the symptoms occur as a result of depletion of one of the brain chemicals – dopamine – in this area, which in turn interferes with the transmission of nerve impulses involved in the co-ordination of muscle action.

The incidence of Parkinson's disease increases significantly in elderly people, rising to 1 in 100 over the age of 65, and 1 in 50 over the age of 80. Symptoms tend to come on gradually and typically include a coarse tremor in the hands, muscle stiffness, difficulty starting and stopping movements such as walking, and a fixed facial expression with staring eyes. Sufferers tend to stoop forward and walk with a shuffling gait.

Several different drugs may be tried before the symptoms are brought under reasonable control. The amount of drug and the timing of each dose have to be adjusted carefully to suit the individual's response. A great deal of research is under way to develop more effective treatments and one day to find a cure.

Physiotherapy and occupational therapy can help improve mobility and maintain independence to a limited extent but, unfortunately, the condition tends to become more severe with time. For details of a self-help group in your part of the country, write to the Parkinson's Disease Society★.

Peptic ulcer

In older people, a common reason for developing an ulcer in the stomach or duodenum – popularly referred to as a peptic ulcer – is long-term treatment with an anti-inflammatory drug to relieve the symptoms of a painful condition such as arthritis. Another medication that can also cause peptic ulceration when taken on a regular basis is a corticosteroid such as prednisolone, taken to suppress inflammatory and allergic disorders.

Warning symptoms of a peptic ulcer include recurrent attacks of abdominal pain, nausea and vomiting, belching and feeling bloated. Vomiting material that looks like coffee grounds or passing black tarry stools are signs that a peptic ulcer is bleeding.

To reduce the risk of developing a peptic ulcer, try to take an ordinary painkiller such as paracetamol or codeine rather than anti-inflammatory drugs which include aspirin and ibuprofen. Doctors now sometimes prescribe a drug to protect the lining of the stomach and duodenum at the same time as prescribing an anti-inflammatory.

Because a peptic ulcer can cause serious complications, such as profuse bleeding or perforation leading to peritonitis, it is essential to visit the doctor if you develop any of the warning symptoms described above.

Piles (haemorrhoids)

Piles are swollen blood vessels in the lower part of the rectum and anal canal, similar to the varicose veins that many people develop in their legs. As many as 40 per cent of men will suffer from piles at some time in their lives, although many of them will never go for treatment because they are too embarrassed or shy.

The most common cause of piles is thought to be straining while passing stools. The risk is increased if the person is constipated, with hard bowel movements that take more time and effort to pass. Symptoms include:

- bleeding during a bowel movement, which causes spots of blood to appear on the toilet bowl and toilet paper
- irritation around the anus
- slight mucous discharge.

Any bleeding from the anus should be checked out by a doctor. Although it is not usually due to any serious bowel disorder, it could be an early warning sign of bowel cancer, particularly if the blood is mixed in with the stools.

The diagnosis of piles may be obvious if they are visible around the opening to the anus. However, the doctor may insert a small instrument known as a proctoscope just inside the rectum to separate the bowel walls – a simple and painless procedure – to look for internal piles.

To relieve anal irritation due to piles, have daily warm salt baths and ask your pharmacist for a soothing emollient to apply. You may also need to use a course of suppositories (which contain an astringent to shrink the swollen inflamed tissue and a corticosteroid to reduce the inflammation) night and morning and after any bowel movement. It is also important to increase your intake of fluids and high-fibre foods, which, by helping to soften the stools, should reduce the need to strain or sit for long periods on the toilet.

Pneumonia

Pneumonia is a condition where the lungs become inflamed; it is usually as a result of an infection from bacteria or viruses, although there are other causes, such as accidental inhalation of a piece of food or a poisonous gas. Symptoms of pneumonia include a productive cough, discoloured or blood-stained sputum, fever and chills, chest pains and breathlessness.

In elderly people, pneumonia can be extremely serious, either because the immune system which defends the body against infections does not work as efficiently later on in life, or because the pneumonia aggravates an underlying chronic disorder such as heart failure or chronic bronchitis.

Antibiotics will be prescribed for a bacterial pneumonia and also in many cases of viral pneumonia to prevent a secondary bacterial infection of the inflamed lung tissues. Hospital admission may be necessary so that oxygen can be given and, in extreme cases, mechanical ventilation initiated until the infection is brought under control.

Because pneumonia is a fairly common complication of flu in elderly people, an annual flu jab is recommended for everyone over the age of 65, especially anyone with a chronic heart or lung condition. A pneumococcal jab every five to ten years is also advisable.

Prostate enlargement

An enlarged prostate gland is a very common problem among older men, although why it should affect some men more than others is not known. The prostate sits at the base of the bladder and surrounds the urethra, which is the narrow tube that carries urine and, in men, semen to the tip of the penis. The function of the prostate is to produce most of the seminal fluid, secretions which transport and nourish the sperm after ejaculation.

Enlargement of the prostate closes off the upper part of the urethra and, as a result, may cause a variety of urinary symptoms such as difficulty starting the flow, a poor stream, dribbling after urination, having to get up to pass urine during the night and rushing to the toilet frequently during the day. Symptoms should always be investigated as they may indicate more serious problems, such as prostate cancer.

Embarrassment causes many men to delay seeing their doctor until these symptoms become intolerable. However, treatment is usually successful at restoring near-normal urinary function. The usual procedure is a surgical rebore, where a narrow instrument with viewing and cutting devices is passed up the urethra and the obstructing tissue pared away.

New forms of treatment include the inflation of a tiny balloon inside the urethra to relieve the constriction, the use of a microwave beam to heat up the prostate gland and a drug which, by preventing hormonal stimulation of the prostate, shrinks the gland and improves the flow of urine as a result.

Rheumatoid arthritis

Rheumatoid arthritis (RA) affects roughly one million people in the UK. It is a severe form of arthritis and, although the exact cause is unknown, is believed to be an autoimmune disease where the body's immune system starts to attack the joints. The resulting inflammation causes pain, tenderness, swelling, redness and warmth in many joints, usually in a symmetrical pattern on either side of the body.

Other symptoms of RA include severe joint stiffness which is typically worse in the early morning, loss of grip strength and some-times fever, generalised weakness and malaise.

Although RA is popularly thought to be a disease of old age, it usually strikes people first in their thirties. The condition then commonly flares up intermittently, with periods of remission which may last several months, even years. Also, many sufferers develop only a mild disability and are able to remain mobile and independent.

In the past, RA used to cause severe joint deformities in those people who were seriously affected by the disease. By the time they reached their 60s and beyond, even though the arthritis often seemed to burn itself out, they would be left housebound and possibly in a wheelchair. However, with the development of powerful drugs, which can slow down the disease and limit the amount of damage to the joints, the risk of permanent disability in these more severe cases has been reduced considerably.

Various aids are available to help people with RA cope with everyday tasks. Artificial joints can now be used to replace knees, fingers and shoulders as well as the hips, if they have been left very stiff or uncomfortable. The Arthritis Research Campaign* can supply more information; and see also Chapter 12 on exercise.

Sexual problems

A common myth about growing older is that an active sex life should end at 60. However, for many couples, love-making actually improves once they become free from the pressures of work and the menopause has removed the worry of an unwanted pregnancy. Some couples may prefer to cease their love-making, while others would like to continue demonstrating their mutual love in a physical way, but encounter some difficulty such as discomfort or impotence.

For any sexual problem, the first step is to talk openly with your partner. The family doctor is usually the best person to consult next. There may be an underlying medical reason which can be corrected, for example a change in medication if a particular drug is thought to be the cause of impotence; or application of a vaginal lubricant or oestrogen cream, if discomfort is due to post-menopausal inflammation of the vaginal lining.

Men who find their erections become infrequent or not good enough for satisfying sex can use various products to help. Family doctors can prescribe a range of drugs, including Sildenafil (Viagra). This works by helping to relax the blood vessels in the penis, allowing blood to flow into the penis and causing an erection. You can't take Viagra if you take drugs called nitrates that are used to treat angina. The family doctor can also arrange referral to a specialist who can advise about other options for treating erectile dysfunction.

If a medical disorder such as heart failure or osteoarthritis is causing love-making to be uncomfortable because of breathlessness or joint pain respectively, the doctor may be able to recommend alternative positions for sexual intercourse which are less stressful. Referral to a professional counsellor, usually through the organisation Relate*, can help a couple learn to communicate better and resolve any sexual fears or anxieties.

Skin problems

All older people can expect to see some changes to their skin as a result of the ageing process. Older people who have been regularly exposed to the ultraviolet radiation of strong sunlight earlier in life without taking appropriate precautions, such as wearing a broad-brimmed sunhat, putting on a sunscreen and keeping out of the midday sun, are much more likely to develop the three characteristic changes that occur in the skins of older people: severe wrinkling, thickened and roughened skin and large numbers of brown spots (also known as age spots) that typically appear on the face and the backs of the hands.

To treat skin-ageing, there is now an effective cream which contains retinoic acid (a derivative of vitamin A). Retinoic acid, which is available on prescription, can reduce wrinkling and roughening of the skin, as well as causing the age spots to fade. A new form of laser therapy has also been developed to remove unsightly age spots from exposed areas of skin.

WARNING

See your doctor if you develop any new blemish on your skin; or if a mole or blemish changes size, colour or shape, itches, bleeds, crusts over or becomes painful. This may signify a skin cancer and the earlier it is treated, the greater the chance of a successful cure.

Stroke

A stroke is caused by the interruption of the normal blood supply to part of the brain, resulting in damage to those brain cells deprived of oxygen for more than a few minutes. The three main types of stroke are a cerebral thrombosis, where a blood clot (thrombus) obstructs one of the main arteries in the brain; a cerebral embolism, where a fragment of blood clot that has broken off from a thrombus elsewhere in the circulation blocks a brain artery; and a cerebral haemorrhage, where a blood vessel in the brain ruptures.

Symptoms from a stroke depend primarily on which part of the brain has been damaged, as each brain area controls specific functions related to particular parts of the body. Typical symptoms may include sudden onset of numbness or weakness (usually on one side of the body), loss of speech or slurring of words, a sudden severe headache, unexplained dizziness, a sudden fall, or blurred vision.

Measures to reduce the risk of a stroke include not smoking, cutting down on foods high in cholesterol and saturated fats and taking regular exercise. Also, have your blood pressure checked regularly as a high level that goes untreated may cause a stroke without any warning symptoms.

If a stroke has occurred, the main part of therapy is a rehabilitation programme that may need to include speech therapy, as well as physiotherapy and occupational therapy. Recovery is unpredictable, but progress may continue to be made for over a year or even longer. For information and practical advice, contact the Stroke Association*.

Transient ischaemic attacks

A transient ischaemic attack (TIA) is a mini-stroke which causes similar symptoms to a normal stroke, but, because there is no permanent damage to the brain, these symptoms resolve completely within 24 hours, leaving no additional disability.

Even if the TIA symptoms disappear within minutes, it is still essential to see your doctor for a full check-up as a TIA is a warning signal that a major stroke could be on the way. Around 10 per cent of strokes are preceded by one or more TIAs, with perhaps a few days or even several months between them.

For some people who have had a TIA, the doctor may recommend aspirin or anticoagulant therapy, or surgery to remove fatty deposits from one of the brain arteries, as a way of reducing the chance of a future stroke.

Varicose veins

Around 20 per cent of the population suffer from varicose veins – bulging, twisted swollen veins usually confined to the lower legs. For most sufferers, the symptoms they cause are only mild and can be eased by wearing elastic support hosiery and not standing still for long periods. The typical symptoms are aching legs, swelling of the feet and ankles and a few visible swollen veins on the calves and thighs.

Varicose veins are generally caused by damaged valves inside the veins, which allow a backflow of blood down the leg and from the deep veins out into the superficial veins that run just under the skin. This pooling of blood in the veins causes them to swell under pressure.

Anyone with mild varicose veins should take various precautions to try to avoid making them worse, such as wearing elastic support stockings or socks, not crossing the legs or ankles, not standing for a long time, and never putting on a garter or elastic stocking top that presses into the thigh and obstructs the circulation. In addition to keeping weight within normal limits, you should ask your GP to recommend a programme of leg exercises to help the circulation through the veins.

Complications from more severe varicose veins include thrombophlebitis (painful tender swelling along a vein) as well as leg ulceration, both of which should be treated as soon as possible by your doctor.

Part 4

Planning ahead

Chapter 14

Becoming a carer

While retirement can bring the bonuses of more leisure you can find yourself facing new responsibilities and challenges, not all of them entirely welcome. This section contains information that you might find useful one day, on ways a house can be adapted to make it easier for an older person to carry on living there and practical information on grants and benefits that might be available.

This section will also be relevant if you find yourself becoming a carer; something that's increasingly likely now that one in six households in the UK contains a carer. Older people make up a significant proportion of carers – over a quarter of people who care for someone in their own home for 20 hours or more a week are themselves aged over 65. You may become a carer for a parent or other relative or for your partner. Sometimes this can happen suddenly as illness strikes or one parent dies, leaving the other unable to cope. At worst the situation may arise when, for example, you yourself are at a stage where you have your own family, health or financial problems to deal with.

There's no need to try to cross all the bridges before you come to them, but a certain amount of forward-planning is wise, and could save time, money and problems later on, whether you are already a carer or think that you might one day become one.

Taking decisions

If you think you may become a carer one day, you should try to talk through what level of support you would be able to offer should the need arise, with the people your decision will affect. This might include your partner, your siblings or your children as well as the person you'd be caring for. You may have to take into account your own health and ability to cope with any stress that might occur as a consequence of becoming a carer. The temptation to try to 'take over' the life of the person you are caring for may be difficult to resist, but as far as possible the decisions should be theirs.

Moving home?

Chapter 1 covers points to consider if you or someone you may be caring for is considering a move, whether this means moving closer to family, or even moving in together. As outlined in that chapter, there is a wide range of gadgets and adaptations that can make it easier to care for someone at home – you'll find more detailed information about these in Chapter 15.

If you are considering living with an older relative you are caring for and are buying a house together or building an extension, take professional advice to make sure you know about any possible implications if the person later needs to enter a care home.

Practical support and minimising stress

Giving compassionate care to another person is an extremely worthwhile job and should be recognised as such, but at times it can also be very stressful. Causes of stress can be very small – irritating mannerisms and reactions repeated on a day-to-day basis can be frustrating – or far more serious if the person you are caring for needs constant physical help and emotional support.

Dealing with stress

Carers UK*, the national charity for carers, says that it is not uncommon for carers to feel frustration, resentment, guilt, anger, fear, loneliness or depression at times. Its advice on dealing with these feelings includes:

- write a list of particular triggers of stress for you, to see if you can identify practical ways to deal with them

---

- think what you'd say to another carer who came to you for advice – it can be easier to see solutions to other people's problems than your own
- try to talk it over with someone. If you find it hard to talk to someone you know, you could try getting counselling (see page 140)
- having some time to yourself is essential – time to do relaxation exercises, yoga or any form of physical activity is particularly valuable
- if you feel you are reaching a crisis, you can call the Samaritans at any time on (08457) 909090 (or (01850) 609090 in Northern Ireland).

The following are some sources of help and support that can help cut down the stress for you and your family.

Local Social Services

Local authorities have a duty to carry out a needs assessment of anyone who seems to need the local authority's services. The Social Services department (Social Work Departments in Scotland, Health and Social Services Boards in Northern Ireland) will carry this out. The person's needs should be assessed without reference to their ability to pay. But whether the local authority will fund the services required will usually depend on means-testing (except for personal care services in Scotland). If you feel an assessment is unfair, you can complain – ask the Social Services department for a copy of its complaints procedure.

Depending on the area you live in, there may be a waiting time to be assessed and there has been considerable variation across the country in charges and criteria for means-testing. However, new government guidelines came into effect from April 2003 to try to reduce these variations.

Carers can also ask their local authority for an assessment of their own needs, and Social Services may provide carers with a range of services; again there may be means-tested charges for these services.

These are some of the services that might be available:

- Meals on Wheels – or similar for people who cannot cook for themselves

- help with household tasks from care workers or care assistants (who used to be known as home helps)
- laundry service for linen
- a social or community alarm (see pages 228–9 for more details)
- aids such as ramps, rails, bath aids – these are normally provided free of charge. Your local branch of the British Red Cross can also provide items on short-term loans which can be useful while you're waiting for an assessment
- provision of respite or short-term residential care (see below)
- a sitter or care attendants (see below), who can take over from a carer who is looking after someone at home.

As an alternative to the local authority arranging for services, the authority can pay money direct to the person who needs care, to enable him or her to shop around and select service providers that suit them best. Contact your local Social Services department for information on all the services it offers.

Local health services

Talk to your GP (or the GP of the person you are caring for) to find out more about services that might be available in your area – for instance, visits from a district nurse to change dressings or give injections.

Breaks, respite care and holidays

All carers need breaks from the responsibility of care. This might be a regular short break of a few hours or it might mean a proper holiday. However, taking a break can be easier said than done; you may be able to ask friends or family for help but try also organisations that can supply assistance. The charities Crossroads – Caring for Carers★ and Leonard Cheshire UK★ are two important providers of these respite services.

Care attendants and sitting service schemes

These services may be provided by the health service, local authority or voluntary organisations, or jointly. Voluntary organisations may use volunteers to help provide these services, but they should have had some training and will often have had first-hand experience of being a carer.

Day care and lunch clubs

Contact your local Social Services department for details of day centres in your area; these are usually run by local authorities or voluntary organisations and provide an opportunity for the person you are caring for to socialise with other people and take part in organised activities. Lunch or other social clubs may also be suitable; again, ask Social Services or a local organisation like Age Concern★. If the person you are caring for needs more specialised treatment or care, ask your GP about day hospitals in your area.

Residential breaks

A residential break means that the person you are caring for stays away from home temporarily. Vouchers for breaks might be available from your local Social Services, and allow you and the person you care for to choose where you want to go. Some residential and nursing homes will take people in for a short stay. You may also get respite health care in a hospital or hospice. There are also schemes where people are cared for in another family's home. Ask your GP in the first instance about respite health care, and contact Social Services to find out about other types of respite care.

Holiday Care★ gives free information on which holidays would best suit elderly people or those with disabilities, according to their needs. It can also provide information on schemes for volunteer helpers to accompany someone with a disability and has a directory of respite care facilities in the UK.

Paying for private care

Paying privately may be the only way you can get exactly the help you need. If you can afford to do this, you can either use an agency or recruit someone yourself. Using a specialist agency may be more expensive but the agency should also take care of the paperwork, National Insurance and tax, and check the worker's references. The UK Home Care Association★ is a professional body for agencies that provide this type of service.

If you decide to recruit someone yourself, you could put an ad in a shop window, local paper or Job Centre. For full-time or live-in positions, you could also advertise in *The Lady* magazine. You should ask for – and check – references before employing someone and you should find out about your legal and tax responsibilities.

Your local Citizen's Advice Bureau should be able to help, and you can also find more information in the *Which? Guide to Help in the Home.*

Support groups

Talking to other people who understand what it's like to be a carer can be a great help. A local support organisation will have invaluable expertise about local services and the best way to access them. Contact Carers UK★ to find out where the nearest local branch is to you or, if the person you are caring for has a particular medical condition, there may also be a specific support group he or she, or you, can join.

If caring is becoming too stressful

If you have tried the suggestions above and taken advice from local carers's groups and Social Services but still find you are constantly stressed, it might be time to review your situation. If you don't think you can carry on, try not to feel you have failed in any way. You will already have done a very valuable job and it's better to be realistic than continue until you reach breaking point and your own health suffers. It may be time to think about residential care – see pages 235–8 for more details.

Case history: Julia

Julia has been caring for her widowed mother for the last five years, a role which has taken up more and more of her time as her mother's health has deteriorated. 'After a while I did get a bit resentful. It seemed that I was picking up all the pieces, because I lived locally. Then my brother David came to stay and I think he was shocked by how stressed I was. We sat down and really tried to talk through it all. David understands better now – and we've shared the responsibility. There are things he can do, even though geographically he's further away. And if my husband and I are planning to go on holiday, I no longer feel I have to ask him to come and look after Mum as "a favour." If he and his wife can't come to take my place, then he'll take responsibility for making suitable arrangements.'

Financial and legal matters

Benefits

The benefits system is complicated. If you're not sure whether you might be entitled to a particular benefit, rather than try to struggle through the maze on your own, it makes sense to get advice from organisations which have experience of cases like yours and know how the system works. Your local Citizen's Advice Bureau, a disability organisation or carers' group are all good places to try. You will also find more information about benefits in the companion volume to this book, the *Which? Guide to Money in Retirement.*

Three of the most important benefits you or the person you are caring for may be entitled to are listed below:

- **Disability Living Allowance (DLA)** is the main disability benefit for people who are under 65 when they first claim. There are two components: a care component and a mobility component, payable at a variety of rates. If someone meets the relevant criteria he or she receives both components. Alternatively he or she might receive just one of the components. It is not means-tested.
- **Attendance Allowance** is the main disability benefit for people who are over 65 when they first claim. It is not means-tested and may be available to people who need frequent help throughout the day with personal care, continual supervision throughout the day or prolonged attention at night. It is paid at two rates depending on whether care is needed during both the day and night.
- **Carer's Allowance** (known as invalid carer allowance until April 2003) may be available to people who spend 35 hours a week or more looking after someone who gets the middle or higher rate of DLA, Attendance Allowance or some other disability benefits. In the past, carers aged over 65 did not qualify for this, but since October 2002 the rules have changed. Your pension and other benefits may affect whether you get the allowance, but if you are entitled to it, you may also qualify for the Carer Premium. For more information or a claim form, call (01253) 856123.

You can claim any of these benefits through your local Social Security office. Carers UK* also has a step-by-step programme on its website that you can use to see if you are eligible for Carer's Allowance.

Power of attorney

An 'enduring power of attorney' gives a person the right to manage another person's financial affairs and property in the event of his or her becoming mentally incapable of doing so. In the right circumstances this is a sensible measure but even so, it may be unwelcome to someone who still feels in full control. An acceptable compromise might be to enter into an arrangement where cheques are signed jointly. The deed must be drawn up while the person concerned can still understand the implications, and it can be modified, if preferred, to take effect only if and when they can no longer cope. In Scotland, the Adults with Incapacity Act 2000 also sets out ways in which other people can take decisions for adults who are unable to make decisions for themselves. For further information, consult a solicitor.

Medical issues

If you are caring for someone, whether or not you're living with him or her, you'll be on the alert for health problems. You may have to ensure that medical check-ups – at the optician, dentist, chiropodist and so on – take place regularly and the person you're caring for has an adequate and nutritious diet.

Remember that some symptoms which are often put down simply to 'getting old' are in fact signs of treatable illness which can be, if not cured, at least alleviated. In some cases an uncharacteristic change in personality such as irritability, rudeness and difficult behaviour or extreme withdrawal and gentleness may indicate the onset of illness. Common illnesses such as bad colds or flu can be serious in elderly people, and a sudden lack of energy or extreme tiredness should be taken seriously. It is better to see the doctor if in doubt, rather than dismissing such things as minor ailments. See Chapter 13 for more on health problems.

Medication

If medication is prescribed, you may need to help ensure it is taken regularly, especially if a hospital stay has meant new and unfamiliar medication has been prescribed. There are various memory aids to help people take their medication at the right time. Ask the pharmacist for more details; he or she can also advise about any possible contra-indications between prescribed medicine and over-the-counter remedies.

In England, everyone over 75 should have a review of any medication they've been prescribed each year, or every six months if they take more than four prescriptions. See also 'Medication problems', pages 200–01.

Incontinence

Many forms of incontinence can be cured so you should always get medical advice. The district nurse should be a good first point of contact and may be able to put you in touch with a specialist continence nurse. A patient may also be referred to a specialist physiotherapist.

Social Services may also help with a laundry service for linen, and a local continence adviser or district nurse can offer practical advice on obtaining a commode, other appliances, incontinence pads, bed-protectors and so on. The Continence Foundation* can give you further information through its helpline or series of factsheets. Ricability* also produces a leaflet *Choosing products for bladder and bowel control.*

Alzheimer's disease

Chapter 13 has more information about specific medical problems, but Alzheimer's disease deserves a special word in this chapter as it is the cause of so much worry and stress. Most cases of Alzheimer's develop later in life. Below the age of 65 the risk is roughly one in 1,000. But one in 50 people between the ages of 65 and 70 have some form of dementia and the risk rises to one person in five by the age of 80.

As we grow older, we can all become muddle-headed from time to time and less 'sharp' than we once were. This can make it difficult to distinguish between the 'normal' forgetfulness of old age and early signs of Alzheimer's disease. If you are concerned about your own or a relative's confusion, you should talk to your GP. Early symptoms of Alzheimer's can include forgetfulness (not being able to remember the right word, not recognising familiar faces, becoming mixed up over dates or times, for example), wandering off, and having fixed delusions and gradual changes in personality. Symptoms that occur suddenly signal a need for urgent medical attention.

Alzheimer's disease can, more than almost any other problem for carers, cause immense distress. To see someone who you love and rely on become a different person, who may not even recognise close members of the family, is enormously upsetting. However, it is essential for carers to protect their emotional state; first of all, by doing everything practical to help and then accepting that the present condition is brought about by illness and that the real affectionate, loving and competent person is the one they remember before the illness struck. Nevertheless, carers will need all the emotional as well as practical support that can be called upon. The Alzheimer's Society★ is an excellent source of information and support for people with dementia and their carers.

After a bereavement

You may feel a whole range of emotions when you experience a bereavement, particularly if you have been a carer for the person who has died. How you react will be very individual and personal. Cruse Bereavement Care★, the national charity that offers support to anyone suffering from a bereavement, can give you information, advice or counselling through its telephone helpline or its network of local branches. It runs local support groups and will also come and visit you in your home. It also provides a range of booklets and other publications that can help people come to terms with their grief.

Practical issues for later on

In the case of a widow or widower, the spouse's death is often a major factor in dictating a change of lifestyle. However, this is a decision which should not be taken hastily and any new long-term arrangements should be carefully organised. Once the funeral and sorting out of legal and financial matters are over, there may be a feeling of flatness or restlessness as well as grief. This is not the best time to make radical decisions or move house.

It's common for a couple to split domestic chores between them, with one taking care of cooking and cleaning, say, and the other being responsible for DIY or managing finances. If this has happened to your parents and you're now trying to help the widowed spouse, try to think through practical solutions without taking over if possible. Taking full responsibility for the activity could be a big time commitment for you and it might turn out to be an activity your surviving parent begins to enjoy. If you've seen this happen to your parents, it might also make you re-evaluate the way you share chores in your own household.

Cooking and eating alone may not be the pleasure that it was as a shared activity, but a balanced diet is important for good health. Check Chapter 11 for more information on choosing a healthy diet. One practical way to approach this is to suggest taking turns to provide lunch every week with a friend who lives nearby. Alternatively you could find out about local lunch clubs. As well as being provided by Social Services departments, lunch clubs are often run by voluntary organisations. Ask your local Age Concern★ group or Social Services department about clubs in your area.

The social life of couples can be very different from that of a single partner; old friends may appear not to want to meet a widow or widower. Often people feel embarrassed or afraid of saying the wrong thing. It can help if the partners in a couple have cultivated individual interests, hobbies and friendships over the years. Try re-reading Chapter 6 for ideas for new social activities. Many people find reminiscence work or writing can be particularly enjoyable, as can gardening or any physical activity.

Chapter 15

Adapting your home

If you find it's not as easy to get around your house as it used to be or you are having trouble with some day-to-day activities, don't just struggle on. There are countless ways a home can be adapted to suit the needs of the person who lives there, and almost all of these are far less hassle than moving. If you live on your own, you may enjoy your independence but occasionally be concerned about what would happen if you had an accident and needed help. This chapter also contains information about alarm systems that mean you can call for help quickly and easily should you ever need it. You don't need to live in sheltered housing to use this kind of alarm; they're widely available and can help bring peace of mind.

Making everyday activities easier

There's a lot you can do to make your home more convenient to live in. These tips are all relatively inexpensive and easy to implement. Contact the Disabled Living Foundation* for more details about buying the special products mentioned, and see also Chapter 3 for more specific advice on home security and safety.

- Think laterally. If there's a particular task that you find difficult, are there other ways round it? For instance, can your ironing board be left up in a spare bedroom, rather than being folded up and put away in an inconvenient cupboard each time? If you find your vacuum heavy or awkward to carry upstairs, could you keep a carpet sweeper on the first floor and use that instead?

- Make sure the layout of your house helps rathers than hinders you. Are items stored in the most logical place? If you find you have to bend to pick up items you use regularly or stretch overhead, look for a more accessible place for that item.

- A whole host of kitchen equipment is available, from tippers to pour water from a kettle safely to devices to help open milk or juice cartons.

- You can get special controls for the oven, but also consider using a microwave oven instead. As well as being more economical to use, a microwave means you can use lighter plastic containers, the food cooks only for a pre-set time, and many models have touch controls which may be easier if you have limited dexterity.

- If you find yourself putting pans on to boil and forgetting about them, get into the habit of always using a timer. You can get models that pin to your clothes.

- Door knobs can be hard to manage. On doors inside your house, you may find it easier to have lever handles or fit a 'sleeve' over the knob to make turning easier. On external doors, the handle on a Yale lock can be increased with a special knob that fits over the existing one.

- If you find it awkward to bend down to put plugs in sockets, ask an electrician to raise sockets that you use regularly to waist height. You can also get plugs with hand grips to make it easier to take them in and out.

- One-handed trays with anti-slip mats can be useful for carrying items from room to room while leaving one hand free for a stick or grab rail.

- Grab rails can be placed in bathrooms, on stairs or anywhere where you need a bit of extra support.

If you have hearing difficulties

The Royal National Institute for Deaf people (RNID)* should be your first port of call for information on equipment for people who are deaf or hard of hearing, whether you use a hearing aid or not. It can tell you about products that let you know when your phone, doorbell or alarm clock is ringing, and also explain about listening equipment to help you hear the TV, radio or conversation. It also has a sales catalogue and online shop and a database of over 400 items of specially designed equipment.

If you have sight problems

The Royal National Institute of the Blind (RNIB)★ is an excellent source of information and advice for people with sight problems. It also sells a good range of products that can make life easier if you have poor sight, such as talking scales and microwaves, products that can help you watch TV more easily and audio-described videos.

Further information

It's well worth getting advice from an occupational therapist (OT) before putting the suggestions in the box on pages 226–7 into action. OTs can advise on alternative approaches to household activities and suggest equipment that will suit your particular circumstances. After assessing your needs, the OT may be able to provide the equipment you need on loan. If you live at home and are not currently receiving hospital treatment, you will need to contact your local Social Services department to get an assessment.

An alternative, particularly if you have difficulty getting an OT assessment or the wait is too long, is to go to your nearest Disabled Living Centre★. These do not sell equipment, but display and demonstrate it with experienced staff to give you advice and information.

Ricability★ and the Disabled Living Foundation★ are two other excellent sources of detailed information and advice. Both have a range of booklets and factsheets describing equipment that may help. Ricability's booklet *Adapting Your Home* is a particularly useful source of information on equipment and tips to make your home easier to live in.

Community or social alarms

A community or social alarm is a means of getting help quickly if it's needed and can bring real peace of mind, especially if you live alone. Many local authorities run schemes, usually through their housing or Social Services departments, for both local authority tenants and home owners.

To use a community alarm you need to wear a small pushbutton on a neckcord or wristband, or clipped to clothing. Pressing this button sends a radio signal to a base unit which acts like a telephone to call for help. With local authority schemes, the call will go through to a 24-hour communication centre where, depending on the service offered, the operator will try to speak to the user through the system (most of the units have loudspeakers built in). However, you don't have to be able to talk to someone to tell them you need help – just pressing the button will alert them to the fact that help is needed. Depending on the service and the reason you've called, some centres have staff who will come to help, otherwise they will phone the relatives, friends or neighbours you have nominated so they can come to your aid. All centres will contact the emergency services if necessary. Some local authorities will take on people who live outside their area and have bought a compatible alarm.

Most local authorities charge for the service and have eligibility rules, but if you are over 75 and live alone, you are very likely to qualify. If not, there are other options. Many housing associations offer similar schemes, as do many other companies including the trading arms of Age Concern★ and Help the Aged★. Alternatively, you can buy alarms that can be programmed to dial friends' numbers direct. These will call more than one number if the first one doesn't answer, but you need to be sure that there will always be someone on your list of nominated people who will be there to take the call if you need them.

For further information, see the Disabled Living Foundation★ factsheet *Choosing a personal alarm system*.

Larger-scale adaptations

You may be considering larger adaptations to your house. This might include a stair-lift, installing a bathroom downstairs, or adapting or extending a house to enable two generations of a family to live together.

Stairlifts and other electrical mobility aids such beds and chairs can be expensive, and an investigation by *Which?* magazine in April 2002 found that some people buying these types of mobility aids felt let down by the advice they received from salespeople. If you're considering buying one, make sure you get independent advice from an occupational therapist (see page 140), the Disabled Living Foundation★ or your nearest Disabled Living Centre★.

Building on an extension and/or creating a 'granny flat' could improve the value of the house, but take professional advice if creating a flat with a completely separate entrance. This could leave you liable for capital gains tax when the property is eventually sold. See below for information on how to find out about the grants that may be available to help fund the work. See Chapter 4 for more information on getting work done on your home and remember to check with your local authority's planning and building control departments about any planning permission you will need.

Financial help and grants

There may be grants or other financial help you can get to help with the cost of home repairs or adaptations, but you must apply to your local authority and get its approval for the work before you start.

The grants are slightly different in England, Scotland, Northern Ireland and Wales but in general grants are currently available for renovation work and large-scale improvements, for adaptions to make a disabled person's home suit their needs, and for smaller but essential repairs. The system is due to change by the end of 2003, but local authorities will still be required to advise and support vulnerable and older home owners with repairs and improvements to their homes. Local authorities will have more flexibility in how they assist people who require repairs and improvements to their home, including new powers to give loans as well as grants.

The best source of advice and information on grants or other sources of funding that may be available and how to apply are the network of advice centres, usually called Home Improvement Agencies (HIAs), Care and Repair or Staying Put across the UK. These can give specialist advice to older home owners on getting repairs done and can often offer practical help too, such as arranging a survey, getting estimates and applying for grants or loans. To find out where your nearest HIA is, contact the relevant regional organisation listed at the back of the book under Home Improvement Agency★.

Don't forget that Social Services may also provide funding for some types of adaptations; usually this is for more minor adaptations such as grab rails which do not require structural work. And if you need help with insulation, heating or draught-proofing there are a large number of grants and other schemes on offer. See pages 31–2 for more information.

You might also be considering equity release or home reversion schemes to raise money on the value of your house. However, it is essential to take legal and independent financial advice before making any commitment of this kind. For more details, see *The Which? Guide to Money in Retirement*, from Which? Books★.

Case history: Marianne

Marianne's father, Ivan, has always prized his independence. He is 85 and lives on his own. 'He's really fit and active – his house is immaculate and I only wish our lawn was as well kept as his. He's got good neighbours, but I do worry sometimes that we live so far away,' Marianne says. Ivan recently joined his local authority's community alarm scheme. This has given Marianne peace of mind: 'He jokes that he only did it to stop me worrying. I know he's taking care of himself, but I sleep better knowing that he could get help quickly if he needed it – and I'm sure he must feel that too.'

Chapter 16

Sheltered housing and care homes

There is a host of gadgets and adaptations available, as well as care services that can help people stay in their own home as long as possible. You can read more about these in Chapters 14 and 15. However, if remaining in your own home is no longer an option for you or for a person you are caring for, you may be considering a move into sheltered housing or perhaps a care home.

Sheltered housing is for older people who are still active and independent – it offers the benefit of being designed to be small and easy to manage, and the added peace of mind of having a warden and alarm system on hand. It may also provide more social opportunities, with a resident's lounge and social events.

Care homes used to be called either residential homes or nursing homes, depending on the services they offered. These terms are still often used, although officially they are both now called care homes – either care homes for personal care (i.e. homes which provide help with things such as dressing, getting up and going to bed) or care homes for personal and nursing care. Care homes which offer nursing care must be run by a doctor or qualified nurse and have enough qualified staff on duty to provide round-the-clock nursing care for residents.

Sheltered housing

Sheltered housing (sometimes known as retirement housing) is developments of flats, bungalows or houses intended for people only above a certain age (usually 55 or 60). The developments are usually meant for residents who can look after themselves, although there is generally also a manager or warden and an alarm system in each home which means residents can call for help if they need it.

Local authorities and housing associations often provide sheltered housing to rent; contact the housing department of your local authority for information on local schemes including any eligibility criteria and costs. There are also many private developments, where the property is generally sold on a leasehold basis. Some housing associations administer schemes where you part buy and part rent sheltered housing. If you are having trouble selling your current home, some developments may offer part-exchange on the one you want to buy. Take legal advice before agreeing to this – it can be convenient but you may be paying for the convenience by selling below the market value.

In sheltered housing developments you pay a service charge to cover things like the warden's salary, the emergency alarm, upkeep of communal areas and repair and maintenance. Usually this is for the external structure and communal areas only and you'll still be responsible for the maintenance of your home. In addition you'll have to pay ground rent as laid out in your lease.

The warden (nowadays often called the 'scheme manager' or 'house manager') is an important part of making sheltered housing a success, so try to find out how well the development is managed. Also check whether there is a residents' association or some system of regular meetings between the residents and warden to ensure residents' views are taken into account in managing the development.

Here are some points to look out for when choosing sheltered housing.

- If you're buying a property in a new development you should make sure the developer is registered with the National House Building Council* (NHBC). This will ensure that residents' rights are protected by a legally binding management agreement between the developer or freeholder and the management organisation.
- Whether the property is new or second-hand, you should make sure the builder is also registered with the NHBC. This will mean that the builder has had to comply with the NHBC's Sheltered Housing Code of Practice.

- If you are buying leasehold, the terms of the lease are crucial – if any of it is unclear, make sure your solicitor explains the details to you fully. (If you're buying freehold, check the management deed). Make sure you know what rights the management company has over you, particularly if you were to become frail or ill.
- If it is not a new development, find out what the increases in services charges have been in previous years.
- All leasehold schemes have a sinking fund to cover the cost of long-term repairs; contributions to this may be included in the service charge or may be deferred until the property is sold. If they are deferred, ask how major repairs will be funded if they are needed before there's enough money in the fund.
- If you're buying a property, check the management company belongs to the Association of Retirement Housing Managers*, which has a code of practice for members and aims to promote best practice in the management of private sheltered housing schemes.
- Communal facilities can be one of the real bonuses of sheltered housing. If there are coffee mornings or similar in a shared lounge, see if you can attend one as a guest to find out what the atmosphere is like.
- Is there guest accommodation so you can have friends or family to stay? At many developments there are guest bedrooms which can be rented when needed.
- Is the location right? Is it near to shops, post offices, parks, libraries or whatever facilities you enjoy using? What public transport is available?
- Check accessibility. Even though the housing should be designed for older people, some developments have first-floor flats without a lift.
- The alarm system should be linked to the warden and there should be a 24-hour covering service when the warden is off-duty.
- Find out exactly what the warden's responsibilities involve. It's important that you're clear about what is and isn't included. Some wardens live on site, some don't.

Sheltered housing if you become frail

If you live in sheltered housing and become too ill or frail to manage on your own, there may be provision in the terms of your lease to end the lease. Management organisations would usually need a court order to enforce this and they would usually take this step only if the situation was severely disrupting the life of the rest of the community. If the care you require can be provided to you in your home, any good management organisation should be willing for you to make arrangements to be treated at home if this is possible.

Further information

Elderly Accommodation Counsel* produces a list of sheltered housing developments. Help the Aged* has a factsheet, *Sheltered housing*, and Age Concern* publishes *A buyer's guide to retirement housing* and a factsheet *Retirement housing for sale*. You can also get specialist advice from the Advice Information and Mediation Service (AIMS)*, for retirement housing which is run in association with Age Concern.

Care homes

There may come a point where someone needs more care than can be provided in his or her own home. It's only natural to want to stay in your own home as long as possible and it's tempting to try to avoid discussing this with someone. It can be a good idea to involve someone outside the family to help and advise. A talk with a social worker or someone from a local branch of a carers' organisation or Age Concern* could help in the formulation of a decision acceptable to everyone.

While it may be difficult to begin this sort of discussion, it may be better to find out about options and preferences earlier rather than later. People can often find themselves precipitated into looking for a care home after a crisis, and research published in *Which?* in February 2003 suggests that it can be difficult to find a place available for immediate occupation – there may well be waiting lists at the place you like best.

Choosing a home

If you're looking on behalf of another person, make sure you involve him or her as fully as possible right from the start. You can save some legwork by phoning round with preliminary questions to shortlist the homes before visiting them. Everyone will have their own priorities when choosing a care home, but note these points.

- Can you have your own room? Can you have a phone in your room and can you bring your own furniture, pictures or plants to personalise it?
- Is the home within easy walking distance of local facilities? Is public transport available or does the home have its own transport service? Is the home in a pleasant area with not too much noise from main roads?
- Do the other residents seem congenial and reasonably active? What is the male to female ratio (this may matter to you if you are a man since most care home residents are female)?
- What training do staff have? What is the ratio of staff to residents?
- What choice of meals is available? How does the home cope with special diets and individual tastes?
- What outings or other social activities are arranged?
- Are pets allowed? (The Elderly Accommodation Counsel* can give you information about homes that accept pets).
- How much independence are residents allowed? Can you choose when you get up and go to bed?
- Are visitors welcome at any time? Can they stay for a meal or overnight?

Care home fees

Current estimates put residential care fees at around £284 a week and nursing care fees at £400, depending on where you live. You may be able to get some help with these fees.

If possible, whether you're at home or in hospital, you should be offered a joint NHS/Social Services care assessment before you go into a care home. If you are at home and have not already had a care assessment, contact your local Social Services department to ask for one.

Case history: Care homes – residents have their say

In February 1999 *Which?* reported the results of interviews it carried out with residents of ten care homes. This may have been a self-selecting sample to some extent, as *Which?* had to contact 166 homes to find ten that were willing for their residents to take part – but overall the results painted a positive picture.

When they first went into the care home, people generally had low expectations. Unsurprisingly, all would have preferred to be able to stay in their own homes. Many residents said that their families had generally found out about the different homes available and that this had made them feel left out of the decisions and sometimes led to resentment. However, generally the residents were pleased with the level of care they received.

'The first six months are the hardest,' said one resident. 'It's far better than I ever thought it would be,' said another. 'You can call it home really.' Even the food was better than people had expected. 'I expected the food to be institutional but it's superb.'

If you are assessed as needing continuing NHS healthcare (i.e. you may need accommodation and personal care but your primary need is for healthcare), you could be eligible to get your care home fees paid in full by the NHS. NHS services are provided according to clinical need, not your ability to pay. However, to be eligible for continuing NHS healthcare, your healthcare needs will be compared against set eligibility criteria, which can vary according to where you live.

In England, Wales and Scotland the state pays for nursing care even if you are well off. However, it's important to realise that this is meant to cover the time a registered nurse spends on caring for you or supervising your care – it won't include the cost of any other staff who are involved in providing your care. In Scotland, personal care is also paid for by the state but elsewhere it is means-tested.

In England, you are assessed by a nurse to see which band of nursing care you need. Currently, depending on the band you are in, your nursing home receives £40, £75 or £120 a week to help pay for your care. In Wales there is only one band, which currently pays £100 a week.

Where state help is means-tested, you won't get help with fees unless your income is low and your savings and other capital come to no more than a set amount, currently £19,500. The value of your home will not be counted as part of your capital if one or more of the following people continue to live there: your spouse or partner, a dependent child, a relative over 60 or a relative who is incapacitated.

Further information

For more information about paying for a care home, see the companion volume to this book, *The Which? Guide to Money in Retirement*. The charities Age Concern★, Elderly Accommodation Counsel★ and Help the Aged★ can offer free advice or information about choosing and financing a place in a care home. You can also get the Department of Health's booklet *NHS funded nursing care in nursing homes – What it means for you* by ringing (08701) 555455, or if you have Internet access you can download it from *www.doh.gov.uk*.

Addresses

Accident Line
Abbey Legal Protection Limited
1st Floor, 17 Lansdown Road
Croydon
Surrey CR0 2BX
Tel: (0800) 192939
Email: info@accidentlinedirect.co.uk
Website: www.accidentlinedirect.co.uk

Age Concern Information Line
Tel: (0800) 009966

Age Concern England
Astral House
1268 London Road
London SW16 4ER
Tel: 020-8765 7200
ActivAge Unit: 020-8765 7231
Email: ace@ace.org.uk
Website: www.ageconcern.org.uk

Age Concern Cymru
4th floor, 1 Cathedral Road
Cardiff CF11 9SD
Tel: 029-2037 1566
Email: enquiries@accymru.org.uk
Website: www.accymru.org.uk

Age Concern Northern Ireland
3 Lower Crescent
Belfast BT7 1NR
Tel: 028-9024 5729
Email: info@ageconcernni.org
Website: www.ageconcernni.org

Age Concern Scotland
Leonard Small House
113 Rose Street
Edinburgh EH2 3DT
Tel: 0131-220 3345
Email: enquiries@acscot.org.uk
Email for INNIS Retirement Housing Advice:
innis@acscot.org.uk
Website: www.ageconcernscotland.org.uk

Age Exchange
The Reminiscence Centre
11 Blackheath Village
London SE3 9LA
Tel: 020-8318 9105
Email: administrator@age-exchange.org.uk
Website: www.age-exchange.org.uk

Advice Information and Mediation Service (AIMS)
Astral House
1268 London Road
London SW16 4ER
Tel: (0845) 600 2001
Email: aims@ace.org.uk
Website: www.ageconcern.org.uk/aims
In Scotland contact INNIS: Retirement Housing Advice Service at Age Concern Scotland (see above)

Alzheimer's Society
Gordon House
10 Greencoat Place
London SW1P 1PH
Helpline: (0845) 300 0336
Email: enquiries@alzheimers.org.uk
Website: www.alzheimers.org.uk

Alzheimer's Scotland
22 Drumsheugh Gardens
Edinburgh EH3 7RN
Tel: 0131-243 1453
Email: alzheimer@alzscot.org
Website: www.alzscot.org

Arthritis Research Campaign
Copeman House
St Mary's Court
St Mary's Gate
Chesterfield
Derbyshire S41 7TD
Tel: (01246) 558033
Email: info@arc.org.uk
Website: www.arc.org.uk

Association of British Travel Agents (ABTA)
68–71 Newman Street
London W1T 3AH
Tel: 020-7637 2444
Email: abta@abta.com
Website: www.abta.com

Association of Independent Tour Operators (AITO)
133A St Margaret's Road
Twickenham
Middlesex TW1 1RG
Tel: 020-7844 9280
Email: info@aito.co.uk
Website: www.aito.co.uk

Association of Personal Injury Lawyers
11 Castle Quay
Castle Boulevard
Nottingham NG7 1FW
Tel: 0115-958 0585
Email: mail@apil.com
Website: www.apil.com

Association of Retirement Housing Managers
3rd Floor, 89 Albert Embankment
London SE1 7TP
Tel: 020-7820 1839
Email: enquiries@arhm.org
Website: www.arhm.org

Automobile Association (AA)
AA Contact Centre
Carr Ellison House
William Armstrong Drive
Newcastle-upon-Tyne NE4 7YA
Car Inspections: (0800) 085 3007
Used Car Data Check: (0800) 234 999
Website: www.theaa.com

BackCare Association
16 Elmtree Road
Teddington
Middlesex TW11 8ST
Tel: 020-8977 5474
Email: website@backcare.org.uk
Website: www.backpain.org

British Association of Cancer United Patients (BACUP)
3 Bath Place
Rivington Street
London EC2A 3JR
Tel: 020-7696 9003
Website: www.cancerbacup.org.uk

British Association for Counselling and Psychotherapy
BACP House
35–37 Albert Street
Rugby CV21 2SG
Tel: (0870) 443 5219
Email: bacp@bacp.co.uk
Website: www.bacp.co.uk

British Deaf Association (BDA)
1–3 Worship Street
London EC2A 2AB
Tel: 020-7588 3520
Email: helpline@bda.org.uk
Website: www.bda.org.uk

British Diabetics Association
10 Parkway
London NW1 7AA
Tel: 020-7424 1000
Email: info@diabetes.org.uk
Website: www.diabetes.org.uk

British Executive Service Overseas (BESO)
164 Vauxhall Bridge Road
London SW1V 2RA
Tel: 020-7630 0644
Email: team@beso.org
Website: www.beso.org

The British Heart Foundation National Centre for Physical Activity and Health
Loughborough University
Loughborough
Leicester LE11 3TU
Tel: (01509) 223259
Email: bhfactive@lists.lboro.ac.uk
Website: www.bhfactive.org.uk

British Psychological Society
St Andrews House
48 Princess Road East
Leicester LE1 7DR
Tel: 0116-254 9568
Email: enquiry@bps.org.uk
Website: www.bps.org.uk

British Telecom (BT)
Complaints Review Service
Tel: (0800) 545458
Customer Services: 150
Directory Enquiries: 118500
Line Faults: 151
Website: www.bt.com

British Trust for Conservation Volunteers (BTCV)
36 St Mary's Street
Wallingford
Oxfordshire OX10 0EU
Tel: (01491) 821600
Email: information@btcv.org.uk
Website: www.btcv.org

Business Connect (Wales)
Tregormen Business Park
Nelson Road
Ystrad Mynach
CF82 7FN
Tel: (0845) 796 9798
Website: www.businessconnect.org.uk

Business Link Signpost Line
Tel: (0845) 604 5678
Email: info@b14london.com
Website: www.businesslink.org
240 Business Links open throughout England

Camping and Caravanning Club
Greenfields House
Westwood Way
Coventry CV4 8JH
Tel: 024-7669 4995
Website:
www.campingandcaravanningclub.co.uk

Carers UK
20–25 Glasshouse Yard
London EC1A 4JT
Carers line: (0808) 808 7777
Email: info@ukcarers.org
Website: www.carersonline.org.uk

Charity and Fundraising Appointments
Lloyds Court
1 Goodman's Yard
London E1 8AT
Tel: 020-7953 1190
Email: enquiries@cfappointments.com
Website: www.cfappointments.com

Chartered Society of Physiotherapy
14 Bedford Row
London WC1R 4ED
Tel: 020-7306 6666
Website: www.csp.org.uk

Citizen's Advice Bureau (CAB)
Website: www.citizensadvice.org.uk
Look in the phone book for details of your local CAB

Community Fund
Chiltern House
St Nicholas Court
25–27 Castle Gate
Nottingham NG1 7AR
Tel: 0115-934 2950
Email: strategicgrants@community-fund.org.uk
Website: www.community-fund.org.uk

Community Legal Service
Tel: (0845) 608 1122
Leaflet line: (0845) 300 0343
Website: www.justask.org.uk

Community Service Volunteers
Retired and Seniors Volunteer Programme
237 Pentonville Road
London N1 9NJ
Tel: 020-7643 1385
Email: info@rsvp.org.uk
Website: www.csv-rsvp.org.uk

Community Transport Association
Highbank, Halton Street
Hyde
Cheshire SK14 2NY
Advice line: 0161-367 8780
Email: ctauk@communitytransport.com
Website: www.communitytransport.com

Consumers' Association
2 Marylebone Road
London NW1 4DF
Customer Services: (0800) 252100
Tel: 020-7770 7000
Email: which@which.net
Website: www.which.net

Contact the Elderly
2nd Floor, 15 Henrietta Street
Covent Garden
London WC2E 8QG
Tel: (0800) 716 543
Email: info@contact-the-elderly.org
Website: www.contact-the-elderly.org

The Continence Foundation
307 Hatton Square
16 Baldwins Gardens
London EC1N 7RJ
Helpline: (0845) 345 0165
(9.30am–1pm weekdays)
Email: continence-help@dial.pipex.com
Website: www.continence-foundation.org.uk

Council for the Advancement of Communication with Deaf People (CACDP)
Durham University Science Park
Block 4, Stockton Road
Durham DH1 3UZ
Tel: 0191-383 1155
Email: durham@cacdp.org.uk
Website: www.cacdp.org.uk

CORGI *(The Council for Registered Gas Installers)*
1 Elmwood
Chineham Business Park
Crockford Lane
Basingstoke
Hants RG24 8WG
Tel: (01256) 372200
Email: enquiries@corgi-group.com
Website: www.corgi-group.com

Council for British Archaeology
Bowes Morell House
111 Walmgate
York YO1 9WA
Tel: (01904) 671417
Email: info@britarch.ac.uk
Website: www.britarch.co.uk

Crisis
64 Commercial Street
London E1 6LT
Tel: (0870) 011 3335
Email: enquiries@crisis.org.uk
Website: www.crisis.org.uk

Crossroads – Caring for Carers
10 Regent Place
Rugby, Warwickshire CV21 2PN
Tel: (0845) 450 0350
Website: www.crossroads.org.uk

Cruse Bereavement Care
Cruse House
126 Sheen Road
Richmond
Surrey TW9 1UR
Helpline: (0870) 167 1677
Email: info@crusebereavementcare.org.uk
Website: www.crusebereavementcare.org.uk

Dark Horse Venture
Kelton, Woodlands Road
Liverpool L17 0AN
Tel: 0151-729 0092
Email: helpdesk@dhv.org.uk
Website: www.dhv.org.uk

Department of Health
Richmond House
79 Whitehall
London SW1A 2NS
Tel: 020-7210 4850
Email: dhmail@doh.gsi.gov.uk
Website: www.doh.gsi.gov.uk

Department of Trade and Industry
DTI Enquiry Unit,
1 Victoria Street
London SW1H OET
Tel: 020-7215 5000
Email: dti.enquiries@dti.gsi.gov.uk
Website: www.dti.gov.uk

Department for Transport
Great Minster House
76 Marsham Street
London SW1P 4DR
Tel: 020-7944 8300
Website: www.dft.gov.uk

Department for Work and Pensions
Age Positive Team
Room W8d
Moorfoot
Sheffield S1 4PQ
Email: agepositive@dwp.gsi.gov.uk
Website: www.agepositive.gov.uk

Pensions and Overseas Benefits Directorate
Tyneview Park
Whitley Road
Benton
Newcastle-upon-Tyne NE98 1BA
Tel: 0191-218 2000
Website: www.dwp.gov.uk

Disability Sport England
Unit 4G, N17 Studios
784–788 High Road
Tottenham N17 ODA
Tel: 020-8801 4466
Email: info@dse.org.uk
Web: www.disabilitysport.org.uk

Disabled Living Centres
Disabled Living Centres Council
Redbank House
4 St Chad's Street
Cheetham
Manchester M8 8QA
Tel: 0161-834 1044
Email: dlcc@dlcc.org.uk
Website: www.dlcc.org.uk

Disabled Living Foundation (DLF)
Advice Department
380–384 Harrow Road
London W9 2HU
Helpline: (0845) 130 9177 *(10am–1pm weekdays)*
Website: www.dlf.org.uk

Drinking Water Inspectorate (DWI)
Floor 2/A1, Ashdown House
123 Victoria Street
London SW1E 6DE
Tel: 020-7944 5956
Email: dwi.enquiries@defra.gsi.gov.uk
Website: www.dwi.gov.uk

Driver and Vehicle Licensing Agency (DVLA)
Customer Enquiry Department
Longview Road, Morriston
Swansea SA6 7JL
Tel: (0870) 240 0009
Website: www.dvla.gov.uk

Elderly Accommodation Counsel
3rd Floor, 89 Albert Embankment
London SE1 7PT
Tel: 020-7820 1343
Email: enquiries@e-a-c.demon.co.uk
Website: www.housingcare.org

Energy Efficiency Advice Centres
Tel: (0800) 512012
for details of your local Energy Efficiency Advice Centre

Energy Saving Trust (EST)
21 Dartmouth Street
London SW1H 9BP
Tel: 020-7222 0101
Energy efficiency helpline: (0845) 727 7200
Website: www.saveenergy.co.uk

energywatch
4th Floor, Artillery House
Artillery Row
London SW1P 1RT
Tel: (0845) 906 0708
Email: enquiries@energywatch.org.uk
Website: www.energywatch.org.uk

Farmstay UK
National Agricultural Centre
Stoneleigh Park
Warwickshire CV8 2LG
Tel: 024-7669 6909
Email: info@farmstayuk.co.uk
Website: www.farmstayuk.co.uk

Fellowship of Depressives Anonymous
Box FDA, Self Help Nottingham
Ormiston House
32–36 Pellam Street
Nottingham NG1 2EG
Tel: (01702) 433838
Email: fdainfo@aol.com
Website: www.depressionanon.co.uk

Hairnet
Little Tufton House
3 Dean Trench Street
London SW1P 3HB
Tel: (0870) 241 5091
Email: info@hairnet.org
Website: www.hairnet.org

Hedgeline
1 Applebees Meadow
Hinckley LE10 0FL
Tel: (0870) 240 0627
Website: www.hedgeline.org
Send an sae for information

Help the Aged
207–221 Pentonville Road
London N1 9UZ
Tel: 020-7278 1114
HandyVan Services: (01255) 473999
Senior Link Services: (0808) 800 6565
Email: info@helptheaged.org.uk
Website: www.helptheaged.org.uk

Holiday Care
Information Unit
7th Floor, Sunley House
4 Bedford Park
Croydon
Surrey CR0 2AP
Tel: (0845) 124 9971
Email: holiday.care@virgin.net
Website: www.holidaycare.org.uk

Home Improvement Agencies
England
Foundations
Bleaklow House
Howard Town Mill
Glossop SK13 8HT
Tel: (01457) 891909
Website: www.foundations.uk.com

Wales
Care & Repair Cymru
Norbury House
Norbury Road
Cardiff CF5 3AS
Tel: 029-2057 6286
Email: enquiries@careandrepair.org.uk
Website: www.careandrepair.org.uk

Scotland
Care & Repair Scotland
236 Clyde Street
Glasgow G1 4JH
Tel: 0141-221 9879
Email: forum@care-repair-scot.org.uk

Northern Ireland
Fold Housing Association
3 Redburn Square
Holywood BT18 9HZ
Tel: 028-9042 8314
Email: info@foldgroup.co.uk
Website: www.foldgroup.co.uk

HPI Register
HPI Ltd
Dolphin House
New Street
Salisbury
Wiltshire SP1 2PH
Tel: (01722) 422422
Website: www.hpi.co.uk

Independent Healthcare Association (IHA)
Westminster Tower
3 Albert Embankment
London SE1 7SP
Email: info@iha.org.uk
Website: www.iha.org.uk

Inland Revenue
Leaflet orderline: (0845) 900 0404
Website: www.inlandrevenue.gov.uk

Institute of Advanced Motorists (IAM)
510 Chiswick High Road
London W4 5RG
Tel: 020-8996 9600
Website: www.iam.org.uk

International Co-operation for Development
Catholic Institute for International Relations
Unit 3, Canonbury Yard
190a New North Road
London N1 7BJ
Tel: 020-7354 0883
Email: ciir@ciir.org
Website: www.ciir.org

International Voluntary Service (IVS)
IVS Head Office
Old Hall
East Bergholt
Colchester CO7 6TQ
Tel: (01206) 298215 (*10am–4pm weekdays*)
Email: ivs@ivsgbsouth.demon.co.uk
Website: www.ivsgbn.demon.co.uk

Interval International Ltd
Coombe Hill House
Beverley Way
London SW20 0AR
Tel: 020-8336 9300
Website: www.intervalworld.com

Joint Contracts Tribunal (JCT)
9 Cavendish Place
London W1G 0QD
Email: stanform@jctltd.co.uk
Website: www.jctltd.co.uk

Kingston Communications
Carr Lane
Kingston upon Hull
HU1 3KE
Tel: (01482) 602100
Email: publicrelations@kcom.com
Website: www.kcom.com

Law Society of England and Wales
Law Society Hall
113 Chancery Lane
London WC2A 1PL
Tel: 020-7242 1222
Website: www.lawsociety.org.uk

Law Society of Northern Ireland
Law Society House
98 Victoria Street
Belfast BT1 3JX
Tel: 028-9023 1614
Website: www.lawsoc-ni.org

Law Society of Scotland
26 Drumsheugh Gardens
Edinburgh EH3 7YR
Tel: 0131-226 7411
Website: www.lawscot.org.uk

Learndirect
PO Box 900
Manchester M60 3LE
Learning advice line: (0800) 100900
Information on Learndirect courses:
(0800) 101901
Website: www.learndirect.co.uk

Learndirect Scotland
Freepost SCO5775
PO Box 25249
Glasgow G3 8XN
Tel: (0808) 100 9000
Email: info@learndirectscotland.com
Website: www.learndirectscotland.com

Leasehold Advisory Service
70–74 City Road
London EC1Y 2BJ
Tel: (0845) 345 1993
Email: info@lease-advice.org
Website: www.lease-advice.org

Leonard Cheshire UK
30 Millbank
London SW1P 4QD
Tel: 020-7802 8200
Email: info@london.leonard-cheshire.org.uk
Website: www.leonard-cheshire.org

Listening Books
12 Lant Street
London SE1 1QH
Tel: 020-7407 9417
Email: info@listening-books.org.uk
Website: www.listening-books.org.uk

Mediation UK
Alexander House
Telephone Avenue
Bristol BS1 4BS
Tel: 0117-904 6661
Email: enquiry@mediationuk.org.uk
Website: www.mediationuk.org.uk

Mobility Centres
Forum of Mobility Centres
Room GN35
Quarry House
Leeds LS2 7UA
Tel: 0113-232 4797
Website: www.justmobility.co.uk/forum

Mobility Information Service (MIS)
National Mobility Centre
Unit B1, Greenwood Court
Cartmel Drive
Shrewsbury SY1 3TB
Tel: (01743) 463072
Email: mis@nmcuk.freeserve.co.uk
Website: www.mis.org.uk

Motability
Goodman House
Station Approach
Harlow
Essex CM20 2ET
Helpline: (01279) 635666
Website: www.motability.co.uk

National Association for Mental Health (MIND)
Granta House
15–19 Broadway
London E15 4BQ
Tel: 020-8519 2122
Email: contact@mind.org.uk
Website: www.mind.org.uk

National Association of Widows
National Office
48 Queens Road
Coventry CV1 3EH
Tel: 024-7663 4848
Email:office@nawidows.org.uk
Website: www.widows.uk.net

National Care Standards Commission
St Nicholas Building
St Nicholas Street
Newcastle NE1 1NB
Tel: 0191-233 3600
Email: enquiries@ncsc.gsi.gov.uk
Website: www.carestandards.org

National Express Ltd
Head Office
Ensign Court
4 Vicarage Road
Edgbaston
Birmingham B15 3ES
Tel: 0121-625 1122
Bookings/enquiries: (08705) 808080
Website: www.nationalexpress.com

National Extension College (NEC)
Michael Young Centre
Purbeck Road
Cambridge CB2 2HN
Tel: (01223) 400200
Email: info@nec.ac.uk
Website: www.nec.ac.uk

National House Building Council (NHBC)
Buildmark House
Chiltern Avenue
Amersham
Bucks HP6 5AP
Tel: (01494) 434477
Website: www.nhbc.co.uk

National Osteoporosis Society
Camerton
Bath BA2 OPJ
Tel: (01761) 471771
Email: info@nos.org.uk

National Society for Clean Air and Environmental Protection
44 Grand Parade
Brighton
East Sussex BN2 9QA
Tel: (01273) 878770
Email: admin@nsca.org.uk
Website: www.nsca.org.uk

National Trust
Rowan Kembrey Park
Swindon SN2 8YL
General enquiries: (0870) 458 4000
Working Holidays enquiries: (0870) 429 2429
Community Learning and Volunteering
enquiries: (0870) 609 5383
Website: www.nationaltrust.org.uk

NHS Direct
England and Wales
NHS Direct Helpline: (0845) 46 47
Website: www.nhsdirect.nhs.uk

Scotland
NHS24 Helpline: (0845) 424 2424
Website: www.nhs24.com
or
NHS Helpline: (0800) 224 488
Website: www.show.scot.nhs.uk

Northern Ireland
Website: www.n-i.nhs.uk

Northern Ireland Advisory Committee on Telecommunications (NIACT)
NIACT Secretariat
22 Great Victoria Street
Belfast BT2 7QA
Tel: (0845) 714 5000
Email: niact@acts.org.uk
Website: www.acts.org.uk

Northern Ireland Water Service
Northland House
3 Frederick Street
Belfast BT1 2NR
Tel: (0845) 744 0088
Website: www.waterni.gov.uk

NTL
Bartley Wood Business Park
Bartley Way
Hook
Hampshire
RG27 9UP
Tel: (01256) 752000
Website: www.ntl.com

O2
Customer Services
O2 online
Dummers Lane
Bury BL9 9QL
Website: www.o2.co.uk

Ofcom
Ofcom Press Office
Office of Communications
Riverside House
2A Southwark Bridge Road
London SE1 9HA
Tel: 020-7981 3000
Email: wwwenq@ofcom.org.uk
Website: www.ofcom.org.uk

Office of Fair Trading
Fleetbank House
2–6 Salisbury Square
London EC4Y 8JX
Tel: (0845) 722 4499
Email: enquiries@oft.gov.uk
Website: www.oft.gov.uk

Ofgem
9 Millbank
London SW1P 3GE
Tel: 020-7901 7000
Website: www.ofgem.gov.uk

Ofreg
Brookmount Building
42 Fountain Street
Belfast BT1 5EE
Tel: 028-9031 1575
Website: ofreg.nics.gov.uk

Office of Fair Trading (OFT)
Fleetbank House
2–6 Salisbury Square
London EC4Y 8JX
Tel: (0845) 722 4499
Email: enquiries@oft.gsi.gov.uk
Website: www.oft.gov.uk

Oftel
50 Ludgate Hill
London EC4M 7JJ
Tel: (0845) 714 5000
Website: www.oftel.gov.uk

Ofwat
Centre City Tower
7 Hill Street
Birmingham B5 4UA
Tel: 0121-625 1300
Email: enquiries@ofwat.gsi.gov.uk
Website: www.ofwat.gov.uk

Open and Distance Learning Quality Council
16 Park Crescent
London W1B 1AH
Tel: 020-7612 7090
Email: info@odlqc.org.uk
Website: www.odlqc.org.uk

Open College of the Arts
Unit 1B
Redbrook Business Park
Wilthorpe Road
Barnsley S75 1JN
Tel: (01226) 730495
Email: open.arts@ukonline.co.uk
Website: www.oca-uk.com

Open University (OU)
Course Information and Advice Centre
Walton Hall
Milton Keynes MK7 6AA
Tel: (01908) 653231
Email: general-enquiries@open.ac.uk
Website: www.open.ac.uk

Orange
Customer Services
PO Box 10
Patchway
Bristol BS32 4BQ
Tel: (07973) 100150
Website: www.orange.co.uk

Organisation for Timeshare in Europe
Rue Defacqz 78–80
1060 Brussels
Tel (Consumers): 0032 (0) 2533 3069
Email: info@ote-info.com
Website: www.ote-info.com

Otelo
Office of the Telecommunications
Ombudsman
Wilderspool Park
Warrington WA4 6HL
Tel: (0845) 050 1614
Email: enquiries@otelo.org.uk
Website: www.otelo.org.uk

Parkinson's Disease Society
215 Vauxhall Bridge Road
London SW1V 1EJ
Tel: 020-7931 8080
Email: enquiries@parkinsons.org.uk
Website: www.parkinsons.org.uk

Public Appointments Unit
Cabinet Office
Admiralty Arch
The Mall
London SW1A 2WH
Tel: (0845) 000 0040
Email: public.appointments.unit@cabinet-office.x.gsi.gov.uk
Website: www.publicappointments.gov.uk

Quality Mark
PO Box 445
Tower Court
Foleshill Enterprise Park
Foleshill Road
Coventry CV6 5NX
Tel: (0845) 300 80 40
Email: qualitymarkscheme@capita.co.uk
Website: www.qualitymark.org.uk

RAC
RAC Motoring Services
RAC House
1 Forest Road
Feltham TW13 7RR
Inspections: (0870) 533 3660
Website: www.rac.co.uk

RCI Europe Ltd
Kettering Parkway
Kettering
Northamptonshire NN15 6EY
Tel: (01536) 310101
Website: www.rci.com

Reach
89 Albert Embankment
London SE1 7TP
Tel: 020-7582 6543
Email: info@reach-online.org.uk
Website: www.reach-online.org.uk

Relate
Central Office
Herbert Gray College
Little Church Street
Rugby
Warwickshire CV21 2AP
Tel: (01788) 573241
Website: www.relate.org.uk

Remap
Hazeldene
Ightham
Sevenoaks
Kent TN15 9AD
Tel: (0845) 130 0456
Email: info@remap.org.uk
Website: www.remap.org.uk

Ricability
30 Angel Gate
City Road
London EC1V 2PT
Tel: 020-7427 2460
Textphone: 020-7427 2469
Email: mail@ricability.org.uk
Website: www.ricability.org.uk

Royal Institute of British Architects (RIBA)
66 Portland Place
London W1B 1AD
Tel: 020-7580 5533
Email: info@inst.riba.org
Website: www.architecture.com

Royal National Institute of the Blind (RNIB)
105 Judd Street
London WC1H 9NE
Helpline: (0845) 766 9999
Email: helpline@rnib.org.uk
Website: www.rnib.org.uk

Royal National Institute for Deaf People (RNID)
19–23 Featherstone Street
London EC1Y 8SL
Tel: (0808) 808 0123
Textphone: (0808) 808 9000
Email: informationline@rnid.org.uk
Website: www.rnid.org.uk

Royal Society for the Prevention of Accidents (RoSPA)
Edgbaston Park
353 Bristol Road
Birmingham B5 7ST
Tel: 0121-248 2099
Email: help@rospa.co.uk
Website: www.rospa.co.uk

Royal Society for the Protection of Birds (RSPB)
The Lodge
Sandy
Bedfordshire SG19 2DL
Tel: (01767) 680551
Email: enquiries@rspb.org.uk
Website: www.rspb.org.uk

Scottish Advisory Committee on Telecommunications
28 Thistle Street
Edinburgh EH2 1EN
Tel: 0131-226 7275
Email: sacot@acts.org.uk
Website: www.acts.org.uk

Scottish Building Contract Committee
7 Manor Place
Edinburgh EH3 7DN
Tel: 0131-240 0832
Website: www.sbcconline.com

Scottish Enterprise
5 Atlantic Quay
150 Broomielaw
Glasgow G2 8LU
Tel: (0845) 607 8787
Email: network.helpline@scotent.co.uk
Website: www.scottish-enterprise.com

Servista
32–38 Saffron Hill
London EC1N 8FH
Tel: (0870) 241 2732
Email: support@servista.com
Website: www.servista.com

Skillshare International
Skills Development Unit
126 New Walk
Leicester LE1 7JA
Tel: 0116-254 1862
Email: info@skillshare.org
Website: www.skillshare.org

Society of Chiropodists and Podiatrists
1 Fellmonger's Path
Tower Bridge Road
London SE1 3LY
Tel: (0845) 450 3720
Email: enq@scpod.org
Website: www.feetforlife.org

Society for the Protection of Ancient Buildings
37 Spital Square
London E1 6DY
Tel: 020-7377 1644
Email: info@spab.org.uk
Website: www.spab.org.uk

Sport England
16 Upper Woburn Place
London WC1 0QP
Tel: 020-7273 1500
Email: info@sportengland.org
Website: www.sportengland.org

Stroke Association
Stroke House
240 City Road
London EC1V 2PR
Tel: 020-7566 0300
Email: stroke@stroke.org.uk
Website: www.stroke.org.uk

T-Mobile (UK)
Customer Services
Elstree Tower
Borehamwood
Hertfordshire WD6 1DT
Customer Services: (0845) 412 5000
Website: www.t-mobile.co.uk

Telewest
Customer services: (0845) 142 0000
Website: www.telewest.co.uk

Third Age Challenge
39 Hawkins Street
Rodbourne
Swindon SN2 2AQ
Tel: (01793) 533370
Email: office@thirdagers.net
Website: www.thirdagers.net

Third Age Employment Network
207–221 Pentonville Road
London N1 9UZ
Tel: 020-7843 1590
Email: taen@helptheaged.org.uk
Website: www.taen.org.uk

Thrive
Geoffrey Udall Centre
Beech Hill
Reading RG7 2AT
Tel: 0118-988 5688
Email: info@thrive.org.uk
Website: www.thrive.org.uk
www.carryongardening.org.uk
(for information about gardening for older people or those with disabilities)

Tripscope
The Vassall Centre
Gill Avenue
Bristol BS16 2QQ
Tel: (0845) 758 5641
Email: enquiries@triscope.org.uk
Website: www.tripscope.org.uk

TV Licensing
Bristol BS98 1TL
Tel: (0870) 241 5590
Website: www.tvlicensing.co.uk

UK Home Care Association
42b Banstead Road
Carshalton Beeches
Surrey SM5 3NW
Tel: 020-8288 1551
Email: enquiries@ukhca.co.uk
Website: www.ukhca.co.uk

United Kingdom Council for Psychotherapy
167–169 Great Portland Street
London W1W 5PF
Tel: 020-7436 3002
Email: ukcp@psychotherapy.org.uk
Website: www.psychotherapy.org.uk

University of the Third Age (U3A)
Third Age Trust
Old Municipal Buildings
19 East Street
Bromley
Kent BR1 1QH
Tel: 020-8466 6139
Email: enquiries@u3a.org.uk
Website: www.u3a.org.uk

Virgin Mobile
Willow Grove House
PO Box 2692
Trowbridge
West Wiltshire BA14 0TQ
Tel: (0845) 600 0070
Website: www.virginmobile.com

Vodafone
Customer Services
PO Box 549
Croydon CR9 3WB
Tel: (07836) 191 191
Website: www.vodafone.co.uk

Voluntary Service Overseas (VSO)
317 Putney Bridge Road
Putney
London SW15 2PN
Tel: 020-8780 7500
Email: enquiry@vso.org.uk
Website: www.vso.org.uk

Water Industry Commissioner for Scotland
Ochil House
Springkerse Business Park
Stirling FK7 7XE
Tel: (01786) 430200
Email: enquiries@watercommissioner.co.uk
Website: www.watercommissioner.co.uk

Which? Books
Castlemead
Gascoyne Way
Hertford X
SG14 1LH
Tel: (0800) 252100

Which? Legal Service
Castlemead
Gascoyne Way
Hertford X
SG14 1LH
Tel: (01992) 822828

The Winged Fellowship Trust
Angel House
20–32 Pentonville Road
London N1 9XD
Tel: 020-7833 2594
Email:wftholidays@wft.org.uk
Website: www.wft.org.uk

Women's Institute's Denman College
Marcham
Abingdon
Oxfordshire OX13 6NW
Tel (01865) 391991
Email: info@denman.org.uk
Website: www.womens-institute.co.uk

Workers' Educational Association (WEA)
Temple House
17 Victoria Park Square
London E2 9PB
Tel: 020-8983 1515
Email: national@wea.org.uk
Website: www.wea.org.uk

Index

abroad
   healthcare 19, 127–8
   holidays 123–5
   moving 19–22
   pension arrangements 20
   property search 20–1
   social security benefits 20
   tax 20
   train travel 116
   voluntary work 83
acupuncture 142
age discrimination 75
age spots 209, 210
ageing process 164, 176
air travel 117–19
alcohol 160, 186, 188
Alzheimer's disease 186, 223–4
angina 142, 175, 177
anxiety 178
appetite loss 157
archaeological digs 82
arteriosclerosis 178, 196
arthritis 167
asthma 166
atherosclerosis 177, 178
Attendance Allowance 221

back pain 166–7, 179–80
bathrooms and toilets 14, 52, 53
bed-and-breakfast business 15
bereavement 180, 224–5
blind and visually impaired people 89, 92, 180–1, 228
blood pressure, high 154, 160, 166, 175, 196, 210
Blue Badge parking scheme 113
bonfires 62–3
book clubs 90

boundaries 64–6
breast cancer 183
bronchitis 166, 181–2
building work 67–70
   approved tradespeople 43, 68
   estimates and quotations 68
   overcharging 69
   quality 69
   stage payments 68
   time factor 69–70
   written contracts 67
burglar alarms 35, 46–7
burglaries 42, 43–4, 48
buses 117

calcium 156, 159, 176, 204
calluses and corns 192
cancer 142, 160, 174, 175, 182–3, 210
caravanning 122
carbon monoxide (CO) poisoning 54
care assistants 139
care homes 232, 235–8
   choosing 236
   fees 237–8
   short stays 219
carers 215–25
   breaks, respite care and holidays 218–19
   financial and legal matters 221–2
   medical issues 222–4
   needs assessments 217
   paying for private care 219–20
   sitting service schemes 218
   stress 216–17, 220, 224
   support 215–16, 217–20
Carer's Allowance 221
cars and driving 104–14
   abandoned vehicles 67

Blue Badge parking scheme 113
depreciation 106
disabled drivers 110, 112–14
doing without 104
driving skills and tests 111, 112
economical driving 106
features 107–8
fuel economy 105
imported cars 108
inspection services 109
insurance 106–7
licence renewal 110
Motability Scheme 114
new cars 107–9
road tax 106
road tax exemptions 114
running costs 104, 105–7
safer driving 110–12
second-hand cars 109–10
servicing and repairs 105
cataracts 181, 191
chiropodists 140, 192–3
chiropractic 142
cholesterol 152, 165, 175
claims assessors 72
closed circuit TV (CCTV) systems 45
coach travel 116–17
cod liver oil 160
cold weather payments 32
colds and flu 183–4, 222
community mental health nurses 140
community projects 81–2
community or social alarms 35, 228–9, 231
complementary therapies 142
computers 93–103
    after-sales support 96
    buying 95–6
    hardware 94–5
    Internet 26, 28, 96–103
    library access 93–4
    modems 95, 97
    older users 93
    training courses 93, 94
    warranties 96
constipation 184–5, 198
counsellors 140, 217
'country smells' 62
Crime Prevention Officers (CPOs) 44, 67

deafness 37–8, 185, 227–8
deep vein thrombosis (DVT) 118
dementia 174, 186–7, 223–4
dental problems 187–8
dentists 136–9

continuing care registration 137
Dental Access Services 137
dental insurance 138–9
home visits 137
NHS treatment 136, 137, 138, 188
private treatment 136, 137, 138–9
treatment costs 138–9, 188
depression 188
diabetes 139, 175, 181, 188–9, 193, 200
dial-a-ride schemes 119, 143
Disability Living Allowance (DLA) 113, 114, 221
disabled people
    car drivers 110, 112–14
    exercise and sport 172
    food preparation 159
    housing 24, 25
    leisure activities 92
    mobility problems 119–20
    public transport 115–16, 117
    telephones 37–8, 40
district nurses 140
dizziness 175
doors
    handles and knobs 227
    locks and chains 44–5
    reinforced 45
    viewers 43, 45
driving see cars and driving

education and recreation 84–92
    computer courses 93, 94
    distance learning 85–7
    full-time study 88–9
    home study groups 90
    library resources 89
    miscellaneous activities 91–2
    neighbourhood classes 84–5, 87, 89
    reminiscence sessions 90–1
    residential courses 87–8
    scrap-booking 91
electric blankets 56
electricity
    deals 28–9
    difficulties paying bills 40
    disconnection 40
    electrical safety 52–3
    repair work 41
    suppliers 27
    visual wiring check 52
emphysema 166, 189–90
employment 75–8
    consultancy and freelance work 76–7
    continuing working 75–6
    finding 76
    home businesses 77–8

see also voluntary work
energy efficiency 21, 30–1
environmental health officers (EHOs) 61
equity release schemes 15, 231
estate agents 22, 23
exercise 165–72
    activities 171–2
    aerobic 164, 170
    classes 170
    disabled people 172
    health benefits 165–7, 173
    psychological benefits 167–8
    safety 168
    starting 168–9
    venues 169
    videos and audio tapes 170
    warming up/down 169
eye problems 190–1
eye tests 139, 191

falls 51–2, 167, 175, 191–2
farm holidays 122
fats, dietary 152–3
ferries 119
fibre (roughage) 152, 155–6, 185
fire safety 44, 55–7
    electric blankets 56
    escape routes 56
    Fire Brigade advice 57
    fire extinguishers 56–7
    heaters, fires and candles 55–6
    smoke alarms 55
    smoking 56
    tackling fires 56–7
fitness 163–72, 173
    fitness gap 163
    mental fitness 174
    stamina 164, 169, 173
    strength and endurance 164–5, 169
    suppleness 165
    see also exercise
flats 16–17, 18
    building management 16, 17
    freehold 16–17
    granny flats 15, 230
    leases 16
flu jabs 135, 175, 184, 190, 207
fluid intake 160
fly-tipping 67
food labels 161
food safety 161–2
foot problems 192–3

gardens 16
    overgrown neighbour gardens 63
    security 50–1

sheds 51
Thrive (horticultural charity) 92
gas
    appliance checks and servicing 53, 54
    carbon monoxide (CO) detector 54
    deals 28–9
    difficulties paying bills 40
    disconnection 40
    repair work 41
    safety 27, 29, 53–4
    suppliers 27
glasses and contact lenses 139, 191
glaucoma 181, 191
gout 193
GPs (family doctors) 134–6
    changing GPs 135
    complaints 147
    registering with 135
    temporary patients 135
graffiti 67
granny flats 15, 230

haemorrhoids *see* piles
hair loss 194
health problems 173–212
health services 17, 133–48
    annual health check-ups 136
    care assistants 140
    chiropodists 139, 192–3
    community dieticians 140
    community mental health nurses 140
    complementary therapies 141–2
    counsellors, psychotherapists and
        psychologists 140, 217
    dentists 136–9
    district nurses 140
    flu jabs 135, 175, 184, 190, 207
    free prescriptions 136
    hospital treatment 142–7
    medical appointments 134
    medicine reviews 136, 201
    nursing specialists 141
    occupational therapists (OTs) 140,
        228
    opticians 139
    overseas 19, 127–8
    pharmacists 136
    physiotherapists 140–1, 173
    speech and language therapists 141
    standards 133
    vaccinations 135
    see also National Health Service
        (NHS); private healthcare
healthy eating 149–62, 176, 203, 225
    catering for one 158
    community dieticians 140

cooking skills and equipment 158–9
fat, sugar, salt and fibre 152–6
fluid and alcohol 160
food safety 161–2
fruit, vegetables and salads 150–1
government recommendations 149
meat, fish and dairy products 151–2
microwave cooking 227
starchy foods 150
storecupboard items 158
vitamin and mineral supplements
    157, 159–60
weight control 156–7
healthy lifestyle 176
hearing aids 185
heart attack 194–5
heart disease 154, 165–6, 174, 175
hedges *see* trees and hedges
herbal medicine 142
hernias 195
holiday homes 17
holidays 121–9
    abroad 123–5
    bed-and-breakfasting 121
    in Britain 121–2
    caravanning 122
    complaints 128–9
    farm holidays 122
    health 127–8
    home security 49, 127
    hotels 121
    insurance 126–7
    money and valuables 126
    package holidays 121
    respite care 219
    self-catering 121–2, 123
    timeshare 124–5
    travel websites 115, 123
    travel-club schemes 125
    working holidays 82
home
    adaptations 14, 18, 216, 226–31
    bed-and-breakfast business 15
    conversions and extensions 15, 18,
        216, 230
    equity release schemes 15, 231
    gardens 16
    grants and funding for improvements
        230–1
    holiday homes 17
    home gadgets 227–8
    living space 13–14
    local authority/housing authority
        tenants 24–5
    lodgers 15
    staying put 13–14, 215–31

    see also building work; flats; moving
        house; sheltered housing
hormone replacement therapy (HRT)
    202
hospital treatment 142–7
    complaints 147, 148
    NHS 142–3, 144
    pensions and 143
    private treatment 143–7
    travel costs and services 142–3
    waiting times 142
hypothermia 196–7

impotence 209
Income Support 32, 76, 138, 143
incontinence 197–8, 223
indigestion 198–9
injury 70–2
    claims assessors 72
    compensation 70
    legal advice 71–2
    negligence claims 70–1
insomnia 199–200
insurance
    cars 106–7
    dental 138–9
    holiday absence and 49
    holidays 126–7
    home insurance discounts 42, 44, 47
    legal expenses 71, 72
    private medical insurance (PMI) 19,
        144, 146–7
Internet 96–103
    computer requirements 97
    costs 99
    Internet service provider (ISP) 97,
        99–100
    popular websites 102–3
    security 100–2
    shopping online 100–2, 103
    surfing tips 98

Jobseeker's Allowance 76

keys, spare 46

leg ulcers 200
legal expenses insurance 71, 72
leisure
    concessions and discounts 84
    disabled people and 92
    TV licences 92
    see also education and recreation
libraries 89, 93–4
lightbulbs 31, 32
lighting, exterior 49–50

litter problems 66–7
local authority and housing authority
   tenants 25
   neighbour disputes 60
   sheltered housing 24, 25, 233
locks and bolts 44–6
   changing 46
   door locks and chains 44–5
   window locks 14, 45–6
lodgers 15
luncheon clubs 158, 219, 225

Macmillan nurses 141
macular degeneration 181, 191
Marie Curie nurses 141
Meals on Wheels 158, 217
Mediation UK 60
medication 200–1, 223
menopause 201–2
mental fitness 174
Minimum Income Guarantee see Income
   Support
mobile phones 38–40
mobility aids and schemes 119–20,
   229–30
mortgages 22, 24
moving house 15–25
   d-i-y conveyancing 24
   estate agents 22, 23
   from house to flat 16–17
   handling your own sale 23
   mortgages 22, 24
   moving abroad 19–22
   moving in with family or friends
      17–18
   pros and cons 17
   reasons for 13
   removal companies 23
   surveys 22–3
   to a new area 17

National Extension College (NEC) 86
National Health Service (NHS) 133–4
   complaints 147
   GPs 134–6
   hospital treatment 142–3, 144
   NHS Direct 141
   primary care 133, 134–41
   Primary Care Trusts (PCTs) 134
   secondary care 133–4, 142–7
   Walk-in centres 141
National Trust
   discounted subscriptions 84
   working holidays 82
neighbour disputes 58–66
   access for repair work 66

bonfires 62–3
boundaries 64–6
   court action 60–1
   high hedges 64
   local authority intervention 60, 62, 63
   mediation 60
   noise 59, 61–2
   'nuisance' 61, 63
   overgrown gardens 63
   overhanging branches 63–4
   pets and livestock 65
   smells 62
   tree roots 64
   trespass 64–5
   walls and fences 65–6
neighbourhood nuisances 66–7
   abandoned vehicles 67
   fly-tipping 67
   graffiti 67
   litter problems 66–7
Neighbourhood Watch schemes 48
noise 59, 61–2
nursing homes see care homes

obesity 202–3
occupational therapists (OTs) 140, 228
Open College of the Arts 86, 87
Open University (OU) 86, 90
opticians 139
osteoarthritis 179, 203
osteopathy 142
osteoporosis 159, 167, 203–4

Parkinson's disease 186, 204–5
pavements, unsafe 70–1
pensions
   abroad 20
   hospital stays 143
peptic ulcer 205
pharmacists 135
physiotherapists 140–1, 173
piles (haemorrhoids) 206
pneumonia 175, 184, 206–7
podiatrists see chiropodists
power of attorney 222
practice nurses 141
presbyopia 190–1
prescriptions
   free 136
   pre-payment certificates 136
private healthcare 143–7
   complaints 147–8
   dentists 136, 137, 138–9
   private medical insurance (PMI) 19,
      144, 146–7
   self-pay healthcare 145–6

property marking kits 48, 49
prostate enlargement 197, 207–8
psychotherapists and psychologists 140
public transport 114–19
    air travel 117–19
    buses 117
    coach travel 116–17
    disabled people 17, 115–16
    ferries 119
    train travel 114–16

reflexology 142
reminiscence sessions 90–1
rent-a-room scheme 15
residential homes *see* care homes
rheumatoid arthritis 208
Royal Mail Keepsafe service 49

safety in the home 51–7
    electrical safety 52–3
    falls 51–2, 175, 191–2
    fire safety 44, 55–7
    gas safety 27, 29, 53–4
    see also security in the home
salt intake 154–5
scooters and buggies 119–20
scrap-booking 91
security in the home 42–51
    burglar alarms 46–7
    burglaries 42, 43–4, 48
    closed circuit TV (CCTV) systems 45
    community or social alarms 228–9,
        231
    emergency phone numbers 42–3
    exterior lighting 49–50
    fire safety 44, 55–7
    gardens 50–1
    help with costs 51
    holiday periods 49, 127
    house sales 23
    locks and bolts 14, 44–6
    Neighbourhood Watch schemes 48
    police advice 44
    spare keys 46
    tradespeople 43
    unannounced callers 43
    valuables 48, 49
    Victim Support schemes 51
    see also safety in the home
sexual problems 209
sheltered housing 24, 232–5
    communal facilities 234
    frail residents 235
    leasehold schemes 234
    local authority developments 24, 25,
        233

    management 233, 234
    service charges 233
    shared ownership schemes 24, 233
    TV licences 92
shopmobility schemes 119
skin cancer 210
skin problems 209–10
small claims procedure 129
smoke alarms 55
smoking 56, 175, 182, 190
social security benefits 221–2
    abroad 20
    see also individual benefits
sockets 14, 53, 227
speech and language therapists 141
stairlifts 229–30
stress 216–17, 220
stroke 174, 175, 181, 186, 210–11
sugar consumption 154
surveys, house 22–3

talking book services 89
taps 14
taxation abroad 20
taxi-card schemes 119
telephones 34–40
    carrier pre-selection 35
    companies 34
    comparing tariffs 35
    complaints 38
    difficulties paying bills 40
    disabled users 37–8
    disconnection 40
    discount schemes 35–6
    handsets 36–7
    help with costs 37
    indirect operators 34, 35, 36
    mobile phones 38–40
    repair work 41
    service accessibility 37–8
timeshare 124–5
tradespeople 43, 68
train travel 114–16
transient ischaemic attacks (TIAs) 211
travel 17, 104–20
    cars 104–14
    disabled people 115–16, 117
    hospital visits 142–3
    mobility problems 119–20
    public transport 114–19
travel-club schemes 125
trees and hedges
    high hedges 64
    overhanging branches 63–4
    Tree Preservation Orders 63–4
    tree roots 64

trespass 64–5
tutoring 77
TV licences 92

ulcers
  leg ulcers 200
  peptic ulcer 205
university courses 86, 88
University of the Third Age (U3A) 85,
  169
utilities 26–41
  complaints 30, 33–4, 38
  deals for older people 28–9
  difficulties paying bills 40
  direct-debit payments 29
  dual fuel deals 28
  energy efficiency 30–1
  help with costs 31–2
  home calls 43
  pre-payment meters 29
  price-comparison websites 26, 28, 35,
    39
  Priority Service Register 29–30
  repair work 41
  see also electricity; gas; telephones;
    water companies

vaccinations 135
  see also flu jabs
varicose veins 200, 211–12
vermin 63
Viagra 209
Victim Support schemes 51
vitamin D 160, 204

vitamin and mineral supplements 157,
  159–60
voluntary work 78–81
  abroad 83
  community projects 81–2
  conservation and environmental
    work 80, 82
  office and business skills 79
  practical skills 80
  public appointment opportunities 79
  working with people 79–80

walls and fences 65–6
  new construction 66
  positioning 65
  repairs to neighbour's fence 66
  upkeep 65, 66
water companies 32–4
  complaints 33–4
  difficulties paying bills 40
  discounts on bills 33
  repair work 41
  service accessibility 33
  water meters 32–3
weight
  gain/loss 156–7, 164
  maintaining your weight 157
  obesity 166, 202–3
window locks 45–6
winter fuel payments 31–2
Witness Service 51
Workers' Educational Association (WEA)
  85
wrinkles 209–10